NUBIAN PHARAOHS AND MEROITIC KINGS

THE KINGDOM OF KUSH

BY

NECIA DESIREE HARKLESS

Bloomington, IN  Milton Keynes, UK

authorHOUSE®

AuthorHouse™
1663 Liberty Drive, Suite 200
Bloomington, IN 47403
www.authorhouse.com
Phone: 1-800-839-8640

AuthorHouse™ UK Ltd.
500 Avebury Boulevard
Central Milton Keynes, MK9 2BE
www.authorhouse.co.uk
Phone: 08001974150

First published by AuthorHouse 9/12/2006

ISBN: 1-4259-4496-5 (sc)

Library of Congress Control Number: 2006907292

Printed in the United States of America
Bloomington, Indiana

This book is printed on acid-free paper.

To

James Mc Connell Harkless
and Ethel Williams Harkless

My deceased parents

ACKNOWLEDGEMENTS

To all my friends, students, and well- wishers who have been apart of my Nubian Odyssey since its inception almost a quarter of a century ago, I wish to thank you for your concerns and support for my passion. My brother, James Mc Connell Harkless Esq. and my sister, Gwendolyn Hogue were my earliest champions. Sharon Pitts, my niece, was my fervent supporter in 1988 to do my research at the British Museum in London, University of Khartoum and the National Museum, University of Warsaw in Poland, Museums in Turin, Italy and Madrid, Spain. She was intrigued with the scholars that we met and the conversations on end. Wlodezimierz Godlewski and Stephan Jacobielski helped us to understand the Polish spirit and a deeper understanding of the Faras Wall hangings. I especially wish to thank my mentor, professor, friend and colleague William Y. Adams, Anthropologist, Salvage Archaeologist who wrote the definitive classic, *Nubia: Corridor to Africa in 1974.* Although out of print at this time, an Arabic translation was recently released. My indebtedness to Karl-Heinz Priese, director at the Egyptian Museum, Berlin, for special access to "The Gold of Meroe" under his guidance, is still immeasurable.

The following know why I am especially grateful to them: Ruth Carney. Brenda Rein, Arturo Alonzo Sandoval, Anthony Gay, Daud Watts, Frances Henry, Anna Margaret Hamilton, Wanda Thomas, Dr. Harvey Thomas, Dr. Jim Pitts, Dr. Abbey Marlatt, Ed Wilson, Kay Garner, Rev. Robert L. Sessum, Father P. Giovanni Vantini and Dr. Timothy Kendall, and Ann Wright.

LIST OF ILLUSTRATIONS

LOCATION OF MODERN NUBIA CONTIGUOUS COUNTRIES AND AREA OF ANCIENT KINGDOM OF KUSH   2

TEMPLE OF ISIS AT THE ISLAND OF PHILAE   3

ISIS SUCKLING HER SON HORUS   3

THE NILE AT THE SECOND CATARACT   4

THE SHADUF, A WATER-LIFTING DEVICE   4

NATIVE BED FOR BURIAL, FOUND AT KERMA   68

FOOT OF BED LEG, BRONZE   68

PYRAMID COMPLEX AT NURI   69

SPHINX OF TAHARQA, NUBIAN PHARAOH, XXV DYN.   69

NORTH PYRAMIDS AT MEROE   94

JEBEL BARKAL, THE HOLY MOUNTAIN   94

MUSAWWARET   95

LION FRIEZE   95

WARRIOR   96

QUEEN AMANITERE IN FULL REGALIA REAR WALL OF LION TEMPLE   96

LION GOD APEDEMAK   97

STAND OF KING ATLANERSA   97

STAND OF KING ATLANERSA   98

MEROITIC SCRIPT WITH PHONETIC VALUES   166

KERMA POTTERY   167

ROPED JUG   167

BEADED NECKLACE   168

SILVER MIRRORS OF KING NASTASEN   168

GOLD ARM BRACELET   169

MADONNA PROTECTING THE NUBIAN PRINCESS PAINTING OF A FRESCO FROM THE FARAS CATHEDRAL   191

PREFACE

This book is the result of a long quest to find answers to a poem I wrote in the wee hours of the morning of November 28, 1982.

> Ageless I stepped out of the sky
> Touched down into the sea
> Saw my image in the reflection of the sun.
> I was masked in shells to hide my essence
> Until cowries became a measure of exchange.
> One shell I gave for salt
> Another for honey and bread
> Many shells I gave to cover my dead.
> I leaped from cowries to gold in several eons
> Built temples and streets emblazoned in gold
> My totem from Tyre to Timbuktu
> Ages flung me across the seas
> My Diaspora won and diapason sung
> On Beale street in Bahia and Benin.
> Ageless I spun back into the sky
> Touched the moon dust and proclaimed
> I am One!

The intervening years of copious reading, travel in Israel, Egypt and Rome, and classes in Egyptian Art History, did not satisfy all my questions. It was not until my directed studies with Professor Adams at University of Kentucky that I knew my quest had really begun. My assumptions for pursuing and independent study of Nubia's historical and cultural evolution through archaeological and textual evidence were based on the following perceptions:

1. The search of the literature on Nubia and cursory readings indicated that there was a new interest in the reconstruction of Nubian history.

2. I found that the foundation of Nubia and her contributions to the Pharaonic culture and that of the Sudan has been obscured by the complexity of historical and archaeological evidence.

3. Further, comparative analysis or the examination of the cultural stages of development has brought a fresh approach to the understanding of Nubia as a pre-literate society with dynastic dimensions.

Although Nubia's history reaches to the Neolithic age, I have chosen to concentrate on the period between the seventh century B.C. and the fourth century A.D. when Nubians played an important part in the Mediterranean-Red Sea world as Pharaohs of Egypt and Kings of Meroe. Hence, the title "Nubian Pharaohs and Meroitic Kings: The Kingdom of Kush." This to me is a very important endeavor because the rulers are no longer mythical but are historical. When the history books of the twenty-first century are written, Nubia will no longer remain on the periphery of history of ancient civilizations.

Pliny, the ancient Greek historian, said centuries ago that out of Africa comes something new. In our country because of the efforts of the numerous archaeological campaigns and their spectacular results, we can begin to speak of the new disciplines of Nubiology and Meroitics. Just as Herodotus, the father of history presented a new view of Nubian culture and its peoples, Professor Adams presented a new perspective from the result of twenty years work in the Nile valley when he wrote:

> "... to tell the story of Nubia in a new way; as a continuous narrative of development of a single people in which the coming and goings of particular actors have been unimportant. Migrations there have undoubtedly been, but they have been for the most part migrations within Nubia: rearrangements of peoples all drawing on a common experience. Such comings and goings have temporarily disturbed but never I believe, permanently altered the on-going process of cultural evolution.
>
> My point of view differs from many of my colleagues and predecessors in other aspects as well. Students of Nubian history from Budge and Reisner to Emery have been mostly Egyptologists, whose involvement in Nubia has been a by-product of their primary commitment to Egypt and its civilization. It is almost inevitable that they should view Nubian history chiefly as a reflection (usually a pale reflection) of the events and condition in the northern country, and should dwell upon the similarities rather than the differences between Nubia and Egypt. Their attitude may perhaps be justly compared to the typical English view of the Irish." [1]

My own rendition of the cultural, social, political history of Nubia will focus on this single people as actors on the world stage as they act out their destinies in the cradle of civilization. As the Greek and Egyptian poets, priests, scribes and augurs were the portenders of the future and preservers of the past; so too were the modern anthropologists, philologists and men of letters. Janus-like our modern archaeologists can pull back the earth and read and decipher the mysteries that it has held over the millennia. Homer and Virgil, Herodotus, and Strabo were the reputed poets and prophets of the beginning of our historic age, particularly the time capsule that contained the "mysterious Kushites" or Homer's "beloved Ethiopians." Homer, the bard, was the singer of Greek stories of the gods in the sky and of God's men on earth, and Virgil was his Latin counterpart.

The underlying purpose of my book is to reconstruct the collective efforts of the past and present Nubian archaeological campaigns and their collaborative scholarship so that African American as well all Americans can begin to understand the contributions of Nubia to the civilization of Africa and Asia as a continuous historical entity. Amadou Mahtar M'Bow, former Director- General of UNESCO (1974-87), points out:

> "In fact, there was a refusal to see Africans as the creators of original cultures
> which flowered ands survived over the centuries in patterns of their own making
> and which historians are unable to grasp unless they forego their prejudices and
> rethink their approach.

> Furthermore, the continent of Africa was hardly ever looked upon as a
> historical entity. On the contrary, emphasis was laid on everything likely to lend
> credence to the idea that a split had existed, from time immemorial, between
> 'white Africa' and a 'black Africa', each unaware of the other's existence. The
> Sahara was often presented an impenetrable space preventing the intermingling
> of ethnic groups and peoples or any exchange of goods, beliefs, customs, and ideas
> between the societies that had grown upon either side of the desert. Hermetic
> frontiers were drawn between the civilizations of Ancient Nubia and those of the
> people of the Sahara".[2]

The time frame to be highlighted here will be from the early seventh and eight centuries B.C. to the third and fourth centuries A.D. So it is that he tale to be told will be perceived though the eyes of the myth-makers of old who scanned the skies and watched the earth for some sense of order and balance, and the modern archaeologists and scholars who unsealed the mysteries of the muted earth. You will read this book as a play on the words and works of the men of Kush as well as all men who "strut and strive on the stage of life and are no more." It will speak of Nubian struggles with godship and kingship.

Part I, the Prologue, includes Chapters 1-7. Chapter 1 will shed some light on Afrocentrism and Nubian scholarship. Chapter 2 begins with the opening curtain revealing the tapestry of time with its warp and woof of oral tradition, classical tradition, historical tradition and biblical tradition. Chapter 3 will explore the Nubian odyssey through the archaeological adventurers and the gentlemen and gentlewomen explorers of the nineteenth century.

Chapter 4 explores the first salvage campaigns of the twentieth century under Reisner and ends with the campaigns to save the cultural heritage of Nubia that was to be submerged by the building of the Aswan High Dam.

In Chapter 5, you will marvel at the ancient Nubian temples and tombs rooted in the valley of the Nile. Chapter 6 and 7 build on the symbiotic nature of Nubia and the Nile through her geology, topology, and geography. In addition, the ethnography of her people and their contiguous influences are explored.

Part II. The Entr'acte, beginning in Chapter 7, is the interlude that offers the readers time to orient themselves with the chronological framework of the main protagonists, Nubia and Egypt. Their economic, cultural, political, and religious developments are discussed in Chapters 8 and 9.

Part III includes Chapters 10-14 as the drama unfolds through godship, kingship and queenship. The curtain falls in on Part IV as the vestiges of greatness of the Nubian Pharaohs and Meroitic Kings are recounted in Chapter15-16. The Kingdom of Kush is placed within the framework of the Mediterranean Sea world, which included Africa, the Middle East and the Orient.

TABLE OF CONTENTS

ACKNOWLEDGEMENTS   VII
LIST OF ILLUSTRATIONS   IX
PREFACE   XI

I.   PROLOGUE

1. AFROCENTRISM AND NUBIAN SCHOLARSHIP   5
2. ETHIOPIA (NUBIA) AND THE GREAT TRADITIONS   10
3. NUBIAN ODYSSEY AND CONSERVATION   20
4. CAMPAIGNS OF THE TWENTIETH CENTURY   27
5. NUBIAN TEMPLES AND ROYAL TOMBS:
    ANCIENT ROOTS OF THE NILE   38
6. NUBIA AND THE NURTURING NILE   46
7. INVISIBLE NUBIANS MADE VISIBLE   61

II.   ENTR'ACTE

8. EGYPTIAN CHRONOLOGY   70
9. NUBIAN CHRONOLOGY   82

III. GODSHIP, KINGSHIP, AND QUEENSHIP

10. CONCEPTS OF GODSHIP AND KINGSHIP   99
11. GODSHIP: ORIGINS OF THE KINGDOM OF KUSH   113
12. GODSHIP: THE ETHIOPIAN DYNASTY   124
13. KINGSHIP: MEROITIC PHASE - THE LONG DENOUEMENT   136
14. ROYAL TOMBS, CEMETERIES, AND CITIES   151

IV.   FINALE: VESTIGES OF GREATNESS

15. THE RESTORATION OF PHARAONIC GREATNESS   170
16. THE LEGACY OF THE KINGDOMS OF KUSH   182

BIBLIOGRAPHY   197
ENDNOTES   201
INDEX   207

I.

PROLOGUE

"I sing of arms and a man." Virgil

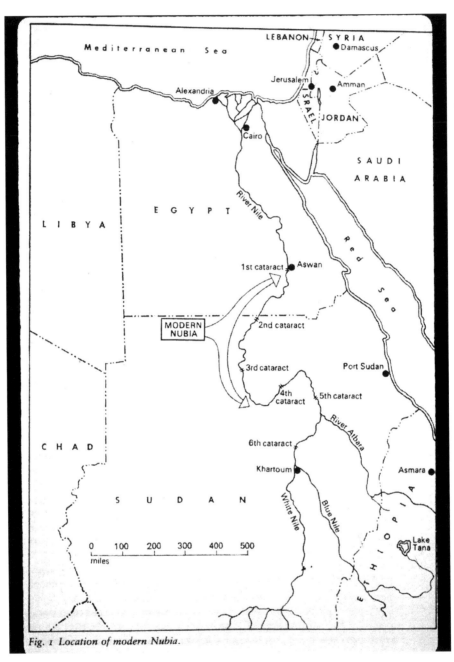

Fig. 1 *Location of modern Nubia.*

LOCATION OF MODERN NUBIA CONTIGUOUS COUNTRIES
AND AREA OF ANCIENT KINGDOM OF KUSH

TEMPLE OF ISIS AT THE ISLAND OF PHILAE

ISIS SUCKLING HER SON HORUS

The Nile at the Second Cataract

The Shaduf, a water-lifting device

CHAPTER 1.
AFROCENTRISM AND NUBIAN SCHOLARSHIP[3]

Afrocentrism is a response to the tradition created by non-Africans that Africa is a continent without history. It was perceived as a land of mystery and barbarism with the potential for exploitation and expansion, derived from the myths and legends about the land of gold. Charles H. Wesley, the noted Black historian, stated that "the history of European expansion in Africa was written and published as African history, and it was assumed that there was no history of any value among black men prior to the arrival of white men".[4] The African American scholars, known as revisionists, have within the last two decades found allies in various fields to confirm their own views that Africa was a cradle of civilization and Egypt was fundamentally African.

Scholarship is a way of articulating and working out some of the issues which one confronts. Because of the culture one lives in, many answers exist between historians, anthropologists, archaeologists, linguists, semanticists, and those in religion and mythology. The approach found in this chapter will focus on African and African American historians, psychologists, mathematicians, scientists, educators, and ethnologists. Nubian scholarship will include Egyptian Nubia, the lower Nile Valley and Sudanese Nubia in the Middle Nile Valley. Afrocentric scholarship includes the Nile Valley culture of Ancient Egypt. The Afrocentric scholars to honor the traditions of "the ancestors" by calling them by their name have substituted the name Kemet for Egypt. Kemet (KMT) is a phonetic rendition of the name that the people called their country....the formal name seems to have been Tawy (The Two Lands) but the commonly used name was Kemet that means the black land along the banks of the Nile River. The people called themselves the Kemites (The Black Ones) [5]

The ferment of African American scholarship on Egypt reached a groundswell in 1984 with two historic conferences. The Black Nationalists convened the First Annual Ancient Egyptian Studies Conference in February 1984, at Los Angeles "to reconstruct and to construct, pose and put in place an African paradigm for both our liberation and ever higher levels of human life."[6] The Nile Valley Conference held on September 26-30, 1984 in Atlanta, Georgia was dedicated to the celebration of the founding of the Morehouse College Chapel. It was also dedicated to Dr. Benjamin Mays who was the president of Morehouse for twenty- seven years. The purpose was to bring into focus the research of the last fifteen years on the Nile Valley "which has changed forever the ideas about who created the Nile Valley civilizations, what they achieved, and the impact they left on Africa and the world...."[7].

THE COLONIAL PERIOD, 1850-1950

The black scholars of this period represent both the Afrocentric and Eurocentric views prevalent during the colonial industrializing period. Martin R. Delaney, the first known black ethnologist, represents both the American and British world view, when he recorded that blacks had no place in the creation of early civilizations. Delaney was a physician, surgeon and practitioner in the diseases of women and children. Delaney was also a member of the International Statistical Congress of London, a member of the social Science Congress of Glasgow, Major in the United States Army and one of the Justices of Charleston, South Carolina. In 1880, he wrote *Principia of Ethnology: The Origin of Races and Color, with A Compendium of Ethiopian and Egyptian Civilization.*

Delaney used the known classical texts of Diodorus, Pliny and others to establish the primacy of the Ethiopian in the creation of civilization, the bible to establish the dispersion of mankind after the flood, and archaeology to confirm biblical beliefs. As for the races and color, Delaney wrote about three pure races and the effects of miscegenation. After extolling the Ethiopians and the Egyptians, he wrote, "the African race should not be adjudged by those portions of the race found out of Africa...The race is a noble one and worthy to emulate the noble Caucasian and Anglo-Saxon.[8]

The Association for the Study of Negro Life and History has been active in the field of research and publication since 1915. W.E.B. Dubois was one of the first black scholars to challenge the view of Africans having no history before the coming of the Europeans to Africa. His book, *The Negro,* published in 1915, was an attempt to outline African history from an African American perspective, which set and early framework for viewing the unity of the African people throughout the Diaspora. Dubois wrote" when Asia overwhelmed by Egypt, Egypt sought refuge in Ethiopia (Nubia) as a child who returns to its mother, and Ethiopia then dominated Egypt and successfully invaded Asia.

Drusilla Dunjee Houston, founder of Mc Alister Seminary in Oklahoma, as a journalist was inspired by Dubois and also her father's extensive library, which she called "dry bones of history". In 1926, she published *Wonderful Ethiopians of the Ancient Kushite Empire, Vol. I* which takes the reader on a glorious pilgrimage beginning with the origin of civilization into ancient Egypt and Ethiopia, establishing linkages among the ancient blacks who inhabited the populations of Arabia, Persia, Babylonia, and India.

William Leo Hansberry taught history at Howard University, one of the leading black colleges for twenty- seven years. During his tenure, he laid the foundation for the systematic study of African culture and peoples. In 1931, Hansberry wrote *Sources for the Study of Ethiopian History. "Ancient Kush, Old Aethiopia, and the Balad es Sudan"* was published in the Journal of Human

Relations, vol. 8, 1960. According to Dr. John Henrike Clarke, retired professor of Black and Puerto Rican Studies at Hunter College, New York, the articles of Professor Hansberry appeared throughout the world in journals and conference papers; but he only published two books: *Africa and Africans Seen by Classical Writers,* 1977 and *Pillars in Ethiopian History,* 1974, Howard University Press.

Since the establishment of the organization for the Study of Negro History in 1915, the Afrocentric view has prevailed. Many of the ideas that were ignited by the radical concepts of the British author, Gerald Massey and E.A. Budge, the Egyptologist helped to reverse the trend of European scholarship. Massey's basic premise was Africa was the source of the world's people, languages, religion, and myths and Egypt was Africa's mouthpiece. Budge through his research reached the conclusion that Egypt could only be understood by references to its African underlay. The research of Reisner also encouraged African and African American scholarship.

THE PERIOD OF TRANSITION: 1950-60

The period represents the movement for liberation and independence both in Africa and America. Following World War II, the need to understand the national movements and the resumption of Archaeological activities in Nubia created new interests on the part of European scholars as well as African American and African scholars. In 1952, Thomas Hodgkin, a fellow at Balliol College, Oxford, stated that it was unfortunate that most of the history was presented from a European point of view and that we must begin to "rid our minds of those preoccupations that influence our thinking on the subject". He further stated, "We shall probably have to wait a little while for the history of Africa to be written by African scholars for an African reading public.[9]

According to many African scholars, revising their histories became even more important in establishing nationhood. African scholars expanded their work on the prehistory of Egypt and Ethiopia based on the report by Dr. Leaky to the Pan African Congress of prehistory in 1959, which reinforced the ideas of origin of civilization in Africa. During this period an obscure Senegalese scholar who had been studying in Paris to become a physicist, began studying Egyptology, linguistics, anthropology and other related subjects, which would later make him a leader in a new field of African Historiography. In the Period of Liberation, this scholar became world renown as Cheikh Anta Diop 'the high priest of New Wave Egyptology' and Afrocentrism.

African American scholarship on Nubia did not emerge until the 'hot summers' cooled after the sixties. The Soviet scholars had already begun to engage in research in Africa to further the Cold War objective and to refute the imperialist propaganda that had always maintained that

African had no history of their own. The first known work in this regard was presented in 1956 at the USSR Academy's Institute of Ethnography.

POST-COLONIAL PERIOD (PERIOD OF LIBERATION) 1960-1990

The Post-Colonial period was one of intense struggle for civil rights by the African American in America and the political independence for many Africans for many African countries on the African continents. In both instances, the search for historical identity by African and African American scholars was critical. Cheikh Anta Diop wrote *The Origin of Civilization: Myth or Reality* in French. It was published in 1974 in English. Diop died in his sleep in 1986.

Martin Bernal, originally in the field of Chinese history, wrote *Black Athena: the Afro-Asiatic of Classical History* in 1987. The same year, Basil Davidson, well known friend, and contemporary of Diop wrote, "It is a profoundly liberating work because it sheers away the murk of racism and is a major attempt to help old history back upon its feet again."[10] *Nubia: Corridor to Africa,* written by W.Y. Adams in 1977 and reprinted in 1984, is a classic study of Nubia and synthesis of the twentieth century archaeological campaigns in Nubia. This work represents the first Nubiocentric view as opposed to the Eurocentric Egyptologists in the field.[11] Bruce Williams, Oriental Institutive, University of Chicago, added some recent research in the Sudan in his 1980 article on "*The Lost Pharaohs of Nubia*". The information that Williams advances is nothing new since black writers have presenting the same view, even more extensively, in the *Destruction of Black Civilizations (Williams, 1976)* and *Introduction to Africa Civilizations,* Jackson, 1980.[12] In essence William states:

> ". . . people in Nubia (sometimes called Kush) had an advanced political organization hundreds of years before the first dynasty of Egypt. What we think of as Egyptian civilization may have moved from the south to north, a concept which is contrary to current thinking on the subject."[13]

According to an article written by Felicity Barringer entitled "Africa's Claim to *Egypt's History Grows More Persistent*" a new generation of Egyptologists "has been increasingly willing to view ancient Egyptian civilization as rooted in Africa instead of the Middle East."[14] Based on the abundance of research on the Nile Valley Civilization, the revisionist view has been presented by a number of black scholars over the past two decades. Frank B. Snowden, Jr. would be considered anachronistic by the revisionists because of his views. As professor emeritus, Department of Classics at Howard University, his career has spanned over fifty -four years since his graduation from Harvard University. During the career of Dr. Snowden, he has explored two worlds, but still clings to his view of color-blindness:

"One existed, as he has shown [in his writing], Before Color Prejudice and "From the Pharaohs to the Fall of The Roman Empire" in The Image of The Black in Literature and Art, which was clearly one of difference without discrimination, where color did not keep a people from being 'counted in'. The other world is our own, marred by an 'acute color consciousness' not found in antiquity nor warranted by reason or revelation."[15]

Papers of the revisionists have been published by Malauna Karanga and Jacob Carruthers in *African World View: Research, Rescue and Restoration,* which represent selected papers of the proceedings of the First and Second Conferences of The Association for the Study of Classical African Civilizations. Governance, history, spirituality, and philosophy and creative production are addressed. Papers are similarly addressed in the publication of the proceedings of the Conference on Nile Valley Civilizations edited by Ivan Van Sertima, editor of the Journal of African Civilizations. This could be the beginning for the establishment of the twin disciplines of Nubiology and Meroitics in American Universities, as it is in some of the European institutions, which could reflect scholarly arguments for a black heritage and the resolution of the debates regarding the ancient views of Egypt.

CHAPTER 2.
ETHIOPIA (NUBIA) AND THE GREAT TRADITIONS

The name of Ethiopia for the modern mind evokes the images of a distant place of famine, distress, and death. It was not so for the peoples of the Mediterranean and Red Sea. They remembered and recounted tales of the noble Ethiopian traditions. The Aethiopes were the first mentioned in the great epic poems of Homer. He described them as the furthest of humanity. Herodotus wrote that the gods attended the banquets in their lands and the sun probably sets in their country.

The distant land of the Ethiopians was an enigmatic land in the minds of all ancient peoples. It was thought to have its beginnings with the creation of the universe. It extended south of Egypt and the Mediterranean basin, far to the east and west, to the ends of the earth, to Arabia, even to India. The Ethiopians gave the doctrine of astrology to all mankind, and their reputation and wisdom was great, being in all else wiser than other men.[16]

THE ORAL TRADITION

The noble tradition of Ethiopia was spread throughout the ancient world by travelers, warriors, sailors, priests, poets and the oracles. The rumors, tales, and legends became the oral corpus of Ethiopian myth and reality. Robert Graves states that "true myth may be defined as the reduction to narrative short-hand of the ritual performed in public festivals and in many cases as recorded on temple walls, vases, seals, bowls, mirrors, chests, shields, tapestries, and the like."[17] The religion, history and drama of the people cannot be understood without its myths that are now our classics, beginning with Virgil and Homer. These myths of over two thousand years accretion have been dismissed as fairy tales of super-mortal and extra-human men. They were fabricated through necessity by fanciful minds to glorify the heroes and gods of a transcendent time.

THE CLASSICAL TRADITION

The Graeco- Roman Mediterranean world has been celebrated over two thousand years through the epic works of the *Iliad* and the *Odyssey* that were based on historical events which occurs about 1250 B.C. Homer composed the Iliad about 750B.C., approximately the time when the Ethiopian (Nubian) Pharaohs were in ascendancy and ruled Egypt. Common tradition states that Homer was the son of Maon, and that in his old age he was blind and poor.

As an Asiatic Greek, Homer enjoyed all the acclaim of a bard, member of a semi-religious craft and served as apprentice in his youth.[18] His poems formed the basis of Greek literature. Single authorship was disputed through the ages. However, it is acknowledged that he was the synthesizer of his time, just as the musical genius of Bach enabled him to bring together the lore of his age that has never been surpassed. Homer's birthplace and date were always matters of dispute. No less than seven cities claimed this ancient bard as a citizen. [19] The epics of Homer, particularly the *Iliad*, have been celebrated as the first literary works of Western Civilization as well as a document of the history of man.

Virgil, the first Latin poet, added to the Homeric corpus with his poem, *Aeneid* that was based on Homer's Aeneas. It is in the Latin Aeneid that the sweeping adventures and the glories of the Trojan War come alive through its hero Aeneas. Aeneas was chosen by Jupiter to found a new race, which was to become the Romans.[20]

Virgil begins the *Aeneid* with "Arma verumque cano" (I sing of arms and a man). Aeneas is everyman speaking for all men of all times, singing of arms, heroes and gods, and the divinity that is the birthright of mankind. Those words still ring clear in my ears from my high school Latin class. My father piqued my interest and curiosity as he filled in the unexplained lines of my translation. I learned first-hand about Virgil's tribute to the Ethiopians who had given aid to Rome's ancestors in the Trojan War. Aside from the mythological elements in the *Iliad*, Virgil's sources were historical. Graves asserted: The Trojan War is historical, and whatever the immediate cause may have been it was a trade war. Troy controlled the valuable Black sea trade in gold, silver, iron, cinnabar, ship's timber, dried fish, oil and Chinese jade. [21]

Carthage was a rival power of Rome until it was sacked by Rome in the third Punic war in 146 B.C. Queen Dido from Tyre founded this seaport town on the north shore of Africa. When Aeneas arrived on the shores of Carthage, he was astounded at the grandeur and opulence of the city. The enormous temple of Queen Dido overwhelmed him as he walked up the bronze steps and crossed the bronze inlaid threshold. Entering the bronze creaking doors, Aeneas marveled at the skill of the Queen's craftsmen:

> "He saw a mural of the Trojan War...
> All its battles in order (so world -renowned
> Become already). There were the Astridae
> And Priam, and their mutual for Achilles...
> He spoke and sighed and pored on the inert picture.
> Tears coursing down his cheeks, reliving the whole scene
> In the depth of his soul. They were back in the thick
> Of the fight round Pergamus, and the Greeks were flying,
> The Trojans hot on their heels. There were the Phrygians

And, hunting them, Achilles in his chariot

His tall crest waving…

There was the battle-line of the Orient

And the standard of swarthy Memnon,

Fire-eating Penthesilea

Was leading her Amazons, with their moonlike shields,

In frenzy among her thousands, her naked breast

Clasped in a golden circle, a war- queen

A maiden against men, and keyed for combat.[22]

In the fourth century, Quintus of Smyrna wrote of the glorious exploits of Memnon and his black Ethiopian soldiers at Troy. They killed many Greeks, arriving in time to help the beleaguered Trojans who nearly succeeded in burning the Greeks ships. Who was this Memnon who had the distinction to be the first black hero to be mentioned in Greek literature?

A Classical Dictionary written for students in 1885 offers the following citation on Memnon:

> "The beautiful son of Tithonus and Eros, was the king of the Ethiopians, and came to the assistance of Priam towards the end of the Trojan War. He wore armor made by Hephaestus at the request of his mother. He slew Antilochus, the son of Hector, but was himself slain by Achilles after a long fierce combat. While the two heroes were fighting, Zeus (Jupiter) weighed their fates, and the scale containing Memnon's sank. To soothe the grief of his mother, Zeus conferred immortality upon Memnon, and caused a number of birds to issue out of the funeral pile, which fought over the ashes of the hero. These birds were called Memnonides, and were said to have visited the tomb of the hero on the Hellespont. The Greeks gave the name the Memnonium to certain ancient buildings or mountains in Europe and Asia, which they supposed to be erected by or in honor of Memnon.
>
> Of these the most celebrated was a great temple of Thebes (present-day Luxor), which was behind a colossal statue (called the statue of Memnon) which when struck by the first rays of sun, was said to give forth a sound like the snapping asunder of a chord. It appears, however that the statue represented in reality the Egyptian King Amenophis.[23]

According to the historian Diodorus, the Egyptians who lived on the border of Egypt maintained that Memnon was a native of their country.

To ignore Quintus in telling the story of the Trojan War was to leave a gap in our knowledge about the denouement of the Trojan War and the achievements of the Greeks, Trojans and the Ethiopians after the defeat of Troy. The poem Quintus is the only surviving link describing what took place between the death of hector and the departure of the Greeks and Ethiopians from Troy. The fact that copies of his works survived the collapse of the ancient world and found persistent readers throughout the Middle Ages and into the Renaissance is proof that there was a need for his work as a commentary on Homer and his works.

The purpose of the poem is expressed in the title "The War on Troy: What Homer Didn't Tell". In his poem, the speech of the characters is so vivid that it allows one to see into the soul and psyche of the characters. In Book Two of the poem, "The Arrival, Deeds, and Death of Memnon", the Trojan soldiers are grief-stricken over the turn of events of the war. The Greek soldiers are reveling over the victories of Achilles. Penthesilea, the Amazon queen and a strong ally of the Trojans are painfully awaiting the arrival of their other ally, Memnon, the King of Ethiopians. Priam, the King of Troy, pleads with his men:

> "My friends, let us not, because of some fear,
> withdraw from our country, nor continue to
> fight the enemy at a distant from the city, but fight
> From the towers and the wall, until strong-spirited
> Memnon comes bringing the countless tribes of
> His peoples who live in Ethiopia, land of the Black
> Men. I really think that by now he is close to our
> Land, since not at all recently, I sent him a message
> in the great distress of my heart. He gladly promised
> that he would come to Troy and do everything I asked.
> I am confident that he is close. Come, endure for a little
> Longer, because it is better to die bravely in battle than
> To run away and live in disgrace among foreigners."[24]

Not long after that Memnon arrived bringing courage and hope to the Trojans. Their greatest hope was that the Ethiopian legions would burn the Greek ships in the harbor. Memnon was overwhelmed with the gifts of gratitude for his arrival and the restoration of hope, which had almost vanished. The Trojans and the Ethiopians conversed about Memnon's conquests along the journey to Troy; they feasted and toasted the gods for their good fortune. Priam held high a huge goblet, as he pledged his friendship to Memnon. As the golden goblet was passed to Memnon, Memnon said:

"a feast is no place for great boasting or for making
promises, but for feasting at one's ease in the halls
and acting to suit the occasion. Whether or not I am
Still brave and strong, you will learn in battle, where
a man's wrath is seen. For the present let us think of
rest and not go on drinking all night long. Unlimited
wine and wretched lack of sleep are a handicap for
A man who is in a hurry to fight. "[25]

THE HISTORICAL TRADITION

Whether it is legend or demi-truth, the Ethiopian side of the story remained buried in the sand until the nineteenth and twentieth centuries. It remained for the historians, archaeologists, and ethnologists to piece the legends together for posterity as a part of the Graeco-Roman Mediterranean mosaic that is called the history of western man. The Ethiopian or Kushite historical reality had its begging when the Napatan Pharaohs became the rulers of Egypt as the XXVth Dynasty.

Herodotus, the Father of History, lived, traveled and wrote about three hundred years after Homer. His travels took him throughout Greece, the northern part of Europe, Asia Minor, Babylonia and Arabia. Herodotus earned the epithet, father of history, when he wrote *The History of the Persian Wars*, not only did he visit Egypt, he went as far as Elephantine (Aswan), which he described as the frontier between Egypt and Ethiopia. By this he meant the Meroitic state known to the Egyptians as Kush. As a result of his travels and observations, Herodotus wrote a complete book on Egypt. While at Aswan, Herodotus gained knowledge from the Meroites and was the first to mention Meroe by name. Earlier writers had used the term "land of the burnt faces". The geographical knowledge of Herodotus was fairly accurate. He described the winding Nile and the necessity for landing at the Fourth Cataract and traveling forty days along the riverbank because of the huge boulders which made river travel almost impossible. Beyond, it was twelve days more to Meroe which was called the capital of the Ethiopians. The capital of Meroe was acclaimed by Herodotus as a great city frequently visited by the gods, Zeus (Amun) and Dionysius (Osisris). The Greeks equated their own gods with those of the Ethiopians whom they thought were the first of humanity.[26]

Meroe became a legend to the peoples and the kings of the southern Mediterranean basin after they became familiar with the temples and the Table of the Sun. The table was described as being in a meadow on the outskirts of Meroe. The magistrates always kept the meadow filled with huge quantities of meat so that very one who came there could eat during the day. It appears that the site was dedicated to the worship of the sun. The wonders of this far -off place caused the Persian King Cambyses, after his conquest of Egypt, to attempt a military reconnaissance into Kush which was unsuccessful.[27]

Diodorus Siculus appeared on the scene of Greek historians approximately four hundred years after the death of Herodotus. He lived in the first century after the birth of Christ, and was a contemporary of Julius Caesar. The travels of Siculus were also extensive, but he only mentioned Egypt and Rome especially. The literate Greeks of his day were indebted to Diodorus for his history of Egypt. When Diodorus was writing the history of Egypt, her history was considered a thing of the past. Egypt's earlier past was more remote to Diodorus than the time of Diodorus is to us. His history covered the period from the beginning of civilization to the conquest of Egypt by Alexander the Great in 332 B.C. Those of us approaching the twenty-first century should also be indebted to Diodorus because he was a prolific and scholarly writer. What has been preserved of ancient history has been credited to Diodorus more than any other writer. He spent thirty years compiling all the historical knowledge in the ancient world. Of the forty books, called his *Library of History,* only the first five books XI-XX are preserved. However, fragments of the twenty- five books have been preserved in the writings of other authors. Diodorus is an invaluable source on the history of Egypt and Ethiopia. What does he say about the Ethiopians?

> "Now the Ethiopians, as historians relate, were the first of all men and proofs of the statement are manifest. For they did not come into their country as immigrants from abroad but were the natives of it and so justly bear the name of Autochone...They that dwell beneath the noonday sun were in all likelihood the first to be generated by the earth... it is reasonable to suppose that the region which was nearest was the first to bring forth living creatures. And they say that they were taught to honor the gods and to hold sacrifices and processions and festivals and other rites by which man honors the deity: and that in consequences their piety was published abroad among all men... they state by reason of their piety towards the deity they manifestly enjoy the favor of the gods, inasmuch as they have never experienced rule of an invader from; for from all time they have enjoyed a state of freedom abroad and peace with the other and though many powerful rulers have made war upon them, not one of them succeeded in this undertaking."[28]

Strabo, the geographer, lived during the whole reign or the Roman emperor, Augustus Caesar, and during the earliest part of the reign of Tiberius, and the reigns of Meroitic Queens Anaishakete and Amanitere and King Natakamani. Strabo was born in Anasia in Asia Minor, although his exact birthdate is unknown. Possibly, it could be placed about 54 B.C., as his death occurred about 24 A.D. Strabo wrote his *Geography* in seventeen books of which the seventh is lost. By his own admission, the *Geography* was written for those who had a good education and those in higher administration particularly. Strabo placed the boundaries of Egypt and Ethiopia (Nubia) beginning from the little cataract above Syene and Elephantine (known today as the First Cataract). He described Meroe as a rather large island enclosed by two rivers, referring to the confluence of the Atbara and the Nile. The city of Meroe, which was named after the island, was placed above the confluence of the Niles. According to Strabo, the island had numerous mountains and large thickets, partly inhabited by nomads and farmers. There are mines of copper, iron, and gold of different kinds.[29]

THE BIBLICAL TRADITION

The human impulse to awe, to wonder, and to seek control of one's destiny has been present since the beginning of time. It was crystallized in the Mediterranean world by the peoples of the Holy Land, from whose mystical, prophetic, and spiritual urges sprang from three of the world's greatest religions. The civilization of the ancient world cannot be understood without some reference to the Holy Bible as well as the Dead Sea Scrolls and the Nag Hammadi Library. Therefore the biblical tradition herein discussed will include those texts that elucidate the role of the Ethiopians or Kushites in the Biblical lands.

In the Creation Story of the Book of Genesis 2:13, the author mentions a river flowing from Eden that is divided into four streams. The second river refers to the Nile. This is the first mention of Kush in the Old Testament. The first Ethiopians who were mentioned in the bible were from the land of Kush (Cush), which according to the biblical tradition was a territory on the Upper Nile, south of Egypt; it was also later known as Nubia. Kush is the name of the eldest son of Noah and the territory inhabited by his descendants. The Kushites are the descendants of Noah who produced the sons: Shem, Ham, and Japhet, each with their own language, clan, and nation. According to Gen. 9:18, the three sons peopled the rest of the earth, which was indicative of the unity of humanity in the ancient mind. Ham's son, Cush, went to Ethiopia; his son, Mizraim, went to Egypt; Canaan went to Canaan; Phut (Pwnt) went to Punt, which in Egyptian records, the fabulous land on the East coast of Africa, source of myrrh (which included present-day Somaliland, perhaps also Arabia. You may refer to Chapter ten of Genesis, also known as the Table of Nations for the continuation of Noah's genealogy.

The Nag Hammadi Library is a collection of religious texts written by early Christians, known as Gnostics, who were excluded from the church as heretics. It is an invaluable source of Coptic lore, buried since 400AD in Nag Hammadi near Luxor in Egypt and discovered in 1945. The

Apocalypse of Adam (v.5), one of the Nag Hammadi tracts cast a new light in the treatment of the flood biblical genealogy.

> "And God will say to Noah- whom all generations will call Deucalon-
> Behold I have protected you in the ark. Therefore I will give the earth to you and your son."
> "Then Noah will divide the whole earth among his sons Ham and Japhet and Shem. He will then say to them, "My sons listen to my words. I have divided the earth among you. But serve Him with all the days of your life. Let not your seed depart from the face of the Almighty."
> "Then others from the seed of Ham and Japhet will come
> Four thousand men, and enter another land and sojourn with those who come from the eternal knowledge. Then the seed of Ham and Japhet will form twelve kingdoms of another people."[30]

There is no reference to slavery to the Canaanites in this version. It is in total opposition to that of the Christian version that has condemned generations of Ham's descendants, even today, to be a slave to the Canaanites.

Egyptian military conquests against Assyria and Israel, aided by Ethiopians are recorded in the Books of Kings, Acts, and the Chronicles. Mention is made of an Ethiopian army assisting Shishak (Sheshonk) who ruled Egypt during the reign of Rehoboam, the King of Judah and the Son of Solomon. Shishak's army swept across the land of Judah, with twelve hundred chariots and sixty thousand men, leaving in his wake fire and destruction. The people of Lubim and Sukkim, and the Ethiopians are further described as a host with many horses and chariots. Subduing the Judeans in the south, Shishak continued north to Jerusalem, taking away the treasures of the king which included all of the gold shields which Solomon had made.[31]

The Ethiopian general, Zerah did not fare as well when he went up against King Asa of Judah, who had destroyed the idolatry of the former Judean kings and was reigning in peace. Although Zerah "had an army of men that bear targets and spears, out of Judah three hundred thousand, and out of Benjamin, that bare shields and drew bows, two hundred and fourscore thousand, all these were men of valor."[32]

The strength of the Ethiopians or Kushites was detested to such a great degree, the prophet Isaiah, an agent of Yahweh (God), issued a proclamation to all:

> Disaster! Land of the whirring locust
> beyond the rivers of Cush,
> who send ambassadors by sea,
> in little reed- boats across the waters!

to a nation tall and bronzed,

a mighty and masterful nation.[33]

The wealth of Egypt and the commerce of Ethiopia is extolled by Isaiah and the gold and topaz of Ethiopia is recorded in Job and Psalms. The first Ethiopian king to be mentioned in the Biblical tradition was Tirhaka, the fifth of the Ethiopian rulers of Egypt, called Taharqa in the Meroitic text. Taharqa, like Memnon, was called upon to lend military assistance to a beleaguered nation. When the Philistines revolted in 70 B.C. and Hezekiah, the king of Judah, joined the rebellion, the people of Enron called on Egypt and Ethiopia for help against the king of Assyria, Sennecherib, they were repulsed by the Assyrians. The practicality of the request was questioned by Sennecherib, who had sent envoys to avert the rebellion. The envoys asked Hezekiah who had consulted him to rely on Ethiopian and Egyptian assistance in rebelling against the house of Assyria. He was also warned "Now behold thou trusted upon a staff of the bruised reed, even upon Egypt, on which if a man lean it will go into his hand and pierce it...[34]

The kings called "Lions of Judah", the Ethiopian (Abyssinian) dynasty centered at Axum are also rooted in biblical history. His Holiness Abuna Phillipos, Archbishop of the Ethiopian Orthodox Church, gives the following citations for their biblical linkage and the fame of their proud emperor and kings of Ethiopia (Abyssinia):

1. Ethiopians should be proud of her dual relations with Jerusalem both material and spiritual and this glorious king is the majesty of her wise and knowledgeable emperors.

2. The source of the wisdom is God and not the cleverness of man. To this effect, "Ethiopia stretches her arm to God" which prophesy was only confirmed by the visit of the Queen of Sheba to Solomon.

3. We are told in the Old Testament when the Queen of Sheba heard of the fame of Solomon concerning the name of the lord; she came to him with questions. Kings 10:11 The queen, who was a virgin and pure, learning about the history of the world, heard of Solomon's wisdom and was curious to see what she had heard about, set on a long journey from Axum to Jerusalem, in those days when land and sea were not controlled by easy transportation. She proved his wisdom both material and spiritual.

4. And God gave her what she desired... and this gift was a conception of Menelik I, the son of Solomon who is from the tribe of Judah, the descendant of Abraham, and this Menelik was to rule after her, hence the motto "The conquering Lion of the Tribes of Judah" which motto is the basis of the country's faith and key to their ancestry. I Kings 10:1-13

5. We are told in the New Testament that our Lord ...has praised her journey she made to hear the Wisdom of Solomon. Luke 11: 13.

6. The history made at the reign of Queen Candace, after the birth of Christ is also one in which Ethiopia takes pride. [35]

The first Ethiopian to be baptized about 37 A.D. was a high official of the royal palace of Meroe. Phillip, the Deacon, encountered him on his return from Jerusalem on official business for the Queen of Ethiopia. At the time he was in his chariot a reading the Greek text of Isaiah, after receiving instructions from Philip he was baptized. Origen, an early African church father, discloses in his writing (250 A.D.) that upon his return of the treasurer to his country, he became the first evangel of Ethiopia. The biblical account of his conversion is recorded in the Acts of the Apostles. He is described as a eunuch and an officer of the Kandake (Candace), or Queen of Ethiopia and was in fact her chief treasurer. Acts 8: 26-36.

Dear Father Vantini, an authority on Nubian Christianity makes the following points about the scripture:

1. Kandake, the Queen of Ethiopia, was in fact, the queen of Meroe/Kabushiya. There are documents that confirm the title-Kandake- which was peculiar to the Queens of the Meroitic kingdom.

2. The eunuch had become familiar with Judaism probably on journeys to Jerusalem. It is worth mentioning that a large Jewish colony was to be found on the island of Elephantine, opposite Aswan.

3. Finally, the eunuch knew the Greek language well for he was reading the Greek text of Isaiah, and the deacon who explained the scripture spoke to him in Greek. This is proof that the Greek language had spread to Nubia among the elite.[36]

CHAPTER 3.
NUBIAN ODYSSEY AND CONSERVATION

ARCHAEOLOGICAL ADVENTURERS OF THE NINETEENTH CENTURY

The Nubian odyssey or fascination with Nubia and its place in history is as old as the world itself. The curiosity of mankind, especially the Greeks and Romans was sparked by the writings of Herodotus, Hecataeus, and Homer when they described the exotic lands Egypt and Nubia. Did not Homer refer to Nubia as the remotest of nations, the most favorite of the Gods and Herodotus call Egypt the Gift of the Nile?

Egypt because of her proximity and her symbiotic relationship with the Nubians knew of gold, glories, and government. It took, however, the spread of myths, legends and travels of the men and women of the Mediterranean and the east to cast the spell that led to the search for the source of life and the fountain- head of the gods and civilization itself. It is the eternal quest as the men and women of the new world are still involved with the mysteries of Nubia and Egypt the lands of the Pharaohs and Kush.

Knowledge of Nubia and Egypt was destined to remain in the hands of the Islamic scholars, travelers, and the Christian monks of Egypt. When the Americas were discovered in the late fifteenth century and the courts of Europe were vying for power in the new world, Nubia and Egypt were still a mysterious pagan world. Their realities were still locked in the ancient lore and tradition of Herodotus and Diodorus Siculus. It was not until the nineteenth century that Islamic scholars were discovered and their geographies and histories of Nubia were translated for European consumption.[37]

The earliest journey of the whole length of Nubia was undertaken by Evliya Celebi, an Ottoman official in 1672-73, prior to this the interest in Egypt on the part of wealthy visitors was fixated on mummies and their medicinal and metaphysical qualities.[38] Gordon Waterfield reports that "as early as 1586, John Sanderson, a member of the Levant Company, visited Egypt and shipped to England five hundred weight of mummy fragments of the to the London Apothecaries."[39] The Arabs sold "mummy powder" mixed with butter as a medicine, supposedly, to cure internal and external ulcers. Sanderson is credited with the discovery of a mummy pit at Memphis. Mummy pit consist of tombs cut back into the rock cliff-filled with embalmed bodies.

Maurice Poncet, doctor of medicine, describes his journey to the 'Land of Kush' in *Voyage to Ethiopia in 1678-1700*.[40] Since his voyage on behalf of The Ethiopian (Abyssinian) court, little knowledge has been gained about Nubia and the Egyptian Sudan. However, in the next few years, journeys were intensified by the Portuguese missionaries, French and German Franciscans. The lures were the converts, a better route to the Red sea, and the treasures of China and India.

The English churchman, Richard Pococke, later to become Bishop of Heath, was to leave a legacy of the first drawings and detailed descriptions of the treasures and monuments of Luxor and Thebes. He published plans for the royal tombs and wrote of the beauty of the frescoes within the tombs. His illustrations predated the illustrious J. L. Burckhardt by seventy-five years. The greatest omission was his failure to describe the famed temple of Queen Hatshepsut that he visited at Deir el Bahri, in the valley of the Queens, during travels in 1737-38.[41]

The Danish Sea captain, Frederick Norden, was to penetrate Nubia just short of Abu Simbel. It was his desire to be the first European to sail beyond Egypt and locate the land of Kush. This wish was thwarted by a native ship owner, who would not go beyond Derr, because of the dangers to life, limb and purse at the hands of the natives and unscrupulous officials. The description of his voyage on behalf of H.M. Christian VI of Denmark in 1737 filled two folio volumes of the plates of antiquities from Aswan to Philae.[42]

James Bruce of Scotland was one of the earliest to visit Meroe where the ancient kingdom of Kush flourished but in his press to find the source of the Nile, he only noted the ancient capital in passing. Bruce represented a world of "the ancestral arm as and the entailed estate, the classical education and the emphasis on manners, the patronage and violent prejudices". He was a formidable horseman and marksman of six foot four inches in height, with a red mane of hair and a loud arrogant voice which stood him well as a gentleman adventurer in his search of the source for the Blue Nile.[43]

Bruce would both repulse and reward the London public who did not understand that rings, according to his custom, belonged in their ears or on their fingers instead of their lips. The raw meat eaters with their blood and honey tonics were a bit overdrawn for genteel tastes. Yet his obsession with becoming the discoverer of the source of the Blue Nile enabled him to leave a legacy of a man who in his vanity discredited other travelers before him and to claim drawings of his travels which he presented to George III as his own. To Burckhardt's credit must remain the fact that he did guess accurately the site of the ancient city of Meroe as he passed it outside of Shendi.

Of interest to those students of the Sudan is Bruce's account of his visit to the queen of the province of Shendi. According to Alan Morehead, Bruce described a beautiful woman of forty, dressed in a purple stole, with hair plaited to her waist, wearing a magnificent crown of gold. Bruce felt that she was "a living reincarnation of the legendary Queen Candace who ruled Meroe and all the Nile North to Egypt in Pharaonic times." [44]

Bruce traveled the route of Norden and Popcocke from Cairo to Aswan and even more tortuous routes to Ethiopia by way of the Red Sea and Jedda, constantly beset by piracy, war, slavery and court intrigue. He found that "Man is the same creature everywhere, although different in colour. The Court of London and that of Abyssinia are in their principles the same." Bruce retired to the continent in 1173 very worn and became embittered after London's reaction to his accounts. The dear Bruce was perceived as a comedic figure given to vainglory and a wild imagination. The French regaled him and followed his accounts with serious interest. He retired to his laird in Scotland and lived as a rich man while indulging his passion as an explorer and writing his memoirs *Travels to Discover the Sources of the Nile in the Years 1768, 1769, 1771, 1772, and 1773,* was dedicated to George III.

It was to become the task of the nineteenth century savants, sailors, and adventurers to further rend the veil that obscured Egypt from European minds. Notwithstanding the zeal of the churchman and the intrepid courage of the agents of the kings and commerce, the sword was mightier than the cross, and guns and mortar a swifter chronicler. It took Napoleon's vision of glory and his 1798 campaign to usher in the age of serious Egyptology.

Napoleon landed on Egyptian soil with a literal institute of modern achievement that included artists, scholars, architects as well as men skilled in artillery and the art of siege. As Napoleon stood before the Sphinx whose silence for centuries stunned and mystified all, his own silence was penetrated as he recalled the notes in his copybook on Raynal and thirty years later they were still indelibly imprinted on his heart.

"In view of the position of Egypt, lying betwixt two seas, second in fact, betwixt the east and the west, Alexander the Great conceived the design of establishing his world-wide vision in that country and making Egypt the center of world -wide commerce. This most enlightened of conquerors had realized that if there was any practicable way of amalgamating his conquests into one consolidated state, it was by use of Egypt, created as a point of union between Africa, Asia, and Europe."[45] Napoleon's sojourn in the land of the Pharaohs was short-lived. Horatio Nelson, commander of the British army, followed quickly, upon the heels of Napoleon, the Egyptian conqueror. Nelson destroyed the French fleet and was rewarded with the title of Viscount Nelson of the Nile. The legacy of Napoleon was to open the door to the savants and adventurers of Europe who began to pierce the darkness of the Nile valley.

The regions of the Nile became an open history book in the early nineteenth as the modern scribes and adventurers began their odyssey. Burckhardt, Caillaiud, and Hoskins were the first to visit Nubia, to record detailed and perceptive accounts of the people and their culture. This was the fist time that Nubia and the Sudan were differentiated.

In 1842-44, Richard Lepsius wrote history detailing Egyptian and Nubian antiquities in twelve volumes. Less than thirty years after Champollion had pierced the mystery of the Rosetta stone and made hieroglyphics readable. Florence Nightingale made a visit to Egypt in 1849. We call her an incurable romantic, daughter of her age, victim of that veiled romanticism which fused her vision of the Arabian nights, her Episcopalian version of Christianity and service to mankind.

Florence was twenty-nine years of age, single and wealthy at the time of her visit. She had yet to become Florence Nightingale of the Crimean war. As a prolific letter writer, we are privy to her personal insights in descriptive prose which were edited and privately published by her sister, Parthenope, in 1854. [46]

In this era before serious travel and paucity of information, Miss Nightingale consulted all the known authorities, before and during her travels. She actually carried thirty volumes of books with her. As an enlightened Victorian scholar, she read the discoveries of Belzoni, Budge, Champollion, Lepsius and other popular books, which reinforced the Graeco- Roman traditions. Even the earlier drawings became Hellenized and lost much of their Egyptian character. Excerpts from her book reflect the thought and habits of modern Europe. [47]

November 19th 1849, Florence penned her first letter from Alexandria:

> "Yes my Dear people, I have set my first footfall in the east, and oh!
> I could tell you the new world of the old poetry, of Bible images, of
> light and life, and beauty, which that word opens. My first day in the
> East, and it has been one of the most striking I am sure, -one I can never
> forget through eternity".

Florence's journey, of more than three months, was 750 miles by boat from Cairo to Abu Simbel. She avoided society and at Thebes she wrote:

> "It is hard to talk by day by the death bed of the greatest race
> and come night at night and talk about quails or London."

About spoils and trinkets which she called rubbish:

> "As for the Egyptian things, unless you carry away
> Memnon's head, like Belzoni I don't know that
> there is anything to be had."

About people in Alexandria:

> "I wish I could describe groups in the Armenian garden, a little triangle of
> children at the gate, eating their dinner out of the porringer of beans, not gobbling
> or messing as European children do, but like little gods with infant dignity slowly
> and majestically dipping their sop in the dish and conversing. On a magnificent,
> broad-shouldered boy of four, resting his little paw upon his knee, with a loose
> shirt on, looking up at us undisturbed, with an attitude like an Apollo at rest;
> another, a little coquette. She the airs of a Juno; and a third, a thing of eighteen,

with his leg stuck straight out, and quite stately as the other two. We do wish for P. to draw it.

Then this group on the well, three Egyptian ladies, in their black silk mantles, which shrouded tem entirely, except the white mantle in front which hangs from their foreheads, only letting their eyes be seen, a tall graceful Nubian behind, entirely robed and shrouded in white, who is not so particular

about her black face..."

At Asyoot, capital of Upper Egypt:

"... looking like the sort of city animal might of built, when they had the possession of the earth as we are told, before man was created, -a collection of mud heaps, except where its thirteen minarets cut the sky. I had read Mungo Park's descriptions of an African village and Bruce's, and had fancied I had understood them, but no description gives the idea of debasement and misery. It is good for man to be here as a nation more powerful than we are, and almost as civilized, 4000 years ago, -for 2000 years already they have been a nation of slaves, -2000 years where shall we be?

Shall we be like them?

At the time of her travels, Burckhardt had been celebrated as the first European to visit Mecca. At the time of this great Swiss explorer's death in his Turkish house in Cairo, he was venerated, by those who knew him, as Jean Louis Burckhardt, dedicated explorer-agent for the African Association.[48] Burckhardt had qualities that set him apart from those of his contemporaries as he exhibited the best qualities of the professional anthropologist and ethnographer. "First of all he was trained for his work. After two and a half years in Syria and a further year in Egypt, he was probably about as well trained, as any outsider could be to travel in Nubia and Arabia- and better trained than many a beginning ethnographer in our time. Second, he had a fluent command of his field in Arabic. Third, in his character as Sheikh Ibrahim ibn Abdullah, he was a kind of participant observer - not precisely in the indigenous societies of Nubia and Arabia but at least in the larger Islamic social system and which both were articulated."[49]

Many of the explorers and travelers drew outlandish and contemptible pictures of the Africans but Burckhardt described the Africans, as he perceived them in his encounters as rascals, kings and knaves. You may find a most revealing account of his travels as well as Bruce and others in *The Blue Nile* by Alan Morehead published in 1962. Other Europeans tried have contributed to the saga of the Nile: Belzoni in 1817-18, Waddington and Hansbury in 1820-21, Cailliaud 1820-22, Linant de Bellefonds in 1821-22, Hoskins in 1833 and Lepsius in 1849-58. However, Burckhardt's legacy to the nineteenth century was his outstanding work as an ethnographer and the first explorer with a cognitive map to accomplish his vision of the exploration of the Nile."[50]

Cailliaud's works, *Voyage a l'Oasis de Thebes* and *Voyage a Meroe* were invaluable not only to Hoskins but to later archaeologists because he documented monuments, with copies of reliefs and inscriptions that no longer exist or in vast deterioration. The career of Cailliaud as an archaeologist and traveler began in 1815 when he spent three years examining the antiquities of Egypt. In 1820, he continued his explorations from Aswan to Khartoum. He had as a guide the advance work of Napoleon and his savants, although they had advanced only to Philae at the southern end of the Second Cataract. The works published in 1926-27 were the most important contribution to archaeology of the Sudan (then called Ethiopia) by his detailed account of the remains of ancient cities and monuments first seen in the nineteenth century. [51]

G.A. Hoskins lured by the accounts of travelers sensationalized in France, Germany, and England, made a journey to the highest places in Ethiopia in 1833. He was considered by Budge a careful and intelligent traveler and suggested that the account of his journey was more valuable from the anthropological viewpoint. His travels were published in 1835 under the rather auspicious title, *Travels in Ethiopia, Above the Second Cataract of the Nile: The State of That Country, And the Various Inhabitants, Under the Dominion of Mohammed Ali: and Illustrating The Antiquities, Arts, and History of the Ancient Kingdom of Meroe.* Hoskins's book is one of importance because he and the artist accompanying him took meticulous pains to validate the work of Cailliaud.

Europe was astonished by the number of antiquities and the grandeur depicted by both of these men. Hoskins was as overjoyed as Cailliaud to find himself in the midst of the great pyramid field, yielding, pyramid after pyramid. Lost in admiration, he stated, "the pyramids of Geezah are magnificent, wonderful from the stupendous magnitude, but for picturesque effect and elegance of architectural design, I infinitely prefer those of Meroe".[52] He enumerated, sketched, measured, photographed and described in detail the rest of the eighty pyramids.

The years between the travels of Burckhardt and those of Hoskins were marked by a scramble for antiquities that was unparalleled for the mixture of characters, bloody intrigue, pyramid battering, and looting in the rush to fill the blossoming museums and the pockets of the adventurers of the nineteenth century. The main characters were the agent Mr. Belzoni, acting on behalf of Henry Salt, the British Consul-General, as well as himself, and the agent Drovetti, representing the French Consul. They were in open siege, with gangs of gun-slinging Arabs and those wielding sticks in order to gain possession of the obelisk stolen from the island of Philae. Belzoni was an Italian giant who gained notoriety in the circus in England before he became an antiquities hound. [53]

James Baikie points out the irony of the British Museum's refusal of a large assignment of antiquities from Salt who later sold them to the Louvre. In the same vein, the French government would not buy Drovetti's collection that was sold to the King of Sardinia who helped to form the Museum of Turin. All was not lost , however, the British Museum is indebted to Belzoni for the colossal head of Thotmes III and that of Ramses II. On the religious note, the French clergy argued vehemently against the purchase, according to Stanley Mayes, because the study of Egyptian antiquities would destroy the Fundamentalist belief in the bible. It was also thought that Egyptian history might alter the established view regarding the date of the appearance of the earth. [54]

BELZONI AND FERLINI

The end of the nineteenth century was a watershed for Egyptian and Nubian archaeology. The museums were hard pressed to explain and exhibit the new finds. The Victorian public needed proof of their perceptions of "Babylon" on the Nile and the Europeans were intrigued with the possibilities of gold to be found in the coffers of the pyramids. The *Denkmaler* of Lepsius provided a copious collection of material for those interested in future archaeology in the Sudan. He also published four Nubian songs in his *Nubische Grammatike*. Auguste Mariette was the first Director of the Service of Antiquities in Egypt, which was established in 1858. He provided the Khedive of Egypt with the plot for the Opera for the opening part of the Suez Canal. The ingenious Mariette, because of his keen and sometimes questionable deals, caused many gruesome stories to surface after his exploits. He earned the title of "the great conservator" based on two of his positions: that excavation in Egypt must be government regulated and that the acquisitions should be under the care of the government with the appropriate setting and not in the hands of private individuals. Notwithstanding, he allowed no one except himself to have supervised thirty -seven sites. [55]

Sir Flinders Petrie is considered the father of archaeology because it fell to him to correct the naiveté, the spoilage and the pillage of the nineteenth century. According to John Wortham, by 1880, Egyptology had become a scholarly discipline, but it still was an 'embryonic science'.[56] Petrie, while in the field, was heartsick because he discovered that there was never a plan, no regularity, and needless destruction with no heed given to preservation or conservation for the future.

CHAPTER 4
CAMPAIGNS OF THE TWENTIETH CENTURY

FIRST ARCHAEOLOGICAL SURVEY, 1901-1911, GEORGE REISNER

The first antiquarian view of Egypt as a source of objet d'art for museums and gentlemen collectors was the prevailing view in the eighteenth century. This view was designated by Professor Adams as a random phase in the history of Egyptian archaeology because of its unscientific approach, looting and sheer destruction of monuments of immeasurable value. In the twentieth century, scientific field archaeology was beginning to get started in conjunction with engineering projects of flood control and industrial progress. This phase has been called the "comprehensive" phrase in the history of archaeological progress. The first phase was designated random as because of its haphazard and completely unscientific looting of treasures of objet d'art. The second phase of excavation is the one in which the sites selected were usually royal tombs, temples, and palaces of imperial or artistic significance. The third phase of field investigation is the comprehensive, which is characterized by action given to smaller sites over a wider range and sample types of remains in every historical age.[57]

The First Archaeological Survey of Nubia (Egypt), 1907-1911 initially directed by George Reisner was a response to the great hue and cry of conservationists to save the temples that were to be destroyed by raising the original Assuan Dam, (1898-1902) near Philae Island. The First Archaeological survey was a benchmark in the history of Egyptian history because it was the first of its kind in the world, and it established the standard for the salvage campaigns. Reisner had to develop methods as he went along because of the unspecified nature of salvage archaeology at the time.

Reisner wrote that the Archaeological Survey of Lower Nubia has been undertaken:

1. for the purpose of ascertaining the value and extent of the historical material found under the soil.
2. for the purpose of making the material available
3. for the construction of the history Nubia and its relation of Nubia to Egypt. The questions of which it is hoped to throw light concerning the successive races and racial mixtures, the extent of the population in different periods, the economical basis of the existence of these populations, the character of their industrial and the source of their civilization.[58]

The First Survey was conducted by Reisner in the first season, and the next three seasons by his successor, C. M. Firth. They covered 95 miles of the Nile Valley just south of the First Cataract and adjacent to Philae. According to their records they excavated 151 cemeteries and over 8,000 individual graves. A few other non-funerary sites were investigated only one fourth of which was investigated thoroughly. Although several archaeologists had visited the great fortress of Ikkur, which could be easily seen as its silhouette filled the skyline, it had never been excavated.

The excavation of the fortress was a highlight of the end of the second season, in March of 1909. It was found to have two systems of fortification which were rectangular in plan with high walls with an inner older canal system consisting of a narrow ditch with its protruding round bastions similar to those later found at the fortresses of Kubban, Aneiba, and Buhen. [59] While Reisner was involved with the First Archaeological Survey, a number of other Egyptologists engaged by the Director of Egyptian Antiquities, Sir Gaston Maspero were planning the temples of Nubia, which were to be inundated, and copying their inscriptions. The Englishman, Aylward Blackman was assigned to the temples of Derr, Dendur and Bigeh. His published works are in three volumes: *The Temples of Dendur* (1911), *The Temple of Derr* (1913), and *The Temple of Bigeh* (1915). The Frenchman, Henri Gauthier, published reports on the Temple of Kalabsha between 1911 and 1914, The Temple of Wadi Sebua in 1912, and of the Temples of Debod and Dakka were published between 1911 and 1913. The German, Gunther Roeder, Gauthier and Blackman published their own work on temple inscriptions in a series of volumes under the collective title *Temples Imerges de la Nubie.*[60]

The Oxford University excavations led by F.Ll. Griffith in 1910-1913 discovered Pharaonic temples, Meroitic and Christian sites, as well as a Napatan temple and cemetery in surrounding areas and at Sanam. He later earned a title Pioneer of Christian Nubian Studies and inaugurated the study of Medieval Nubian texts. Griffith's methodology in the field left something to be desired as he was a contemporary of Reisner but not privy to his archaeological acumen. In 1913, Reisner organized and served as Director of the Harvard-Boston expedition, sponsored jointly by Harvard University and the Boston Museum of Fine Arts. This enabled him to spend the next ten years with different field directors in the north Sudan investigating sites dating from the Dynastic period of Nubian history (Pharaonic, Napatan, and Meroitic). The work of this expedition represents the most outstanding archaeological work carried out in Nubia, and it forms the basis for all later studies of Meroitic history. Adams cites the following accomplishments:

1. Excavation of the Great Egyptian trading emporium and the Nubian Royal Cemetery of Kerma between 1913 and 1916 This was published in the Harvard *African Studies.*
2. Excavations of several of The Second Cataract Forts built during the Middle Kingdom and enlarged in the new Kingdom. This work was carried on inter-mittently over several years under the different field directors. The results have been published in two volumes entitled *Second Cataract Forts.*

3. Excavations of the Napatan and Meroitic Royal cemeteries associated Temples near Kareima and at Meroe.

This was undoubtedly Reisner's chef d'ouvre in the Sudan. From it he constructed the royal succession of the Napatan and Meroitic dynasties, which is still the basic chronological framework for the discussions of this phase of Nubian history. Again, in a series of superbly illustrated volumes prepared by Dows Dunham and collectively called *Royal Cemeteries of Kush*. Dunham also completed *Second Cataract Forts* and in 1970 *The Barkal Temples.*[61]

The ancient kingdom of Kerma is situated just below the Third Cataract. It has now been recognized as the most ancient kingdom in Saharan Africa beginning about 2500 B.C. Kerma was known to the Egyptians, as the land of Yam. The site is about a mile and a half from the Nile. It is composed of the two major areas containing a Western and Upper Defuffa and a large necropolis or Royal Cemetery. The Western Defuffa, a solid rectangular mass of mud brick more than 150 feet long and 75 feet wide, and probably stood to a height considered greater than 60 feet which are stilled preserved, a winding stairway seemed to lead to the top of the structure with the lower steps leading into the guard room . The Lower Defuffa is also of mud brick. The cemetery covers an area about a mile and a half long. Over 3000 have been cited. The grave goods indicate a high degree of wealth in gold, ivory, metal, faience and other exotic items. According to Reisner, the largest of the burial monuments is 300 feet in diameter with interior chambers more extensive than those of the Egyptian Pyramid.

The Second Cataract Fortresses, seven in number and named after the potential enemies, were a series of elaborate fortifications built during the Middle Kingdom and later expanded or enlarged during the New Kingdom. Buhen, a massive fortress was situated at the headwaters of the Second Cataract and 10 miles downstream, guarding the foot of the Second Cataract. Mirgissa, a more massive fortress with the lesser fortresses, is dotted in between. It was during the reign of Senusret III that the Forts in Nubia were completed. The design and distribution of the fortresses suggests that they were to function as a unit. Emery, the excavator, describes Buhen, "as an elaborate series of fortifications built on a rectangular plan, 172 by 160 meters [c.560x525 ft], which enclosed a town containing domestic habitations, barrack buildings, workshops, a temple, and a Governor's palace." [62]

The real purpose of the fortresses for Egypt is a matter of conjecture. They were both for defense and trade. Adams suggests some corollaries to consider:

"First, there must already have exited in the Twelfth Dynasty
a very substantial volume of trade between Egypt and the lands
to the south of Semna, since the Egyptians were at such pains to

control and protect it.

Second, some desert the habit of preying on the riverain 'caravans'…

Third, the Egyptian 'boundary' at Semna, and the effort to enforce a monopoly of trade only below that point, indicate that the upstream origins of the Nile trade were not under Egyptian direct control. If so, this was a genuine international trade."[63]

Finally, the absence of Egyptian forts above Semna (admittedly not as dangerous as those further downstream) suggests the possibility that the Nile was effectively controlled by another power.

T HE SECOND ARCHAEOLOGICAL SURVEY

The original Aswan dam was heightened a second time and the reservoir was enlarged to the total of 235 miles, extending to the Sudanese border. It was again necessary for the Egyptian government to launch the Second Archaeological Survey between 1929 and 1934, to rescue the antiquities in the area. This time the British archaeologists, W.B Emery and L. P. Kirwan could follow the precedence set by Reisner and his colleagues in the first comprehensive field excavations.

Dr.Emery upon his own admission approached his new post as Director of the Archaeological Survey of Nubia with 'some trepidation' as Nubia was an unknown entity for him except for his book knowledge of Nubia. His previous directorship was that of the Mound Excavations of the University of Liverpool at Luxor and Armant, where at Armant, he discovered the tombs of the sacred bulls. Emery's staff and 150 Egyptian workmen, although skilled at excavation, were at the same level of awareness, but were guided by Cecil Firth who has directed apart of the First Survey. He was compensated adequately the six winter months of 1929,1930 and 1931 beginning at Wadi es Sebua and exploring part of Lower Nubia to the Sudan frontier in Adindan. A sum of $165,000 covered the expenses for the Survey and the cost of publication. It is hard to believe that this sum covered all the expenses of two dahabeahs (houseboats), equipment, and food for labor gangs usually 150 a day. Part of the equipment included a number of smaller boats and a cargo sailing boat for all the tentage and baggage for the workmen who followed on a river steamer to their stating destination. The main part of the diet for the workers was bread cooked by their wives that was hard as a brick. It was soaked in water until it was edible.

The Nubian experience for Emery he wrote was not at all like his previous ones. He said time was not a factor and his work site was not a factor. One of his great fortunes was to receive from Firth before he left Cairo a few sheets of type entitled "*The Body Snatchers Vade Mecum* that Emery found Reisner's method with a few modifications the only practical way to excavate cemeteries and fortresses when they contained a detailed account of Reisner's recording method during the First Survey when the expedition was constantly on the move and with little time. Many decisions had to be made which caused him great concern because he thought, "what I miss now will never be recovered, and I have so little time to make sure."[64]

Reisner's notes were extremely important for the details of recording both in the field and recording in base camp. For recording at the base camp, Emery wrote that four essentials must be kept on a day -to- day basis:

1. The diary, which must be written up at the end of each day of excavation by the director. For this purpose each member of the expedition will give him tomb cards and field notes that he made during the day. (Every grave or super structure is numbered, photographed, said markings painted on a stone for identification. The same is done for any grave goods. All information is recorded on cards and notes in the field)

2. Pottery register (in duplicate), with each pot typed according to the Corpus. A Corpus is already in existence from the previous Archaeological Survey 1929-34) and it is the duty of the archaeologist in charge of this section to date by adding any new type, which may occur. The pottery of the Corpus is drawn to a scale of 1.5

3. Object register (in duplicate). With this is included a bead Corpus, which again can be based on the existing Corpus of the Archaeological Survey of 1929-34

4. Photograph register and the attachment of the relevant photographs (when print- ed) to the back of the cards.

The above information is very essential not only to the reader but for the archives in the museums and visitors to understand the description of pottery, beads, skeletons and etc. Again there was emphasis on monuments that filled the gap in the cultural history in the area previously covered. Seventy cemeteries and 2,400 individual graves were examined including the remains of the A, B, C, and X – Groups, the New Kingdom and Christian periods. There were also Meroitic graves, Middle Kingdom Fortresses in Kubban, the C-Group and Meroitic town sites in Wadi Arab. The X- Group Royal tombs of Ballana and Qustul were the greatest discoveries of Kirwan and Emery. Nubian rulers of the 5th centuryB.C. were excavated. It was years after that that Dr. Emery was astonished to find while re-reading *A Thousand Miles Up The Nile,* the uncanny insight of Amelia Edwards regarding the value of the tumuli and objects later to be found in them.

The following excerpt is from her travels in 1874:

"Some way beyond Kalat Abba when Abu Simbel range and the

Palm Island have all vanished into the distant, and the lonely peak

Called The Mountain of the Sun (Gebel esh Shems) have been left behind, we

come upon a new wonder- namely upon the two groups of tumuli, on the eastern

31

bank, one upon the western bank. Not volcanic forms these; not even accidental forms, if anyone may adventure to form an opinion so far. They are of various sizes; some big; all perfectly round and smooth and covered with brownish alluvial soil. How did they come here? Who made them? What did they contain? The Roman ruins nearby- the 240,000 that certainly poured their thousands along the way—the Egyptian and Ethiopian armies might have fought many a battle on this open plain, suggests all kinds of possibilities and fill one's head with visions of buried arms and jewels, and funery urns. We are more than half-mind to stop the boat and land that very moment; we will at least excavate one of the small hillocks on our way back." [65]

Miss Edwards never returned to excavate but Emery and Kirwan found that her speculations were not far off. The grave goods of the tumuli contained an overwhelming array of regal richness, including magnificent crowns, other bejeweled ornaments, mirrors, weapons and tools. Even the horses were buried as regally as the king and queens with invaluable silver harnesses and headgear. The reports and illustrations on these two sites alone were much larger than the previous reports on the 74 sites investigated by the same investigator. Nevertheless, their reports represented the chief advance of The Second Archaeological Survey.

During the same period of 1929-34 salvage operations of the German expedition under the direction of G.A. Steindorf were working at Aniba where they made the most complete examination of the A Group and C Group remains. Ugo Monneret De Villard was invited to make observations that resulted in the four volumes, *La Nubia Mediavale*. It was a synthesis of the archaeological and literary sources available at the time and was seen as the basis of medieval Nubian archaeology.[66]

LATER EXPEDITIONS 1935-59

Archaeological activity in Nubia and the Sudan was greatly reduced because of world wide economic depression in the 30s and as suggested by Adams the inundation of Lower Nubia. Reisner's excavations with the Harvard Boston excavations were suspended in 1932 and fully liquidated some years later. The work of the Egypt Exploration society was suspended during the Second World but refueled by 1947. It was during this period that Shinnie and Fairman found a Pharaonic temple at Amara and Blackman found a town and temple at Sesebi for the Society. The Sudan Antiquities Service acquired Dr. Arkell as a director during 1944-45 found Mesolithic remains at Khartoum and found Neolithic remains at Shaheinab. The director, at the University of Khartoum in 1948 and1957, found neolithic remains. These expeditions were sited in Adams' "Summary of Archaeology Expeditions -1907-58." The expeditions of the many universities around the world are not to be obscured. When UNESCO made its appeal in 1959 to help in the conservation of the treasures in Egyptian and Sudanese Nubia a vast resevoir of knowledge, skill and interest was made available.

ASWAN DAM AND RECENT SALVAGE CAMPAIGNS

The latter half of the twentieth century will be recorded in the history of archaeology as the full bloom of the Comprehensive phase of field archaeology and the greatest challenge to Egyptian Archaeology. The challenge was vigorously pursued by UNESCO (United Nations Educational, Scientific and Cultural Organization) after the appeal of the Egyptian government. Its Nubian cultural heritage was soon to be submerged under the Nile with the construction of the High Dam at Aswan. This was not the first time the temples and monuments were threatened by the need of the Egyptian and Sudanese people. Attempting to survive on a rainless land a few miles on each side of the Nile has been their life- blood for centuries. It was the increased population in Egypt that was forcing this momentous decision. When the dam was heightened in 1934, the Egyptian population had risen to 16 million and was estimated to double by 1961. Rex Keating observed that the critical solution was birth control over water control. The economic and political national gains were as follows:

1. Increasing the present cultivated area about one million Feddan (4,200 sq. meters) and converting 700,000 feddans in Upper Egypt from the basin to perennial irrigation.
2. Guaranteeing water requirements even in the years for low Flood, improving drainage, and guaranteeing the cultivation of one million feddan of rice annually.
3. Protecting the country against the danger of high floods, preseepage and inundation of small islands and riverbanks
4. Improving navigation conditions on the Nile
5. Producing electric power annually about 10,000 million kwh[67]

THE TEXT OF UNESCO'S APPEAL

Victorian Veronese, Director General of UNESCO, made a heart-wrenching world appeal March 9, 1960 which you will feel as you read the text in full:

"Work had begun on the great Aswan Dam. Within five years, the Middle Valley of the Nile will be turned into a vast lake. Wondrous structures, ranking among the most magnificent on earth, are in danger of disappearing beneath the waters. The dam will bring fertility to huge stretches of desert, but the opening fields of fields to tractors, the provision of new sources of power to future factories threaten exact a terrible price.

True, when the welfare of suffering human beings is at stake, then, if need be, images of granite and porphyry must be sacrificed unhesitatingly. But no one forced to make such a choice could contemplate without anguish the necessity of making it.

It is not easy to choose between a heritage of the past and present well–being of a people, living in need in the shadow of one of history's most splendid legacies, it is not easy to choose between temples and crops. I would be sorry for any man who, whatever decision he might reach, could bear the responsibility for that decision without feeling remorse.

It is not surprising, therefore, that the governments of the United Arab Republic and the Sudan have called on an International body, on UNESCO, to save the threatened monuments. These monuments, the loss of which may be tragically near, do not belong solely to the countries who hold them in trust. The whole world has a right to see them endure. They are a part of a common heritage, which com-promises Socrates' message and the Ajanta frescoes, the walls of Axial and Beethoven's symphonies. Treasures of universal values are entitled to universal protection. When a thing of beauty, whose loveliness increases rather than diminishes by being shared, is lost, then all men are the losers. Moreover, it is not merely a question of bringing to light an as yet undiscovered wealth for all in return for the help world gives them, the governments of Cairo and Khartoum will open up the whole of their countries to archaeological excavation and will allow half of whatever works of art maybe unearthed by science or hazard to go to foreign museums. They will even agree to transport, stone by stone certain monuments of Nubia. A new era of magnificent enrichment is thus opened in the field of Egyptology. Instead of the world being deprived of part of its wonders, mankind may hope for a revelation of hither unknown marvels. So noble a response deserves a no less generous response. It therefore, with every confidence that I invite governments, institutions, public or private foundations and men of good will everywhere to contribute to the success of a task, without parallel in history. Services, equipment and money is all needed.

There are innumerable ways in which all can help. It is fitting for land which throughout the centuries, has been the scene of or stake in so many disputes, should spring a convincing proof of international solidarity. "Egypt is the gift of the Nile"; for countless centuries this was the first Greek phrase which they learnt to translate. May the peoples of the world becoming a great source of fertility and power does not bury beneath its waters marvels which we of today have inherited from generations long since vanished."[68] (Translated from the French)

PRESERVATION OF NUBIA'S HERITAGE

The preservation of Nubia's heritage was carried on by some forty archaeological expeditions from Africa, America Asia and Europe over a period of twenty years marked the greatest act of international effort for humanitarian and cultural purposes to date. The financial contributions came to a total of $26 million given by 50 member states of UNESCO. The campaign was sustained by private contributions, revenue from exhibitions and may other fundraising projects. Soderbugh states that the list of private donors ran into many pages listing the sacrifices of those large and small.

The Director General received a letter on the day after the appeal from an eleven- year old girl from Tournus (France) saying, "I do not know what the beautiful temple of Abu Simbel is like, but I do know what Egypt must be like because we have just learned about if in school. I do not want all of these beautiful temples to be lost. I have just broken into my piggy bank and I am sending you what was in it. I am also making a collection at school."[69]

A char -woman from Bordeaux whose husband had been killed during the war wrote: "I have made sacrifices all my life so that my daughter would be educated and cultivated. She is happily married; she has a job and children. And I am sending you what three of my dinners a week would cost, for if I cannot hope to see these Nubian temples. Myself, I want my grandchildren to see them."[70] These letters underscore the depth of the human consciousness.

The doomed temples, fortresses, monuments, ancient town sites, tombs and prehistoric remains of Nubia dotted some two hundred miles along the Nile in Egyptian Nubia and one hundred miles in Sudanese Nubia were marked for a watery grave, with the exception of those that could be saved by relocation. The success of the salvage campaign or preservation of Nubia's heritage was UNESCO's gift to the world and its succeeding generations. Some of the treasures were distributed throughout the world to the Member States of UNESCO as gratuity and valuable recordings of prehistoric remains and of cemeteries are now accessible in archives. Each of the monuments was all dismantled stone by stone and reassembled in others sites. There were three temples and shrines in all. The National Museum of the Sudan in Khartoum and the Nubian Museum in Egypt at Aswan are repositories of Art and monuments for the world to see. Six groups of monuments and temples have been saved in Egypt and the Sudan. The temples sent abroad as grants in return by Egypt were known as "New Ambassadors Extraodinary":

1. Debod in Madrid was built in the 3rd century B.C. when the Ptolemies reigned in Egypt, and the kings of Meroe ruled in the upper part of the Nile valley.

2. Taffa, sent to Leiden in the the Netherlands arrived in 657 blocks, wrapped in plastic for the sea voyage

3. Dendur, now in New York, was built by the Augustus, Roman Emperor to honor two deceased sons of a local Nubian ally and Isis, the goddess of Philae, whose clergy was staffed at the temple.

4. Ellesiya, the small built by Tuthmosis and dedicated to the Nubian God Horus of Miam, was sent to Turin.

The relocated six groups are:

1. The Temples of Philae Island relocated on the Island of Agilka. near the former Aswan Dam.

2. The Temples of Beit el Wali and Kalabsha and the Kiosk of Kertassi, relocated near the High Dam.

3. The Temples of Dakka, Maharraqua and Wadi es Sebua, relocated near the former site of Wadi-es Sebua.

4. The Temples Amada and Derr and Pennut's Tomb at Aniba, relocated near the former site of Amada.

5. The Temples of Abu Simbel, relocated in situ, but 60 miles above their original site.

6. The Temples of Aksha, Buhen, Semna East and Semna West, relocated in the Museum Garden at Khartoum. [71].

The Frescoes of Faras are another wealthy and stunning gift now residing in Warsaw and Khartoum overshadowed most of the finds of the Late Nubian era. Kazamierz Michaelowski and his team of experts skillfully extracted them from the walls of a Nubia Christian Cathedral buried beneath the walls of an Arab Citadel. I was privileged to view the complete collection of 174, in number, half of which are housed in Khartoum and the other half in Warsaw. To view these ancient, yet seemingly immediate finds in both Khartoum and Warsaw was a stunning and humbling experience. However, it is Michalowski and his team that seems to have had the most awesome experience. He describes his discovery:

> "Today Faras lies some 130 feet beneath the water, but in the
> 7th century it was the capital of northern Nubia. During the
> three years of excavations of the Polish expedition succeeded
> in resuscitating a hitherto unknown chapter in Nubian history
> of early Christian Nubia and a large part of its art."
> "Among the most famous works discovered are the head of St.
> Anne with finger to her lips in silence, the Black Bishop Petros
> under the protection of the Apostle Peter, the olive-skinned bishop, Marianos,
> the dark-complexioned Queen Mother Martha, and a vast nativity scene which
> includes the shepherds and the Thee Wise Men."

"It would be impossible at Faras to list all these objects such as the splendid 11th century glass chalice found during the excavations which covered not only the great church but also a whole complex of buildings including an eparch's palace, two monasteries and a second church."

"The Excavations were a race against time. In the course of four seasons each lasting five to six months, the expedition succeeded in salvaging the most important objects, not only of the frescoes of the church that was taken down and packed in cases, but also the bronzes, ceramics, the inscriptions and tombs of the bishop complete with their skeletons. The list of their names which were found on the walls of the church constitutes one of the original documents of Christianity in Nubia,hardly had the expedition finished nailing up the cases for removal when the Nile water reached the level of the hill on which the excavations had taken place. Some months later the tops of a few palm trees emerging from the lake were all that remained to mark the spot where Faras had stood."[72]

CHAPTER 5.
NUBIAN TEMPLES AND ROYAL TOMBS:
ANCIENT ROOTS OF THE NILE

"There is only one action over which indifference and unchanging rivers have no sway. It is the action of man who snatches something from death"

Andre Malraux

The salvage operations of the twentieth century will not be fully appreciated and understood historically and culturally until all of archaeological and literary documentation has been examined and the results made accessible to a wider audience. The results recently obtained with the UNESCO campaign in the 1960s have challenged the minds of the New Wave Egyptologists and Nubiologists and has "proved to be of great importance for our understanding of the cultural history of Nubia and its links with Africa."[73]

Martin Bernal, the iconoclastic scholar, has bruised the sensitivities of many scholars and has tipped the scales of classical discussion towards the Afroasiatic roots of classical civilizations with his proposal of the genesis of Greek civilization Nubia and Egypt. [74] Like beacons in the dark and ancient sentinels, the Nubian temples and tombs have been rescued and brought to a new threshold for all to see and witness the undeniable continuous Nubian past and a hopeful future in their new locations. This chapter will highlight for those temples and sites in Egyptian Nubia in the north to Sudanese Nubia in the south, which have been saved, and relocated, as well as those sent abroad.

TEMPLES OF PHILAE

The Temples of Philae, often called "The Pearl of Egypt" were located on the Island of Philae, today known as Anas-el -Wagud. In antiquity the island was called Pilak, which means the frontier or extremity of Egypt, which at the time was at the First Cataract, four kilometers south of the modern Aswan Dam.[75] The base of the island is solid granite, which has been layered with silt that nurtures the flowering shrubs, shimmering palms and rich vegetation for centuries. The island is small in size, 500 yards long and 150 yards wide. Most of the footage of the island is covered with sacred buildings associated with the Cult of Isis. The beauty of the sculptured pylons and elegant monumental structures and colonnades has caused visitors and pilgrims to experience the ethereal and to leave their imprint on the walls and pylons. The late pagan age

(394-452 A.D.) was prolific with graffiti in hieroglyphs, demotic and hieratic, Greek, Latin and Meroitic (Nubian).[76]

After building the Aswan Low Dam, the temples were submerged for nine months of the year and reappeared above the water during the summer months. Philae temples suffered enormous damage during the double heightening of the Aswan Dam because they had been inadequately protected during the 1900s. These were major losses in artifacts and pottery, which might have filled the gaps in the history of the Nubian peoples.

The Temple of Isis, the principle sanctuary on the island, was consecrated to Isis and her son Horus. The pylons, which seemed in the distance to touch the heavens were much in scale with the size of the island in actuality. They were only 60 feet high and 40 feet high and correspondingly less wide. The Temple of Isis was probably built on the site of a more ancient temple when it was dedicated to the immemorial Earth Mother, Isis, who was the goddess of fertility, and her son Horus. The temple was begun by Ptolemy II (285-246) and largely finished by Ptolemy III (246-221). The decorations were gradually added with some left unfinished. There is an open court, a pronaos, several smaller rooms and the Holy- of-Holies, with decorations representing the Ptolemies of Roman emperors making sacrifices, offerings and other cult ceremonies.[77]

In the front of the Temple of Isis, Ptolemy IV added an entrance to the small side temple built by Arkamani (Ergamenes), a Meroitic King. From this early Meroitic age several blocks from the site of the Arsenuphis temple with scenes and inscriptions of Arkamani. Meriotic inscriptions were also found in the great temple of Isis, "one in the eastern colonnade and the other on the back of the first pylon; as well as the Meroitic chamber with its remarkable sculpture and inscriptions.[78]

The most ancient building on the site was built by King Nectanebo of the 30th dynasty in 350B.C. (blocks discovered in the foundations dated back to Taharqa). This site was a Mecca for the worship of Isis, the "Great Divine Mother", which spread throughout the Mediterranean and northward to Britain, seriously challenging Christianity for a while.[79]

Ptolemy VI built a small temple, dedicated to the Goddess Hathor, to the east of the Temple Of Isis. The forecourt was added in Roman times, containing columns with Hathor (cow-headed) capitals. The best-known building on the island, northeast of the Hathor Temple and on the bank rose the kiosk, which was attributed to Trajan. [80] Wallis Budge in his travels referred to it as "Pharaoh's Bed". The reliefs in this graceful edifice show the emperor making offerings to Isis and Horus, and standing in the presence of Isis and Osiris.

The temples grew in religious importance with the interest of the Greek and Roman pharaohs who may have been inclined toward the occult and esoteric aspects of the Cult of Isis. The cult of Isis was internationalized by the Romans and in time the island was called the "Holy island,

Interior of Heaven" and the "City of Isis".[81] Early images of the Madonna and child were based on representations of Isis and Horus, which have been generally accepted by many writers.

Apuleius, born in 130 A.D., wrote in his Metamorphoseon libri XI (de Asino Aureo) about the moral and religious conditions of his time with a lot of humor and lifelike colors. His book is known as *The Golden Ass of Apuleius.* Apuleius wrote "Only the Ethiopians of both sort, that dwell in the Orient and are enlightened by the rays of the sun, and the Egyptians, which are excellent in all kinds of doctrine and by their proper ceremonies accustom to worship me, do call me by my true name," Queen Isis".[82]

The Temples of Beit el-Wali, Kalabsha, and the Kiosk of Kertassi Rameses II built the Temple of Beit-el Wali a mile and a quarter north of Kalabsha . It consisted of an open court, a hypo-style hall, and a sanctuary cut from rock. On the walls of the court were the typical Ramesside scenes of the victorious battles with the peoples of the south. One scene shows the king in a chariot accompanied by his sons subduing the enemy. Tribute of gold, ring, chairs, elephant tusks, panther skins, ebony and fans also were depicted. One can see some of those highly colored scenes in the British Museum. In the Christian period, the court was transformed into a three -naved church with a vaulted mud brick roof.[83]

The Temple of Kalabsha (Talmis) was originally located some 30 miles south of Aswan and is considered, because of its size, the most important monument in Nubia after Abu Simbel. Since the beginning of the century, the temple was under water most of the time. Alexander built the Great the present temple. It stands immediately on the Tropic of cancer and on an ancient site of an older temple built by Thutmose III about 1600B.C.; Amenhotep II added to it about 158-6 B.C. The temple is reached by means of a stone quay ninety-eight feet long from the Port of Kalabsha and twenty-six feet wide. There are shallow steps leading up to a platform, which is in front of the pylon gateway to the temple. Porticoes on three sides enclose the court between the pylon and the pronaos. On the west side it forms the imposing of the pronaos the gate of which opens in the center. Within the pronaos are twelve columns with floral capitals.[84]

On the facade of the twelve columns are a number of inscriptions important to the Meroitic period in Nubian history. On the second column the Meroitic inscription no.94 has a Greek inscription above and below it. This inscription seems to commemorate a conquest, by one of the Kushite kings, Khamaramazeye. It also gives an account of the transfer of properties for the sub-kings. [85]

Amenhotep is represented on the west wall of the temple making an offering to the God Amsu (Re) and one of the Nubian gods Meral while one of the Ptolemies is making an offering to Isis.[86] The other three walls depict the Emperor before the gods of Talmis and other deities and Mandulis. The Ptolemies and the Romans made considerable restorations and enlargements. Outside the temple is a small chapel from Roman times and behind it is the *mamisi* or "Birth house".

With the introduction of Christianity, the temple was changed into a church. A pagan prayer was inscribed in the courtyard by Decurion Maximos, probably between the 2nd and 3rd centuries A.D.: "Be benevolent, O Mandulis, the son of Zeus, and nod to me in acquiescence! Save me and my beloved and children! I call upon Thee constantly that my companions and the female slaves, free from disease and toil, may return to our country." "How happy is the people which live in the town of Talmis, loved by Mandulis, the son of the Sun god, and which is under the sceptre of Isis, of beautiful and many names."[87] Two Christian texts were inscribed on a pylon when the temple became a church: "I, the priest, Paulos, have rayed here for the first time".

"I, the priest, Paulos, have erected a cross for the first time in this place". [88]

KIOSK OF KERTASSI

The Kiosk of Kertassi is a small elegant Graeco-Roman temple, which was, located some twenty-five miles from Aswan, near quarries that provided the building materials for the temples of Philae. It reminds one of the Kiosk of Trajan at Philae. The larger part of the Kiosk had been demolished by the water, which covered it for several months out of the year.[89]

THE TEMPLE OF DAKKA

On the west side of the Nile was the Temple of Dakka, 68 miles south of Aswan. The Meroitic King Ergamenes built the most beautiful ancient part of the building (222-204B.C.) and his contemporary; Ptolemy IV of Egypt added a forecourt. The Ptolemies sometimes collaborated in the building of the temples with the Meroites because friendly relations had been established under the Ergamenes reign. The Roman emperors later added a pylon and a sanctuary. The temple is parallel to the river, running north and south, which is contrary to the axis of most Nubian temples.

"A large dromos, of which a part of the paving and inscribed blocks remain, lead to the pylon that formed the real entrance to the temple. Each of the pylon's towers is ornamented in high relief and bears numerous graffiti from visitors, mostly Greek, and some in Demotic and Meriotic. Inside the gateway, the king Ergamenes, is represented on the left sacrificing to Thoth, with Tefnut and Hathor above and Isis below. On the facade of the pronaos, the temples have been later converted into a church. Christian paintings were still visible before the temple submerged."

"On he left post of the vestibule door, Philapater is represented by Re, Khnumm and Isis. On the right, he stands before Haredotes and Isis. On the embrasure an emperor is making offerings to the statue of the goddess of Truth (Ma'at), to Thoth and the lion-headed goddess, Tefnut. The sanctuary contained a shrine representing the emperor in the presence of various gods."

"The site of Dakka witnessed the battle the battle that was fought between the Queen of the Sudan Kandaki (Candace) and the Roman forces under Petronius in 23 B.C."[90]

THE TEMPLE OF MAHARRAQA

"The Temple of Maharraqa, also known as the temple of Ofeduine, was located on the west bank of the Nile, some 80 miles from Aswan. The border between the Meroites and the Romans was established at Hierasykaminos (the town of the Sacred Sycamore) or Maharraqa. It was at this site that Seraphis consecrated the temple but it was never finished. There is an open court enclosed on three sides by porticoes. The longitudinal axis of the temple is east and west. Walls between them join the columns. In the middle of the court a gate opens onto a gallery. Most of the temple has been destroyed."[91]

THE TEMPLE OF WADI ES-SEBUA

"Es Sebua ("The Lions") was the third temple built by Rameses II ninety- three moles from Aswan. Part of the temple is cut from rock. Rameses II dedicated the temple to Re- Harakhte and to Amun as he considered he was a god, by this time. He also worshiped in the temple. The entrance to the temple was formed by an avenue of Sphinxes (from which es-Sebua derives its name) that led up to the south pylon before which stood two colossal statues of Rameses II. At the far end of the sanctuary and above the solar bark on which the beetle-headed Re-Harakhte, the solar god is seated under a canopy while he is seated under a canopy while he is being adored on the left by the king and on the right by three baboons. Below is a niche that still shows traces of the three chiseled statues of the temples. Three principal gods are painted over the picture of St. Peter.[92]

THE TEMPLE OF AMADA

Thutmose III built the Temple of Amada, the most ancient and beautiful temple in Nubia, 125 miles south of Aswan. It had experienced many transformations. It was enlarged by his son, Amenhotep II, and later by Thutmose IV. The images of Amun were hammered out under Amenhotep IV and later restored by Seti I. During the Christian period the reliefs were covered with stucco and paintings of that period. Thanks to the ravages of time, sand, and storm the outer covering of stucco had long since fallen only to reveal the majesty of the reliefs.

The dedications are to the sun god. There is a commemorative inscription, which describes the expedition of Mer-en-Ptah against the peoples of the south. The offerings and the adoration of the gods are depicted as in other temples. "On the interior of the Holy of Holies which is approached through the central gateway of the Amada Stele. The upper half shows the oblation scene with Amenhotep II offering wine to the sun god, all in the sacred boat. It was dated in the third year of his reign and he is extolling his father's prowess in Syria with the bow and generosity to his people on his return. "He is the king very mighty of arm, there is not one who can draw his bow among his army among the hill sheiks or among the Retennu, because his strength, so much greater than that of any king who ever existed, raging like a panther when he courses through the battlefield. He is the king with a heart favorable to the buildings of all the gods, being one who builds their temples and fashions their statue. The divine offerings are established for the first time, loaves, and beer in plenty and fowl in multitude as a daily offering... He established revenues for the first time for his fathers to the gods, to be seen by the people, to be known of all."[93]

THE TEMPLE OF DERR

The Temple of Derr is one of two temples built on the east side of the Nile, the other is Ellisiya. It was built by Rameses I 1,162 miles south of Aswan and dedicated also to Re-harakhte. At the entrance are the reliefs showing Rameses II on his campaigns in Nubia and other places. Here he is shown in his chariot accompanied by his pet lion and leading a group of prisoners into the presence of the god. Another scene shows him with drawn bow as his enemies flee before the chariot. The fugitives are seen taking refuge in the mountains with their slain and wounded; also a group of grief stricken shepherds can be seen, surrounded by their flocks. [94]

THE TOMB OF PENNUT

Pennut, Viceroy of Kush, also known as "King's Son of Kush" built a tomb in the cliffs behind Aneiba, which was, located 140 miles south of Aswan. Aneiba was the ancient site of the capital of Nubia (Kush), which was known as Mi'am at the time and was the seat of the governor and the other officials. Professor Steindorff found the tomb during the excavations, which he made at the second raising of the Aswan Dam. In studying the tomb, he found that Pennut served under Rameses VI (20th dyn.). His chief office was "Deputy of Wawat", "Chief of the Quarry Service" and "Steward of Horus, Lord of Mi'am". Nubia appeared to be his native land as two of his relatives held the office of "Treasurer of the Lord of Two Lands of Mi'am" and another was "Scribe of the white House and Mayor of Mi'am". Their tombs have never been found. [95]

The Tomb of Pennut was cut from rock and contained several scenes showing how the Viceroy with members of his royal family adoring various gods. In front of other Rammeside officials, and the King's Sons of Kush. The tomb is famous for the inscriptions that Pennut had inscribed and the invaluable glimpse it affords into the life of a local official, including records of the boundaries, maintenance of the offerings and presents to Rameses VI. Pennut, in his line of duty, had erected a statue of Rameses II at Derr, and as a reward the Pharaoh sent him two vessels of silver. Pictured in a tomb is Pennut's reception of the gifts from the Viceroy receiving the gifts from the Pharaoh to be delivered to Pennut with a message, which is inscribed in the tomb. [96]

THE TEMPLES OF ABU SIMBEL

The greatest works of Rameses II are the two temples consisting of huge carvings on the faces of the cliff; together representing the largest rock sculpture in the known world.

THE GREAT TEMPLE OF ABU SIMBEL

Over the entrance is a picture of the sun god, with a falcon head, worshipped by Rameses II. The following is a continued description of the temple by Professor Save-Soderbergh in his book. *Temples and Tombs of Ancient Nubia* "Again the cult names found on the shoulders of the statues show the identity of the King and god." "Only the last scene alludes to the south, to Nubia."

THE TEMPLE OF HATHOR (THE SMALL TEMPLE)

It could be one of the finest structures in Nubia but the Great Temple overshadows it.

"Rameses II he made (it) as his monument for the Great King's -Wife, beloved of Mutt- a house hewn in the pure mountain of Nubia, of fine, white and enduring sandstone, as eternal work.

"Rameses-Meriamon, beloved of Amon, like Re, forever, made a house of very great monuments, for the Great King' s-Wife, Nefertari.

"His majesty commanded to make a house in Nubia hewn in the mountain." The temple itself is shaped in the form of a pylon with a facade ninety feet long and forty feet wide. Thirty-foot statues of the King and Queen stand in three deep niches on each side of the entrance. The Great temple seems to have more representations of grandeur and conquest while the smaller temple represents the attributes of love and the mysteries of the maternal. The Hathor cow emerges from the papyrus marches, the proverbial Nubia in the 7th century.

It is the hope for the next century that the scholars who ponder the feat of the salvage of the Nubian monuments and sacred sites and burrow through the inscriptions that there will be a Champollion of sort who will decode the Nubian (Meroitic) script and broaden the study of Nubiology and Meroitics.

CHAPTER 6
NUBIA AND THE NURTURING NILE

"They take the flow of the Nile by certain scales i.e.' the pyramid; they know by the height, the lowness, of the mean, if dearth of poison follow. The higher Nilus dwells, the more it promises as it webs, the seeds man is upon the slime and ooze scatters his grain, and shortly comes to harvest." Antony and Cleopatra, 11, 7

NUBIA AND EGYPT, THE GIFT OF THE NILE

The Nile, the oldest river known to the civilized world and known as Hapi, father of the Gods by the ancients, was the barometer by which the Nubians and Egyptians experienced life, They learned from experience, the mood shifts which could bring terror or joy, famine or abundance, hope and despair. Therefore, the reverence paid the Nile was very great because one's wealth, happiness, and prosperity depended upon the waters of the Nile.

Hapi, the god of the Nile, was placed above all gods and addressed as the "Father of the Gods". There is a hymn that indicates if he were to fail "the gods would fall down headlong, and men would perish". They were considered so powerful, according to the hymn, that "he cannot be sculpted in stone; he is not to be seen in the statues on which are seen the crowns of the South and the North; neither service or oblations can be offered unto him on person; and he cannot be brought forth from his secret habitations; the place where he dwelleth is unknown, he is not to be found in the shrines whereon arc inscriptions; no habitation is kluged enough to hold him; and cannot be imagined by thee in thy heart."[97] How did these waters achieve such power and what was their source'?

During the time of Herodotus, the source of the Nile was unknown. By 150 A.D., Ptolemy, the geographer, had correctly formed an opinion from the prevalent myths, stories and idea floating around the Lower Nile at the time. The priests of the islands of Philae made the assumption that the source of the Nile was at Philae and was able to make prophetic pronouncements regarding its inundations During the reign of Rameses II, it was believed that the area of tears of Iris Silsila, which was the border of Egypt and Nubia at the time, was the home of the Nile-god. To honor the god and to remain true to the legion of the region, Rameses ordered an inscription to be placed at Jebel Silsila, to record the celebration of two ancient festivals, which were observed in June and August. Each of the festivals coincided with the rise and fall of the Nile and the Isis and Osiris story. The tears shed by her annually in commemoration of her great grief over the dead body of her husband, Osiris, caused the flood of the Nile each year. During the Second Libyan war

Ramses said, "I am the Hero of Egypt, and I defend her.... I over throw for her every boundary; I am an abundant Nile, supplying her with good things.[98]

John Hanning Speke discovered Lake Victoria (Ripon Falls) where they say that the fisherman still find Nile perch. On a subsequent trip in 1852, he wrote the Royal Geographical Society in London saying that the question of the source of the Nile was settled. Unfortunately, the Nile's true source lay upstream which was almost proved by his rivals, Richard Burton, David Livingstone and Henry Morton Stanley, It was only in this century, that a *German* explorer, Dr. Burckhardt Waldecker, traced the southernmost source of the Nile to the spring in Burundi in 1937. (My own lifetime)[99]The headwaters of the Kagera River are regarded as one of the sources of the White Nile. Its source is some 500 miles southwest of the Lake where the Kagera forms the border between Rwanda and Tanzania. In Burundi at the southern most point, a very tiny trickle of water issues from the earth, and on a weathered metal plaque on a small pyramid stone reads, "Source of the Nile".

The beginning of Lake Albert, is in fabled Mountains of the Moon whose six snow peaked glacial crowns are located on the border of Uganda-Zaire. It is from this point, on the equator that the "glacial melt and more than 75 inches of annual rainfall" cascade down from the peaks in rivulets and streams that feed Lake George, Edward and Albert below. The Nile begins here at 16,763 feet as ice".[100]

Between Victoria and Albert, a distance of 242 miles, begins the White Nile, once known as Somerset River. Lake Victoria is 4,670 feet above the sea and 1,625 feet higher than Lake Albert. Lake Victoria is 160 miles long and 200 miles wide. The White Nile grows to 1,300 feet when it leaves the lake and Ripon Falls; it drops about 13 feet. The passage through the number of swamps, channels and falls causes a reduction in width and an increase in torrential strength. The distance from Lake Victoria to Khartoum by river is about 1,500 miles, from Khartoum to Aswan about 1,165 miles, and from Aswan to the sea 500 miles, making the tributary over 4,000 miles. The rush of the rivers downward seeking the sea, fills the air with torrential roaring of falls, cascades, and the turbulence of rivulets being forced through the narrow passages.[101]

At Khartoum, the Blue Nile with has traveled about 960 miles from the Abyssinian Mountains, joins the White Nile which is about 1,253 mile over sea level and 1800 miles from the sea. This other river because of its continued flow of water from Central Africa is called White Nile, because of the fine white clay that colors its water. The Blue Nile rises in the mountains of Abyssinia and its hue appears almost purple at times with a hue that almost becomes clear in the winter. From June to October, its water is of a reddish -brown hue and is highly charged with alluvium. The green color, far to the north, is due to the decay of vegetation brought down by the White Nile. According to Budge there can be no doubt that the Blue Nile or the Atbara is the true maker of Egypt for during their rapid course from the Abyssinian mountains they carry down with them all the rich alluvial silt and mud which has been deposited down through the ages over the land on each side of the Nile that has formed Egypt and Nubia.

Andre Malraux, the French Minister of State for Cultural Affairs painted the most poetic reflection of Nile as he addressed the citizens of the world on March 6, 1960, when the campaign to save the monuments *was* launched:

"The slow flood of the Nile has reflected the melancholy caravans of the Bible (Tirhaka and the Kings of Kush), the armies of Alexander, the Knights of Byzantium and Islam, the soldiers of Napoleon. No doubt when the sandstorm blows across it, its ancient memory no longer distinguishes the brilliant notes of Rameses' triumph from the pathetic dust that settles again in the wake of the defeated armies. And when the sand is scattered again, the Nile is once more alone with its sculpted mountains, its colossal effigies whose motionless reflection has so long been a part of its echo of eternity."

Through the ages each fellah or prince has looked to the Nile for succor. This was even true in July and August of 1988 when the rains came and the Nile vaulted 52 feet more than it had in forty year. There were several villages under water and 10,000 dead from the flood. In the pillage and disaster, the Nubians looked forward to a better crop. herein lay the character of the Nubian people who had been called the "peaceful Nubians." If the waters of the Nile help to form a mind set of the individuals, the cataracts shape the land space and use of the land.

Nubia, the Land of the Cataracts

In a particular sense, Nubia is the product of the Nile cataracts. The cataracts themselves are a series of swift rapids that can impede communication, commerce, and cultivation. There are six major cataracts in all, ranging from Aswan in Egypt to Khartoum in the Sudan. Five of them were politically in the Sudan. The cataracts are the key to Nubia's special identity according to William Y. Adams. Geography and topography determine the specificity of each region transforms along the Nile by the cataracts.

There are three land formations hich will account for much of the diversity in the land space land use. They are limestone, sandstone and a group of huge igneous rocks (the North African, basement complex), composed largely of granite.

Therefore, the Nubian Nile becomes a nurturer and giver of arable lands in the sandstone zones where the bed of the river is broad and wide and the alluvial flood plains makes its way along one or both sides of the river. The valley is a thing of beauty as the alluvial basins formed from the abandoned river channels make patterns in area of low relief. The pinkish yellow sandstone, from which many of the monuments are made, ripples across the desert landscape becomes bleak, marked by granite stones that pierce the sky with their sharp ridges and fissures, and narrow deep wadis. The Nile is stripped of its nurturing attributes and turns into and avenging god. The cataracts are actually formed by the change in texture of the land formations that are encountered by the waters of the Nile as it makes its way to the sea.

The First Cataract and the Sixth Cataract are in the predominantly sandstone area with outcroppings of granite in specific zones. The Fifth Cataract is in the granite zone and the Fourth Cataract moves from granite to a sandstone area in Kareima. The Third Cataract reenters a granite zone at Kerma and the Second Cataract changes back into sandstone between the First and Second Cataracts. Dr. Adams states, "in general, the decent gradient of the Nile averages one foot in ten miles in the sandstone zones, as against one foot in a half mile in the granite zones". These physiographic zones correspond to distinct Reaches in the Nile: Lower Nubia, the Batn el-Hajar, the Abri-Delgo Reach, the Dongola Reach, the Abu Hamed Reach, and the Shendi Reach.

LOWER NUBIA

Nubia is divided into two parts, designated as Lower and Upper Nubia. Lower Nubia lies almost entirely within Egypt. Lower Nubia is located between the First and Second cataracts. The First Cataract lies between Philae and Aswan and was a little over six miles long. Nubia begins just south of Aswan; the First cataract is a natural barrier formed by the mass of granite which thrusts its igneous rock through the sandstone monsters resting amid the sandstone resembling extraterrestial stone monsters resting amid the choked waters, interspersed with the brilliance of the green luxuriant islands. This granite outcropping extended along the Nile valley upstream as far as Kalabsha Gate (35m.south of Aswan). From that point southward wit the Second Cataract the river cuts a narrow trench through the sandstone to the Second cataract. The stream itself was a rather calm, broad, and easy avenue for navigate river crafts.

Alluvium deposited at the mouth of the wadis supported farming at intervals, which could be seen as ribbons of green growth and patches of sand that grew into bluffs to the west of the river. The suitable and habitable areas were narrow strips a mile or so on either side of the river. The sandstone bluffs were sometimes from one hundred to three hundred feet high, providing irregular protected walls to the desert valley floor. The encroaching deserts were interspersed with wadis and desert jebels (small mesa-like mountains) that sometimes approach the height of jebels but never exceed five hundred feet.

The expanse between the First and Second Cataracts was considered peaceful and somewhat prosperous and an easy plain for expansion or exploitation on the part of the Egyptians. However this area is now under water, as it was closest to the Aswan Dam. Also, it is in this area that most of the treasures of Nubia were in the greatest peril and became the Ambassadors

Extraodinaire. Abu Simbel has been moved to higher ground but remains a testament to ancient grandeur and greatness.

The Second Cataract is a little south of Wadi Halfa. For about fourteen miles, the placidity of Lower Nubia is sharply contrasted by the wild rush of tumbling rapids and swift narrow channels pummeling the glistening rocks and prohibiting reverting travel except at great risk. The rocky barriers became outposts for fortification for the middle Kingdom pharaohs who were fearful of the encroachment fern the peoples of the south and the Nubian and Libyan deserts.

Reference to the famous Second Cataract Forts of the Middle Kingdom was found in papyri from the Ramseum Thebes. There were 14 forts listed in the Second Cataract zone, two were further north with one possibly at Elephantine. Their names betrayed the original motivation for their construction "Khakure (Sesostris Ill) is Powerful", "Warding of the Hostile Bows," "Curbing the Countries", and the like.

The forts were in clusters with Buhen, Mirgissa, and Serra in the northernmost stretch of the Second Cataract. Semna East, West and South, along with Uronarti formed the southern flank of the fortresses along the Nile. Most of the fortresses, which reflected unparallel military architectural genius, have been partially cleared. It was from Buhen that the Temple of Buhen was dismantled and sent to Khartoum. [102]

UPPER NUBIA

The land south of the Second Cataract is known as Upper Nubia. The landscape exhibits several different configurations; from rocky and wild to calm and expansive and is subdivided into regions *called* Reaches which were enumerated above, with the exception of Lower Nubia.

THE BATN EL-HAJAR

The area between the Second and Third Cataracts is included between two regions: Batn el Hajar to the north and Abri-Delgo Reach to the south. The Dahl Cataract is the divider. The more northerly reach is the most formidable. Batn el Hajar means "Belly of the Rock". Without a doubt, the 100 miles stretching south from the Second Cataract is dubbed the "most barren and forbidding landscape of all the Nubian environments."

If one stood on the peak of the Rock of Abu Sir, which is seven miles form Wadi Halfa, a startling view would be beheld. The snarling waters, forming gullies swirling around the bare, glistening granite rocks recall to mind the rocks of Scylla and Charybdis of Homer. There seems to be only patches of vegetation in area where the alluvium endured and tiny hamlets peeked through. The gorge channels and slick, steep riverbanks seemed only for the dogged mountain goat and not for man. Seasonal fluctuation in the water level of the river is so enormous during the slack season that one can stand in his or her own field and peer fifty feet below for a sign of the river stream. The hundred or so mile expanse of the Nile through the Batn el Hajar is punctuated with swift rapids and the islands and shoals seem without end.

The Nubians of the *Upper* Nile were able to shield themselves from penetration from the north for centuries because Batn el Hajar was like a 'granite curtain'. This was another of nature's gifts but time from "The Belly of the Rock". each time that an incursion was attempted by the pharaohs from the north, it was maintained for a very brief period of time.

THE ABRI-DELGO REACH

At the Dal Cataract, about one hundred miles from Wadi Halfa, one begins to experience a mirage. At the cataract, the river drops about five feet while the nearby Jebel Dal is about 1,973 feet. Smaller craft are able to negotiate the waters of the Nile and the minor rapids. From Kosha (113 mi) and points further south there is much cultivated land and very tall palms appear. Tall buttes amidst wide clay plains with some of the tallest peaks more than a 1,000 feet high lend a picturesque, mountainous view. There still exists the basement complex exposed at the surface, but it does not appear as formidable as in the Batn el Hajar.

The desert and river valley is not as clearly distinct. The alluvium in the northern part of Abri-Delgo Reach supports a number of well-populated farming villages. For this reason there were found more monuments and temples in this region than any other in Upper New Nubia. There were the remains of a temple of Rameses II at Amara (118 mi) on the west bank and on the east bank those of a Meroitic temple.

THE DONGOLA REACH

Between the Third and Fourth Cataracts, including the great 'S' bend of the Nile, Dongola Reach which is about 200 miles in length. Dongola Reach is much like the Abri-Delgo Reach from the south. In appearance, it is almost featureless, yet it is unique in other ways. The river is wide, calm and navigable. The annual overflow of the Nile is very nearly like that of Lower Nubia with a high productive yield and expansive vistas.

It was in the lower limit of this Reach that Kerma (2500-2400B.C.), the most ancient indigenous Nubia civilization was found. It attracted Egyptians "conquistadors" during the New Kingdom and later was almost the seat of the great and powerful Nubian Kings and ultimate conquerors of Egypt. As the Nile descends from the Fourth Cataract,

Jebel Barkal, the majestic Holy Mountain, is sighted on the right with ruins of several temples and pyramids in the cemetery of Barkal spread before it. The remains of the City of Sanam and the pyramids of the Royal Cemetery of Napata are on the left bank of the river Nile.

Much later the Dongola Reach spawned yet another medieval kingdom, that of Christian Makouria, (750 A.D.). Aerial photographs again reveal an interesting topography.

The outline of fields and ditches were still visible, indicating thousands of acres under cultivation in which is now the present desert.

THE ABU HAMED REACH

The Abu Hamed Reach, another area of granite, begins at the Fourth Cataract near Kareima and marks the end of the fertile productive Dongola area. The head of the fourth Cataract is near Abu Hamed, 587 miles from Wadi Haifa. Abu Hamed was named after a venerated local sheik buried there. It has been said that the caravans began their treks over the desert at Abu Hamed and those that left any article at the tomb of the sheik at their departure would return and find the article uninjured.

The navigability of the Nile almost ceases because of the cataracts, numerous islands and shoals. This might account for the birth of population in this zone as well as no monuments or areas of archaeological interest. There was limited farming and the land space was also used for limited grazing. It is equally devoid of important remains from the Napatan- Meriotic civilization and from the high period of the medieval kingdoms. Its only conspicuous relics belong to the medieval age of military feudalism, when this area, with its numerous and inaccessible islands, provided a perfect refuge for predatory landlords.

THE SHENDI REACH

The Shendi Reach, like the Abu Hamed, has not been well explored by the archaeologists. The Fifth Cataract, called "the Cataract of Wild Asses" is the natural barrier between Abu flamed and Shendi Reach. It begins at Wadi el-Hamar, 76 miles from Abu Hamed and ends about 88 miles from Abu Hamed. The Nile is practically impassable at this point.

This uppermost Reach of what is considered Nubia south of Berber at the Atbara River extends to the confluence of the Blue and White Niles. The Atbara River reaches the Nile on the east bank about 151 miles from Abu Flamed and 300 miles from Khartoum. The Atbara River, the last major tributary to the Nile, contributes one fifth of the Nile volume during the flood.

In this stretch, Shendi appears like Dongola Reach, only the igneous granite rocks of the basement complex are closer to the surface. The traveler finds little interest in the landscape, and on each bank of the river the torn growths and the grass provide strips of cultivable land on which the people eke out an existence. In the distance the jebels and granite outcroppings mark the valley like sentinels.

Topographically, Shendi is representative of the true Sudan with its semi-desert grasslands and sporadic thorn three which extend south of the Sahara. Pastoral nomads were very much a part of the landscape as they could be seen camped at the deserts' edge in great numbers. The valley between Atbara and Shendi harbors the great numbers. The valley between Atbara and Shendi harbored the great ancient city of Meroe, regaled by Strabo, the geographer, and Herodotus, the historian. It flourished between 300B.C. and 200 A.D. and was located about 44 miles from Atbara and three and one half miles on the east bank of the Nile. Not far from the city and further to the east were the pyramid-tombs of the Meroitic Kings of Kush. Further south, near Shendi about 86 miles from Atbara, in the dry hinterlands are remains of other Meroitic cities. Wad ben Naga, at the Sixth Cataract, known as the Shabaloka Cataract, is about 10 miles long. It is a few miles Musawwarat es Sufra north of Khartoum and about 130 miles from Atbara. The nurturant Nile flows through a channel about 500 feet wide, created out of the granite rocks. There is continual alluvium on both sides of the river that support numerous farming villages and a bountiful population. The islands on the river are filled with crops all the way to Khartoum. At Khartoum the Niles are spotted with passenger boats, steamers, barges and ferries and the joyous population who are industrious and mysterious.

CLIMATE

The adaptation to the climate and the resources of the environment by the indigenous Nubian population was gradual throughout the ages. The Nubians lived in one of the hottest and most arid regions of the world; they also experience one of the most extreme climates on earth. "At Wadi Haifa, on the border between Lower and Upper Nubia, the mean daily temperature from May to September is about 90 degrees; the daily high nearly exceeds 100 degrees, and my reach above 120 degrees. Winter, from November to March, is mild, with mean daily temperatures between 60-70 degrees, and occasional cold spells when the thermometer drops nearly to freezing. Nubia rarely experiences rain. This is especially true of the area between Aswan and Dongola. In addition, a whole generation might pass without rain. Arial rainy season of abut eight to ten weeks duration occurs south of Dongola with one-inch precipitation, increasing to seven inches at Khartoum. The heat following the rain can be very oppressive and humid.

The annual fluctuation of the waters of the Nile between low season and high season is excessive. A minimum of 60 million cubic feet a day is expected the beginning of May, which is low season. An increase of over 1000 can be reached by September, the beginning of the season of high water. The capriciousness of the Nile is accepted by the Nubians as they learned to take advantage of the low and high yield of the soil that in a sense is, neither Egyptian nor Nubian, because it along with the water originates over 2,000 miles away in the Abyssinian highlands. Nubians also learned to patch their mud-brick houses if they were still standing after the floods. I witnessed, that and more during the 1988 floods at Khartoum.

The winds, even though fierce in the winter are, less dreaded than the summer rain. The summer wind is a pleasant relief from the excessive summer heat. The winds are expected to blow constantly over the eastern Sahara desert from the north at least once a month. Nothing is spared in its wake. Fields and houses can be swallowed up forcing, at times, the abandonment of whole villages, particularly on the west (windward) bank of the Nile.

The river navigation can come to a standstill in the absence of the wind. The wind is also a boon to upstream traffic; it follows that the subsistence level and population density are affected by the rigors of the climate and the vagaries of the river.

VEGETATION AND ANIMAL LIFE

Soil, water and rain in reasonable proportions for vegetation, has been the eternal prayer of the patient Nubia for centuries. The desert only blooms with a sufficient amount of rainfall and the banks of the Nile provide three kinds of arable land: Seluka land, and Saqia and Shaduf land Basin land is a depression found between the natural levees of the river and the desert. From Aswan to Dongola the vegetation is dependent upon the annual inundation of the water flowing into the Nile from the Blue and White Niles and other tributaries originating thousands of miles away. The waters are directed into the basins during the High Nile season and then drained off after the lands have been soaked.

The basin system is effective throughout Egypt and Nubia with some variations. It allows water to be passed from higher to lower levels after resting for a predetermined time. The basins in Lower Nubia are larger than the ones in Upper Nubia, which are smaller and simpler. Each basin has a feeder canal with one or more drains and inner divisions. In some area, it appeared like the dyke system in Holland.

Seluka land receives its name from the seluka, a stick used to dig crops, which result in minimal effort and confined to the growing season. Seluka land is found on the banks and islands of the river that have received enough moisture to support a crop without further wetting during the high inundation period. Cultivation varies according to the patches of land available.

Saqia lands are usually well above the watermark and require the water lifting device known as the Saqia or oxen-driven water wheel. The device is a large cogged, wooden wheel with buckets suspended much Ike a Ferris wheel and yoked to one or two draft animals. Since the introduction of the saqia in Hellenistic Egypt, cultivation became more intensive and cost effective. One acre of saqia land can yield 350 bushels of wheat.

The Shaduf, a simpler device, has been used on the land since the new kingdom "It is nothing more than a counter-poised lever with a bucket at one end - easy to construct and worked by hand. It can lift up to 3 meters, but the higher the lift, the fewer strokes and be made per minute. With a lift of 2 meters, a shaduf can water about half a feddan. They are usually used to water vegetable patches during the flood season."

There are three growing seasons: Shitwi, or the winter season from November until March; Seifi, or summer season about April or May and ends just before the floods in late July or August and lasts until November. During the flood season the only food produced is in the saqia fields with millet (durra), beans, and maize as the main crops. Immediately after the flood, according to Burckhardt, millet, also known as fodder food, is planted which lasted the rest of the year. Watermelons, peas, lentils, beans, barley and tobacco also lasted throughout the season.

High above the patches of green produce are the plentiful palm trees and the luxuriant acacias. Near the desert spring are low-growing shrubs, wiry grasses and other trees. The date palms grow in great profusion along the river - bank and amidst the cultivated fields. The Dom palm is a low branching species, which grow in clumps or individually on the edge of the desert. The tamarisk tree appears each year below the high water level of the Nile, in dense carpets, near the dunes of the riverbank. The trunk of the Dom palm and the wood of the acacia, called sunt, are used for building. The Dom palm furnishes the roofs of Nubian houses. The sunt is used for boats, house doors, and windows because the wood is harder. The date palm is the most valued of all the trees because it is one of the principal cash crops of Nubia.

Animal husbandry is an alternative for the Nubian farmer as he adapts to the capriciousness of the Nile floods. Animals graze on the wild grasses and the residue of the floodplain and fodder that is provided during the flood season. The herds of cattle, sheep and goats provide the milk and butter, for the community. The cattle are usually used to power the Saqia and not to plow the fields. Chickens are seen in the courtyards or under foot as women go to the riverbanks or the well. The beasts of transport are the donkey and the camel, the latter of which is known as the ship of the desert: Dogs, although despised, guard the houses; and the skinny cats act like predators about the pyramids.

The exotic animals of the past, such as hippopotami, elephants, giraffes, rhinoceroses, and buffalo, have long sense been displaced in Nubia but can still be seen on the ancient pottery. Neolithic Nubian rock drawings are in the zoo at Khartoum. The animals of the night, namely the jackals, foxes, and hyenas, skulk far from the riverbanks about 30 or more miles inland in the desert wadis.

Nubia is ideal for bird watchers at different seasons along the Nile. The most common are the wild geese portrayed in many of the tombs of the pharaohs as a recreational activity. Graceful egrets and cranes are mirrored in the Nile sometimes as graceful as the feluccas that swoop and swirl below. A coveted sight is that of the colorful hoopoe stalking in the field, continuously bobbing its head. The crows and the sparrows imperil the grain crops.

The fish, an early Christian symbol of life, was certainly for the Nubians an important staple and subsistence activity in its early history. There are still forty known species in existence most of which are edible. Along the Blue Nile, you can see fisherman with huge nets between two buoys dragging the Nile for the catch of the day. Nile perch is highly prized for its succulence.

It is in Upper Nubia that you can find poisonous and semi-poisonous snakes, and the little lizards that scurry about the pavement and the walls of the houses. The other worry bugs, such as flies, mosquitoes, and gnats are inevitable. The real pest is the nimitti is like a miniature gnat, which appears in swarms during the spring and causes irritation from its bite. The scorpion has its aquatic snails which acute "Snail Fever" or bilharzias, a debilitating disease affecting the kidney and other organs.

NUBIA: THE LAND OF GOLD

Nubia, as it has been pointed out, was divided into two parts: Lower Nubia which is literally from the first to the Second cataract: and Upper Nubia which extends beyond the Second Cataract to the Sixth cataract. This corresponds to the modern political division of the United Arab Republic of Egypt and the republic of the Sudan. In Ancient times, Lower Egypt was called Wawat and Upper Nubia was called Kush. The name Nubia was derived from the word Nub meaning Gold.

The Gold of Wawat or Lower Nubia was the bedrock of the Egyptian economy and power of Egypt in Asia during the XVIIIth Dynasty. Egypt's position as a world power depended upon the large amount of gold as extracted from Nubia. "Send me much more gold," writes an Asiatic King to Akhenaton, "in my brother's land gold is as common as dust." When the Napatan and Meroitic empires were in ascendancy, as the XXVth dynasty, the same gold was crucial to their dynastic goals.

The Gold of Wawat or Lower Nubia came from the mouth of the Wadi Allaqi at the Fortress of Kubban. The Gold of Kush was taken from Duweishat district, a few miles from Semna. Gold was expected to be found throughout Nubia, wherever the veins of igneous rock were exposed. The main sources of gold ware were those of the above and the gold found in the Desert of Coptos, located between Upper Egypt and the Red sea. Over eighty-five ancient mines have been located in the northeastern Sudan. Diodorus wrote a detailed account of his visit to the mine -fields in the second century A.D.

Diodorus has preserved his work. The mining technology was reasonably sophisticated for the time. The process included firing the ore to crack the rock which was further broken by pick and hammer, and then reduced to dust by hammer and hand milling. The powder was rinsed to separate the metal, which was finally molded into ingots. In reference to, Nubian mines Vercoutter

(1959) said that only a few mines have permanent installations, huts, washing tables, furnaces, remains of melting pots and slag heaps. In Ramses I records that 'if a few of the caravaneers of the gold washing went thither, it was only half of them that arrived, for they died of thirst on the road, together with the asses which they drove before them." Upper Nubia produced less gold than Wawat, Most of the gold was panned between the Second and Third Cataracts.[103]

The amount of gold extracted in only three of the reign of Thuthmose III totaled 8,682 deben. A deben was equal to approximately twenty pounds of gold and a kidet was a ring of gold weighing five pounds. The 1.710 pounds of gold extracted from Wawat, Upper Egypt and the 120 pounds extracted from Kush in one year amounted to well over three million dollars on the market twenty years ago.

According to the Annals of Thutmose III, gold was not the only resource contributed by Nubia to the coffers of the Egyptian Pharaoh:

Tribute of Wawat

Year 31 92 cattle, 1 harvest

Year 33 20 slaves, 104 cattle, 1 harvest

Year 38 2,844 deben of gold and 1 Kidet of gold; an unknown quantity of slaves, ivory and ebony, and 1 harvest

Year 39 89 cattle, ivory and ebony

Year 41 3,144 deben and 1 Kidet of gold; and unknown quantity of slaves, ivory, ebony, and 1 harvest

The tribute from Kush was equally revealing. Gold was not the first metal that attracted the attention of foreigners to Nubia. Buhen smelted copper ore but its source has never been discovered. Pink granite from Aswan was also a prized commodity for columns, obelisks and stelae. Ivory suggests that elephants were available through the Nubian middleman. The Meroitic residents of Upper Nubia used the elephant as a beast of war. Other resources were ostrich eggs and feathers, various kinds of skins and live animals for recreation and enjoyment.

NUBIA: THE LAND OF THE BOW

For many centuries, the Egyptians seemed to think that the people south of Elephantine was a potential danger. It was a king from the South that united the two countries so the dangerous potential of the south has always existed. Historically, the "Land of the Bow" was the ancient name, for the Egyptian province between Thebes and Aswan. It was long called Ta-Seti and the hieroglyphic documents traditionally apply this term to what we now call Nubia. The fighting prowess of the Nubians and their skill with the bow has won them the name of "pupil-smiters."

They have long fought in the army of the Egyptians as mercenaries. Their handiness with the spear and javelin is also known. There was a model of these men found in a tomb c. 2100 B.C. These men guarded the garrisons of the Second Cataract Forts. One of the forts was named "Warding of the Hostile Bows." The term, bow was used by Strabo, when he referred to the weapons of the Ethiopians (Meroites) or Elephant eaters. He wrote that they used bows four cubits long, and hardened in fire.

The earliest depiction of the Nubian with a bow was in the prehistoric art found at Abkan dated between 7,000 and 4,000 B.C. The rock pictures also included giraffe, orxy, gazelle, hartebeest, wild ass, elephant, hippopotamus, rhinoceros, ostrich and hare. The hunters are depicted with dogs and other various human figures. It appears that the Neolithic wet phase enriched the already well-established hunting-fishing -gathering economy of the Nubians on the Upper Nile.

From another point of view, the "Land of the Bow" was a coveted land. Most of the resources required for empire building were to be found south of The Second cataract: mineral, human, animal and natural resources. The Egyptian incursions into Nubia were always either commercial of military, depending upon the needs of both countries. Nubian mercenaries and Nubian slaves seemed to dictate the relationship between Nubia and Egypt during the pre-dynastic period. Although according to Professor Adams there must have been peaceful exchanges during the First and Second Dynasties. The grave goods found in the A horizon indicated a high degree of Nubian and Egyptian commerce.

However, there are several records that suggest some hostility between the Nubians and the Egyptians. Exhibited in the antiquities Garden of the Sudan national Museum of Khartoum is a text originally engraved on a sandstone slab found near The Second Cataract (Jebel Sheikh Suleiman) .The name of the King Jer of the first Dynasty is engraved and the text is in hieroglyphics and pictogram. The scene shows a Nubian chief bound to the prow of an Egyptian ship. A bound figure on the left bears the curved bow sign, which is the traditional hieroglyph for Lower Nubia. A corpse lies in the water under the boat. The scene is thought to commemorate the conquest of two villages identified by a bird and an unknown sign. The Palermo stone documents a massive slave raid during the Fourth Dynasty where King Sneferu and his armies "hacked" up the Nubians and returned home with "7, 000 prisoners and 200,00 head of cattle."[104]

Peace existed in the "Land of the Bow" during the Sixth dynasty under King Sneferu's enemy was the Bedouin to the north of Sinai instead of the south. However, the commercial potential of the land to the south was not lost on Mernere. The King Menere found his Master of the footstool and saddle bearer Uni, a vigilant, trustworthy servant and elevated him to Governor of the South. According to the biography of Uni, on the walls of his tomb, he was entrusted to secure a false door, offering tables and doorways for the upper chamber of the king's pyramid called Menere-Shines-and-is beautiful. Uni made a trip to the alabaster quarry at Hatnub to bring a huge offering table, which was brought downstream in a cargo boat. Uni built a boat out of acacia wood of 60 cubits in length and 30 cubits wide.[105]

On the next trip to the granite quarry, Uni was ordered to dig five canals through the cataract and to make three more cargo boats, and four tow boats of acacia wood from Wawat, Yam and Mazzoi. The boats were launched and laden with large granite blocks for the king's pyramid. King Menere was so pleased that he visited the chiefs of Nubia who had furnished the wood for his quarry boats. Uni was proud of the mandates that he has fulfilled for his king. The inscription in Uni's tomb was completed with the following paragraph: "I was one beloved of his father, and praised by his mother; first-born-pleasant to his brothers, the count, the real governor of the south, revered by Osiris, Uni."

When Uni was a child, he began his career under Teti, the first king of the sixth Dynasty, as an under-custodian. When Pepi took the throne, Uni served as a judge at the Nekken court and was soon promoted to a superior custodianship of the Royal Domain. Uni was asked by Pepi to organize an army for the campaign against the Bedouin north of the Sinai, the land off the Sand-dwellers and five times saw action in that area... The army was composed "Of many ten thousands; in the entire South, southward to Elephantine and northward to Aphroditopolis; in the Northland, the entire stronghold [was composed] of Nubians from Trthet, Mazoi, Yam, and the land of Temeh."

The soldiers from the "Land of the Bow" were well represented. Harkuf became the next governor of the South or "Land of the Bow" after the death of Uni. He became a highly respected and successful caravan leader and tradesman under King Mernere and his son Pepi II. Pepi I ascended the throne at the age of six and ruled the country for ninety-four years. The inscriptions in the throne of Harkuf lend an invaluable insight into the commercial enterprises beyond the Second and Third Cataracts and the Dongola Reach, Harkuf was fortunate because he was accompanied by his father who could introduce him to the complexities of being a trader, the best routes, his Nubian trading partners and the dangers to be encountered. Harkuf made four journeys into the Southern lands and he had the distinction of being the first caravan -conductor to trade with Yam. The location of Yam has been the source of conjecture. The inscriptions suggest, however; that it was located in or near the Kerma Basin.[106]

It was on Harkuf's fourth trip that he returned with a dwarf, who was a sacred dancer from one of the tribes of inner Africa. Pepi II, only eight years old, was in his second year reign. The child-king was so happy to hear from Harkuf that he had reached the frontier and had in his possession such a prized gift. The letter that Harkuf received from Pepi was engraved on the front of Harkuf's tomb in Aswan, which was evidence of the great favor he enjoyed from Pepi. Upon reaching Yam for his fourth trip, Harkuf made an appropriate ceremonial greeting and was rewarded with "300 asses laden with incense, ebony, heknu, grain, panthers, ivory throw sticks and every good product."[107]

The Yamite prince also provided Harkuf with soldiers for the Egyptian army. The relations with the land of the Bow deteriorated during the later part of Pepi's reign because of the centralization of his power which resulted in the loss of amicable arrangements with the Nubian chiefs of the South. This cycle of economic and military interest was to continue throughout the history of Nubian and Egyptian affairs. However, the relationship between Egypt and Nubia was always either common or else military depending upon the needs of forth comers.

CHAPTER 7.
INVISIBLE NUBIANS MADE VISIBLE

<u>ORIGINS</u>

The peoples of the Nile Valley from the ancient boundary between Nubia and Egypt located at the First Cataract to at least the Sixth Cataract above Khartoum have only been a modest concern since the publications of the sixties. The Eight International Conference of Nubian Studies in Lille, France, September 11-17, 1994 has generated much more information from the continuous archaeological research as reflected by its title "Nubia Thirty Years Later". Multi -disciplinary interest among the scholars across the United States and in Europe has proliferated.

According to William Y. Adams, "In many Continental European Countries today there are separate chairs and departments of the Nubian studies, and since the International Society for Nubian Studies in Great Britain, the United States and Canada remain firmly lodged within the University and Museum, departments of Egyptology. " [107] Since 1992, the Louvre, in Paris, the British Museum, the Boston Museum of Fine Arts, The University of Pennvalnia and the Royal Ontario Museum of Toronto have separated their superb collections to display them in separate galleries. The perceptions of Nubia's place in the historical arena of ancient cultures are changing with new research and new attitudes.

In the last chapter, we explored the riverain view of Nubia and the influence of the Nile.

In this chapter, we will continue to explore the various interpretations of Nubia. At different points in time, the Nubians have been called Ethiopians not modern Abyssinians), or Kushites. The term is interchangeable, as you have noted. The ancient, predynastic Nubians like ancient predynastic Egyptians did not leave written texts, which lend to the obscurity of the word, Nubian. However, these peoples lived in the Nile Valley south of the First cataract, which was the ancient boundary of Egypt, some five hundred miles from the Mediterranean Sea.

The early Egyptian texts and the Bible designated this area as Kush (Cush). The classical Greek, Roman, and early Christian authors consistently referred to this area as Ethiopia. Nubia refers to the same area, which is divided into two sections. Lower Nubia extends from the First Cataract to the Second Cataract and Upper Nubia extends from the Second Cataract to the Sixth Cataract, which is above present day Khartoum. Lower Nubia has been referred to as Egyptian Nubia and Upper Nubia as Sudanese Nubia for political and geographical reasons.

Who are the Nubians (Ethiopians or Kushites)? Where did they originate? Are they an ancient myth rejuvenated, a people appropriated for political ends, or an historical reality that has just been discovered? Homer, the Father of History recounts that these peoples were the first of humanity. What does this mean? Can the ancient Nubians (Ethiopians or Kushites) be defined so that the people of today who have been removed for over eight millennia include them in their historical understanding? Will they be able to take their place with other ancient civilizations? Lastly, can one trace the bio-cultural, political mosaic of Nubian culture backward in a continuous evolution to its autochthonous beginning?

In tracing the origin and identity of the Nubians and other peoples, we can begin with the discovery of mankind or humanity in the east Rift Valley. One can assume continuity as a part of the human aggregates' existence or origin. When the Neanderthals were discovered in Europe less than two hundred years ago, they had been in existence for 100,000 years; but there was no knowledge of human ancestry in Africa. Today it is an accepted fact that the earliest specimen of Homo erectus and *Homo ergaster* fossils are from East Africa. At the Olduvai Gorge, a partial cranium was found dating 1.25 million years old. In 1984, at Lake Turkana, above the Gorge was found a complete *ergaster* skeleton, dating about 1.6 million years ago. When we think of our own species, Homo sapiens came into being 60,000 years ago in Africa.

When one considers that evolution is a complex change in organisms over time and space through the process of adaptation culturally and bio-chemically, we must turn to the latest discoveries in the biochemical evolution. Scientists all over the world are using mitochondrial DNA to recreate the migration of the ancient peoples across and out of Africa. It must be kept in mind that the mitochondrial DNA is inherited only from the mother. Just recently, the Statistical Institute using DNA from a blood sample of thirty different ethnic groups, including an ancient Indian tribe to be a model for the subcontinent.[108]

The data suggests that the populations arrived in India from Africa and then rapidly dispersed and expanded. This may further studies in migration theory. It is the use of Mitochondrial DNA that traces all humanity back to the hypothetical African Eve. The historian, Christopher Ehret, attempts to help the student of today to recognize the mind-set of the cultural past when he writes "in the work of certain mid-century writers who favored the idea of a million-multigenerational evolution of a single species all across the Eastern hemisphere, one can detect, sadly, a more insidious tendency, a difficulty with accepting the idea that all of us might have a common ancestor."[109]

In tracing the identity and origin of Nubian, one would not be stretching the imagination to begin with the discovery of humanity in East Africa. Evidence is not forthcoming at this time to fill the historical gap of several million years. However, the Nubians have continuously existed in the Nile Valley, continuously since 10,000 B.C. There is agreement among most scholars, especially the Nubiologists, at this point. The assertion is based on artifacts uncovered in recent campaigns.

The biocultural evolutionists suggest that the patterns of human evolution began with Homo erectus over a million years ago and evolved through mutation, political adaptation, and diffusion over time. The Nubians have ancestors in this aggregate of humanity. In sum, the other certainty that would apply to the Nubians (Homer's, first of all humanity) is the genetic unity of all humanity.

There is evidence of human activity in Nubia for over a hundred thousand years. However, the archaeologists have not found evidence of cultural continuity until the late Stone Age, which is Neolithic. It was during this period that a great transition from the fishing and hunting economy to a more sedentary life based on the cultivation of food.

CHARACTER

The character of a people may be defined historically, culturally and racially. The lack of empirical evidence can produce a plethora of ambiguities depending upon the eye of the beholder. If viewed from the stance of an outsider, the Nubian is defined not by himself but by the yardstick of another. Such definition is full of economic, cultural and political overtones. The conqueror is concerned with its own dominance or perceived superiority. The vanquished is concerned with the pride of the fallen. The early Egyptians who considered themselves as the only true men saw Nubians less than men, slaves, if you will, to enhance their dynastic gains. The people of Judah saw the Nubians through the eyes of the prophets as the wretched and cursed. The Greeks viewed themselves as descendants of the gods and Homer saw the Nubians as the noblest of men. During classical antiquity, the Greeks and the Romans were the first to classify the other by the by color and the yardstick was the Ethiopian.

Snowden pointed to Manilus, first century A.D., when he mentioned in his poem on Astrology the groups who were to be included most frequently in a Classical "color scheme": Ethiopians, the blackest; Indians, less sunburned; Egyptians mildly dark; and the Mauri (Moors), whose name was derived from the color of their skins. Herodotus explained skin coloring by the rays of the sun. He called the Ethiopian "burnt faces." Snowden also states that Alexander while visiting the Indians, found them to be blacker than all peoples except the Ethiopians; those south of the Ganges were described as browned by the sun but not so black as the Ethiopians, northern Indians resembled the Egyptians.[110]

It is difficult to avoid racial stereotyping as it exists today, as classification by color and race is more virulent because of the shadow of colonialism and the deprecation of Africa and Africans. It is because of preconceived notions of race and cultural conditioning that we are taught how Nubians should look and how all other Africans should look. The irony lies in the fact that they all African.

The character of the Nubian must properly be defined within the context of the historical, linguistic, and racial evidence available to date. Christopher Frye, in his lecture on "Race, Empire and Post Empire" reminds us of the senselessness of the concept of race. "In the ancient Mediterranean world, for instance, the writings, paintings and sculpture of ancient Egypt show that rule and subordination were not assigned according to physical appearances. It was the same in Greece and Rome. In the Roman Empire, slaves were brought in from all directions: from Britain, Eastern Europe, Asia and Africa. They could not be distinguished from their masters in physical appearance. What was significant was the slaves' status, not his physical appearance.[112]

VARIOUS TYPES OF NUBIANS

Racially, both the Nubians and the Egyptians are an admixture of African and Mediterranean types in various proportions. The aggregate of types is seen in the African American whose color ranges from white to ebony. The Nubian is of medium frame and stature, slightly taller than the Egyptian, but decidedly shorter than the Sudanese. I was struck by the beauty and litheness of many of the Nubians as Homer was and also Vergil when he described the ebony swarthiness and beauty of Memnon, the Ethiopian king. Solomon, in the Song of Songs in the Bible, honored the black and beautiful maiden.

The hair of the Nubian varies from soft curls to wiry braids and thick rolls like lambs wool, such as that of Isaiah in the bible. The facial features exhibit the same variation, from lips complimented with noses of the same variety. The mark of beauty for the Nubian or Kushite beauty is her swaying corpulence and it is said that for men corpulence is a sign of wealth. Facial scarification is more apparent in the more southern regions of the Sudan. Scholars say that the early Nubians exhibited the same characteristics.

The ancient Nubian's (Kushite's) physical characteristics, as well as their cultural identity can be rediscovered from the objects and images of them found in their tombs, temples, wall paintings, sculpture, pottery, jewelry and crowns of gold, and rock painting found in the continuing archaeological campaigns.

A figure found in the tomb of Seti (1291-1297 B.C) at Luxor in the Valley of the Kings shows the four branches of man according to the Egyptians. The accompanying hieroglyphs designate from right to left, Egyptians, brown, western Asians, less brown, Nubians, black; Libyans, yellow. There is a rare statuette of a beautiful Nubian concubine in the Boston Museum of Fine Arts dated about 2000-1785 B.C. There are also dolls found in a tomb from the Eleventh dynasty indicating the sensitivity toward the beauty of the Nubian or Kushite woman. The Egyptian Museum of Cairo has a model painted in wood of a troop of Nubian archers representing their mercenary status from 2200B.C. to 2000B.C. when they were heavily involved in the military activities of the Intermediate Period. There is a limestone stela from the same period with traces of paint in the Leiden Museum showing a Nubian Mercenary with his wife.

An ostracon (flake of limestone) representing the Queen of Punt is an example of the contact that queen Hapsepsut had with her neighbor to the south when she sent her expedition to the exotic land of Punt. The queen is very fleshy. Ethnologists point to the similarities of the royal women of Kagagwe in northwest Tanzania and the later depictions of the queens of Meroe. The two wall reliefs in the mortuary temple of Queen Hatshepsut of Deir el Bahri lend more insight into the customs and images of the people, The text shows the march of the elite troops, which formed part of the festival procession, represented on the walls of the uppermost terrace in the queen's temple.

The soldiers are carrying bows and arrows with their right hands and axes with their left. The weaponry is distinctly Nubian. Skin coloring is grayish and their hair is gathered at the neck in tiered locks. The faces are definitely Nubian, confirmed by their features, the lower portions of the faces extend forword, the nasolabial furrows are deeply impressed, and the lips are full. A second relief fragment, also of painted limestone, is featuring Egyptian soldiers. The differentiation from that of the Nubian soldier is indicated by the reddish brown skin color, close-cropped hair, falling to the shoulder and no weapons.

II.

ENTR'ACTE

"Knowledge is the orderly loss of information not piling it on bit by bit."

Boulding

NATIVE BED FOR BURIAL,
FOUND AT KERMA

FOOT OF BED LEG, BRONZE

PYRAMID COMPLEX AT NURI

SPHINX OF TAHARQA, NUBIAN
PHARAOH, XXV DYN.

CHAPTER 8.
EGYPTIAN CHRONOLOGY

Nubian and Egyptian political and cultural history because of contiguity in time and geographical space seem for the Egyptologists to run on a continuum of shared existence based on symbiosis. However, the entity that is Nubia achieved greater historical significance in the twentieth century than it had in previous centuries. To the scholars and adventurers from the early fifteenth century to the end of the nineteenth century Nubia was still in the realm of the exotic and boundaries were to be explored. Yet it was G.A Reisner who was acclaimed the father of Nubiology as discussed in Chapter III. His schema for Nubian cultural history has been largely episodic and followed by the Egyptologists who presented an Egyptocentric continuum.

The chronology of Nubia will consist of the Nubiocentric approach advanced by W.Y. Adams who did not discard the Reisner assumptions of the cultural development of Nubia to define his ubiquitous groups, A, B, C and X. You will find that the X Group will be more clearly defined. Because of fifty years of archaeological investigation and the years (22+) spent by professor Adams in Nubia and the Sudan and the fact that it was no longer "necessary to bring in alien peoples to account for the relatively minor differences between the 'A- Group' and 'C- Group or between Meroitic and 'X-Group'; we can see them as the result of normal on going processes of cultural evolution and diffusion."[112] Adams changes the nomenclature from groups to Horizons in consistency with his belief in the comings and goings of the same peoples over time.

The Egyptian chronology will consist of a historical summary based on the summary report on Pharaonic Egypt in the *General History of Africa* by Vercoutter, diagram by J. Vercoutter, and the Historical Summary of Egypt found in the practical guide "The Egyptian Museum of Turin" and other textual sources. The prevailing view as expressed in the *General History of Africa* is as follows:

"Although Egypt was open to cultural currents coming especially from the East, this volume shows how the Egyptian civilization rests to a great extent on an African foundation and also that Egypt, which was part of Africa, was one of the main centers of universal civilization in ancient times and that a great deal of the scientific knowledge, art, literature emanated from that region, and influenced Greece in particular. In the fields of mathematics (geometry, arithmetic, etc.) astronomy and measurement of time (calendar), medicine, architecture, music and literature (narrative, poetry, tragedy, etc.), Greece received, developed, and transmitted to the West a great part of Egyptian legacy from Pharaonic and Ptolemaic Egypt".

"According to records mentioned in this volume, Nubia has been closely connected with Egypt since earliest times as a result of various factors: physical factors, particularly similar geographical features, especially between Nubia and the extreme southern part of Upper Egypt; historical and political factors, which are important in themselves and were greatly strengthen by the physical aspect which are reflected in culture and religion. Thus, the beginning of the First Egyptian Dynasty, and through the Old Kingdom, the Egyptians paid a great deal of attention to the northern area of Nubia, which they considered as a complimentary part of their own country. They organized a flow of trade with the Nubians, exploited Nubian natural resources and when any Nubian resistance was shown they sent military missions to end it." [113]

The various periods and divisions in Egyptian history as well as the dating need some explanation. The Neolithic age and its influences of perhaps 10,000 years ago appeared in Africa played out in two ways of life of Lower and Upper Egypt during the wet phase, which occurred toward the end of the Neolithic age. According to the Western historians, history begins with the invention of writing. Egyptian history in that period is known as the Dynastic period of Pharaonic age. This period stretches from the Third Millennium (3000B.C.) to the end if the first Millennium, a period well over three thousand years before the Christian era. All the dates therefore will refer to the period before Christ.

By combining the Lunar calendar, dates of the religious festivals, the natural calendar based on the periodicity of the flood of the Nile, dates appearing in the Turin Papyrus and Palermo stone, the beginning of Egyptian history was reckoned at 3000B.C. (-3000). The Palermo Stone, a diorite slab, is carved on both sides with the names of all the Pharaohs who reigned in Egypt from the beginning to the Fifth Dynasty, around -2450. Each Pharaoh is listed with the dates of their sovereignty in the order of their succession and the significant events of each reign. The Turin Papyrus provides only the lists of the rulers, their complete venue, and the number of years, months and days of their reign in chronological order. The complete list ranges from the earliest pharaohs to about 1200 B.C. When examining these chronologies, allowance for a large margin for error should be considered. The periods before the dynastic history are designated, prehistory or pre-dynastic, pro-dynastic or archaic. Although the focus of this book is around the New Kingdom and the end of the Pharaonic age, the significant periods prior to that time will be cited by millennia, dynasty and significant events within each delineation.

NEOLITHIC OR NEW STONE AGE (10,000- 6000B.C.)

Although the activities of humankind can be traced in the Nile valley for over 100,000 years, the agricultural or food producing revolution, nomadic, semi nomadic husbandry, and the wet phase appeared at this time.

PREDYNASTIC PERIOD (5000- 3000B.C.)

The northern cultures (Faiyum and Merimda) were flourishing Neolithic cultures exemplified by organizing social groups around the subsistence needs, fishing and hunting, settlement and coalitions.

NAGADA I NAGADA I (TASA/BADARI/AMRA, 4300-3000B.C.)

These southern cultures continued to exhibit Neolithic influences: blacktopped vase production was begun. The entrenchment of the 'food producing revolution' became apparent in the Delta Neolithic (Merimda and Faiyum) or Northern Cultures of Lower Egypt, and the Badarian culture of Upper Egypt. The other influence was the pastoralism that made life possible in the 'newly inhabitable Sahara.

Petrie and other excavators discovered predynastic cemeteries in Upper Egypt at the end of the nineteenth century. The principal predynastic cultures are distinguished as Naqada I (early) and Naqada II (late). T.G.H. James, former keeper of the department of Egyptian Antiquities, British Museum, warns about the nomenclature in the above instance because they were named after a precedent for the naming of subsequent sites. Amra was named after a village of el-Amra; Badarian after the village of el-Badari. James suggests that the names of Amratian and Gerzean should be discarded because they are merely duplicates for different stages of the Naqada I and Nagada II cultures.

Little is known about the political organization of Egypt during the predynastic period. However, we know that some coalitions were being formed as suggested by earlier literary evidence. The entities or nomes coalesced around certain gods representing different districts. The eastern gnomes of the delta were joined under the god Adjjty; the west followed Horus. The political centers were Naqada (Nubt) in the south with Seth as the chief deity and Behdet in the north with the falcon-good Horus as the chief deity.

DYNASTY I (3000-2600B.C.)

Tradition indicates that Menes was the King from the South who unified the two kingdoms of Upper and Lower Egypt. Archaeological sources identify Menes with Narmer who is shown wearing two crowns, Red and White, on a huge palette in the Cairo Museum. The King of Lower Egypt traditionally wears the Red crown with the Uraeus and the King of Upper Egypt wears the white crown.

The Palermo Stone shows the names of the seven kings fully preserved wearing the Red Crown of Lower Egypt. The main fragment has ten determinatives; six are showing the Double Crown of a united Egypt. They are Narmer, Aha. Djer, Den, Anedjib, Semerkhet, and Qaa (Ka'a) all of three First and Second Dynasties.

DYNASTY II (2800- 2650B.C.)

Memphis, the City of the Great White Wall was founded. The vast cemeteries of Abydos and Sakkara appear. Trade with the Near East encouraged the need for imported wood via mercantile port of Byblos (Lebanon). Biblical students are familiar with the Cedars of Lebanon.

The peril of dissolution is ever present with unification and the aim for single authority is highly significant psychologically and symbolically. The beginning of each reign has the following formula on the Palermo stone: "Unification of Upper and Lower Egypt, Encircling of the Wall". The encircling is in reference to one of the coronation ceremonies and the wall refers to the Great White Wall of the administrative capital at Memphis, which was situated at the junction of Upper and Lower Egypt. The names on the lists of kings in the Second Dynasty suggest some internal turmoil. The first king whose name appears is Hotepsekhemwy, which means, "Two Powers are appeased". The sixth king of the period has a large grey stela bearing his name, Peribsen. His change of allegiance from Horus, the god of unified Egypt, to Seth the god of his divine rival, suggests some internal political change. Peribsen's successor, who ascends to the throne with the Khasekhemui, "the Power has appeared", restored the practice of writing the Horus- falcon over his name. However, he seemed to solve the theological problem, somewhat ironically. He changed his name to Khasekhemui ("the Two powers has appeared". written beneath the Horus-falcon and the set animal. In a tone of mockery or appeasement, he added to his name the phrase, "the two Lords are content in him".

DYNASTY III (2650-2579B.C.)

The foundation of Egypt's divine kingship began in the Third Dynasty and the foundation of Egyptian civilization was firmly established. As crafts and industries expanded, the scribes sharpened their wits and reeds with the demands for accounting and recording. Zoser, the founder of the dynasty, was a strong and able ruler. Zoser and his somewhat shadowy successor, Sakhte, left prospecting records in the Sinai desert. Nefertari and Huny were also members of this dynasty.

The most outstanding undertaking of this period was the amazing funerary complex, which Imhotep designed and constructed at Saqqara (Sakkara) for his Pharaoh, Zoser. The skills of

Imhotep as architect, physician, magician, and weaver of proverbs won for him lasting fame. He was eventually worshiped as a god and was equated by the Greeks to their own god of healing, Asklepios. There is the possibility that Zoser extended the southern boundary of Egypt to the First Cataract.

DYNASTY IV (2570- 2450B.C.)

Pyramid building reached its zenith during this dynasty. Two pyramids were built for Snefru at Dashur; he married the daughter of Huny, the dynast of the Third Dynasty, legitimizing the reign and insuring royal bloodline for his own dynasty. The trio of Pyramids built at Giza was for Cheops (Khufu), Chephre (Khafre), and Mycerinus (Makaure). They stand on a high promontory 10 miles from Cairo. The Cheops pyramid is one of the largest buildings built by, man and is one of the Seven Wonders of the World.

The solar cult of Heliopolis was affirmed and probably the first edition of the body of the "Pyramid Texts". As we know from the Palermo Stone, punitive expeditions were launched by Snefru into Nubia and Libya. The inscriptions left in the diorite quarries in Nubia and mines in the Sinai inform us, that expeditions were made to obtain materials, usually accompanied by a military contingent. The timber trade with Byblos was continued. The nobles or expedition commanders also left biographical inscriptions in their tombs.

DYNASTY V (2450-2300B.C.)

The dynasts of this period included Userkaf, Sahura, Nyuserra and Unas. They made expeditions in Asia and Punt (the Sudanese-Eritrean hinterland of the Red Sea). They constructed solar temples at Abu Garab, a few miles south of Giza. They also built pyramids. The Pyramid Texts began to be recorded in the Pyramid of Unas. The nobles built tombs with lavish wall decorations. The tombs were not clustered around the royal tomb as in the Fourth dynasty, suggesting less dependence on the King for esteem.

DYNASTY VI (2300-2150B.C.)

The dynasty began with Teti who was followed by Pepi I, Merenre, and Pepi II. Decentralization of the administration reduced the effectiveness and finally led to the collapse of the Old Kingdom with death of Pepi II. Expeditions were made to Punt, Palestine, and Nubia with the use of mercenaries. Private tombs were more lavish. Pyramids were built at Saqqara.

THE FIRST INTERMEDIATE PERIOD (2151-2100B.C.)

Dynasties VII -VIII experienced the decadence of central government and division among the Provinces.

Dynasties IX-X, the legitimate monarchy reappeared at Herakleopolis.

DYNASTY XI (2100-1955B.C.)

The princes of Thebes (Luxor), beginning with Mentuhotep I and followed by the Antefs I-III, declared themselves sovereigns. Periods of chaos, anarchy, and civil disobedience follow. Grandiose funerary temples were constructed at Thebes. Mentuhotep II unifies Egypt, conquering the north and putting and end to the Herakleopitan dynasty. Memphis was again the capital and Saqqara the necropolis.

During this period of chaos and uncertainty, there emerged socially significant literature written by the sage, Ipu-wer. He describes the early part of the First Intermediate period, magnified by the absence of a centralized authority. During this chaotic period, the Egyptians began to confront their loss of purpose and sense of order. What evolved was a papyrus from the Tenth dynasty known as the "Protests of the Eloquent Peasant", the story line is that of a poor peasant who has been robbed of his belongings by a very wealthy landowner and he is seeking redress.

DYNASTY XII

There were solid reforms such as co regencies with heir to the throne. "It is even possible that Amenemhat I, the founder of the Twelfth Dynasty and a scion of the princely family of Amenemhat, the vizier of Metuhotep III, had Nubian blood in his veins."[115] Nubia presented a threat throughout the Twelfth Dynasty. When Amenemhat was eighty years old, his son, Senruret who had been his coregent for nine years was forced to overthrow Wawat and restore order between the First and Second Cataract. Lower Nubia was annexed and the First of the Second Cataract Fortresses were built at Buhen. With the completion of the forts, the Egyptians controlled Nubia as far as Semna. Kerma (Yam?) at the Third Cataract threatened aggression. Military campaigns were carried into Punt and Palestine. Also Aegean contacts were pursued and Abydos becomes a cult center. Wisdom texts, hymns, and arts and crafts flourished. The dynasty ends with Sebekneferura, the sister of Amenenhat IV, who also is another shadowy figure

SECOND INTERMEDIATE PERIOD(1640-154B.C.)

DYNASTIES XIII AND XIV (1750-1640B.C.)

The Thirteenth and Fourteenth dynasties were largely contemporaneous with a number of petty kings reigning in obscurity. There was a profound weakening in government with Lower Egypt becoming detached from the Thirteenth Dynasty.

DYNASTIES XV-XVII (1641-1540B.C.)

The "Shepherd Kings" or Hyksos approached Egypt from the north and founded a capital at Avaris in the Delta. Part of the south was subject to a Nubian King at Kerma. Sekenenra and Kamose, Theban Princes, instigated a revolt.

DYNASTY XVIII (1540-1070B.C.)

The New Kingdom was inaugurated by Ahmose (1540-1515) after Kamose had successfully routed the Hyksos with the assistance of the Medjay. It was necessary for the Hyksos King to form an alliance with the Kushite prince to defend himself against the Thebans and their Medjay allies. A large stela found in Karnak in 1954 describes how the followers of Kamose intercepted a message, which never reached its destination and this allowed Ahmose to storm Avaris and drive the Hyksos back to Asia. The Two Lands again united and the capital was again at Thebes. The reconquest of Nubia was begun by Ahmose immediately after his triumphs in Asia and Palestine. Little resistance was offered and the Fortress of Buhen was reoccupied. Thuwwre, a permanent Egyptian Governor of Nubia, was appointed by Ahmose and became the First Viceroy of Kush in the next Reign.

The Kings of the Eighteenth dynasty accomplished the expansion beyond the Second Cataract. The Kings following Ahmose were warriors and great builders. Amenhotep I and the there Thutmose extended their influence militarily both in Asia (Mitanni, Hittites, Assyrians, and Kassites) and Nubia and maybe beyond. In due time, they pressed their fortunes as far as the Fourth Cataract The boundary stelae of Thutmose I (1494- 1482) and Thutmose III (1479-1425) proclaimed their dominion where the Korosko road joined the Nile from the desert. A fortress was erected at Tumbus and named in defiance of Egypt's traditional enemies the "Nine Bows"; "Nobody-Dares-to Look-at- Him -among - the United Nine Bows."

The Fortresses of Buhen, Aniba, Kubban and Ikkur were restored and enlarged. Temple communities were built and the Second Cataract Fortresses became obsolete with the pressure beyond that point. In order to assure fidelity of the Kushites, their young princes were taken and employed in the Pharaonic court. This could possibly be interpreted as the beginning of subjugation, infiltration or Egyptianization.

Queen Hatshepsut (1479-1457) also campaigned in Nubia. Thutmose III, her youthful co-regent and stepson supplanted her. The Queen ruled as a king with ceremonial beard and a firm hand for twenty years. The temple built at Deir el Bahri was the outstanding monument of her reign. The walls display her important trading expedition to Punt. However, it was Thutmose III who extended the Egyptian frontier to the foot of the Holy Mountain at Gebel Barkal at the Fourth Cataract in his 47th regal year. His victory stele at Napata marked his triumph and the extent of the Egyptian frontier and in his temple of Amun-Re, he could boast of his satisfaction in both Egypt and Asia.

Amenhotep II (1427-1401) was a famous sportsman in his youth and carried on the conquest of his father. Thutmose IV (1401-1390) excavated a sphinx and married a Mitanni princess, which strengthened his position in Asia considerably.

Amenhotep III (1390-1352) known as "the Magnificent" marries Tiy, his principal wife, who is of non-royal birth. Her strong Nubian personality left a signal mark on the reign. Amenhotep III built the Colossus of Memnon in honor of himself. The devotion to the arts was unparallel and many great temples were erected. The Temple of Luxor, dedicated to Aten-Re, was built at the height of Egypt's prosperity.

Amenhotep IV (Akhnaten) (1352-1336) was a coregent with his father, Amenhotep the III, during his later reign. Amenhotep changed his name during his reign to Akhnaten, signifying his new devotion to the Sun god Aten, which was in conflict with the Theban god Amun, and the priesthood. The center of government remained at Thebes while Akhnaten moved to Amarna with his beautiful wife Nefertari, and the adherents to the new religion that was a forerunner of Monotheism. Akhnaten built a temple at Karnak in honor of Aten. The gains made abroad were gradually diminished by lack of attention on the home front. The agreement of the factions of Aten and Amun seem to have begun under Semenekhara (1335-1332), who was coregent with Akhnaten for a short period. He was succeeded by Tutankhamon (1332-23) who was successful in returning the splintered worship of Amun to Thebes. The death of Tutankhamon while still a youth made a place for an elderly noble named Ay (1323-1319) who legitimized his claim by marrying the widow of the deceased.

General Horemhab, former advisor to Tutankhamon, may have initiated the marriage so that ay could become the transitional king until Horemhab was ready to seize power. Death was swift and Horemhab became king immediately. (1319-1925). This marked the beginning of military power and the transition to the Nineteenth Dynasty since Horemhab did not belong to the royal family of the Eighteenth Dynasty. Nevertheless, he considered himself the legitimate successor of Amenhotep III and systematically erased the memory of the "heretic king" by erasure of names and the demolition of buildings associated with him.

DYNASTY XIX (1295- 1190B.C.)

During the XIX Dynasty Egypt was at the height of expansion as Rameses I and Seti I began an intensive reconquest of the Asiatic Empire, which had been lost by Akhnaten. The capital was moved to the Eastern Delta at Piramesses under Rameses II. There were intensive contacts with Syria and Palestine. Rameses II, heading four armies, ended the Battle of Kadesh against the Hittites with an international treaty of peace. The marriage to the eldest daughter of the Hittite king was a symbolic union of brother and peace. Rameses II built many monuments and eradicated the monuments of other in his effort that he was the greatest warrior and celebrant of the gods in his victories. His son Merenptah razed Israel and engaged the peoples of Europe for the first time.

The invasion of the Sea peoples was repulsed, but the Sards and the Libyans gained a foothold in Egypt. The stela of Merneptah is a record of his military activities in the Syro-Palestine region, listing a number of the conquered cities and states among which was Canaan, Askalon, Gezer, Yenoam, and Israel. The village of Deir el-Medina prospers but the ephemeral kinglets were too weak to maintain a powerful state.

DYNASTY XX (1190-1070B.C.)

The great foreign powers fell and Setnakt restored order. His son Rameses III, a strong king repulsed. The invaders from the West and the North saved his country and were killed by an assassin. During the reigns of the Rameses IV-XI, power was wrested from them by the Theban priests while Egypt lost prestige abroad.

DYNASTY XXI (1070-945B.C.)

The High Priests of Amon ruled in Thebes and the Princes of Tanis ruled in Tanis. The capital was moved to Tanis as the descendants of the foreigners took over Egypt. A new family of Libyan descent from the Faiyum begins to emerge. Sheshonk, a Libyan family member seized control and began a new dynasty.

DYNASTY XXII (945-715B.C.)

Sheshonk (945-924B.C.)

Osorkon (924-889B.C.)

Takelot (889-874B.C.)

The capital was transferred to Bubastis. The country was divided into feudal kingdoms and the immigrant troops from Libya took over the government. Near the end of this dynasty, the country was the beleaguered by Assyria and a powerful independent country in the Sudan

DYNASTY XXIII (818-715B.C.)

The power of Assyria grows in Asia. This dynasty is spoken of as a rival to the XXII because the kings still maintained the names of the dynasty. "At that time Egypt maintained peaceful relations with Solomon in Jerusalem, who even took an Egyptian princess to wife. In the Fifth year of the reign of Solomon's successor, however, Sheshonk attacked Palestine. Though Egypt, she regained something of her former influence and profited by a greatly increased foreign trade".

DYNASTY XXIV (727- 715B.C.)

"The Twenty-fourth Dynasty had one king only, namely Daken Renef, whom the Greeks called Bocchoris, son of Tefnahkt. Bocchoris endeavored to give support to the king of Israel against the Syrian king, Sargon II, but his army was beaten at Raphia in 720 B.C. His reign was ended when the Sudanese (Nubian) King Shabaka invaded Egypt."

DYNASTY XXV (747-656B.C.): THE ETHIOPIAN (NUBIAN) PHARAOHS

The Ethiopian (Nubian) who were an established, stable monarchy who ruled the Sudan between the First and Sixth Cataracts, invaded Egypt and established the Twenty-Fifth Dynasty of Pharaohs. They reestablished the Middle Kingdom ambiance of Kingship and Godship and restored the sanctity of ancient Egyptian traditions. The Assyrians briefly occupied at least as far as Thebes. The sack of Thebes and the death of Tanutamon marked the end of Nubian supremacy in the northern Nile Valley.

DYNASTY XXVI (664-525B.C.)

PSAMMETICHUS I (664-610B.C.)

Egypt was liberated, from Assyrian domination by Saiite Psammetichus, with the help of Lydian and Greek mercenaries. The famous stela in Cairo records that in the year 665 B.C, Shawnee II, the last Kushite divine consort, adopted the daughter of Psammetichus as her successor. During his dynasty, Psammetichus tried to restore the commercial leadership of Egypt by selling the rich produce of Upper Egypt. The reign of Psammetichus was imperiled by the Persian conquest.

DYNASTY XXVII (525-405B.C.)

The Twenty-seventh Dynasty or the First Persian domination was headed by the Persian Kings Cambyses, Darius I, Xerxes, Artaxerxes, and Darius II, who transformed Egypt into a Satrapy. It was during this time that Herodotus visited Egypt. Cambyses undertook a campaign against "Ethiopia "(Nubia or Kush) after the conquest of Egypt in 525B.C.. Herodotus said that Cambyses had to retreat because his army was destroyed as the result of lack of provisions. In addition, Herodotus that "Ethiopians above Egypt" sent gifts to the Persians every three years (gold, ivory, ebony, five boys) but paid no tribute. In his building inscription found in Susa, Darius mentions that the ivory used in the building of the palace of Susa came from Kushiya".

DYNASTIES XXVIII-XXX (440-341B.C.)

This domination of Egypt was very brief under Artaxerxes III, Axerxes, and Darius III. It was brought to an end by the conquest of Egypt by Alexander the Great in 332 when the Persians met with ignominious defeat at the battle of Issus. Egypt was swallowed up in the vast empire of Alexander which comprised Macedonia, a large part of Asia Minor, the southern shores of the Mediterranean, and as Far East as the Punjab (India). With Alexander's death in 323B.C., three of his generals were poised and sufficiently established to control the empire: "the Antiginids in Macedonia, the Seleucids in Asia and the former Persian empire, and the Ptolemies in Egypt"

PTOLEMAIC (OR LAGID) DYNASTY (403-330B.C.)

Alexander's successors established their capital at Alexandria and an independent Hellenistic monarchy. The Ptolemies ruled Egypt for three centuries. Hellenization was thorough with a syncretization of Egyptian and Greek gods, the usurpation of farms for Royal cultivation at the expense of the fellaheen and the exportation of the coveted products of Nubia.

ANNEXATION TO THE ROMAN EMPIRE

The battle of Actium in 30B.C. and the suicide of Cleopatra was the demise of three hundred years of Ptolemaic rule and a hybrid mixture of Hellenistic and Pharaonic overlay. Egypt became a province of Rome under Augustus Caesar.

CHAPTER 9.
NUBIAN CHRONOLOGY

We shall now plot the rise and fall of Nubian Kingdom who became the legitimate heirs of that great and noble tradition—a rise and fall of which we have long been unaware. The fine bronze head of Augustus at Meroe, the later capital of Kush, is a mute testimony to the keepers of the flame of Kushite Monarchy which stood the test of time in the Valley of the Nile for well over one thousand years.

The Land of the Bow or ancient Nubia was called Ta Seti and found by the ancient travelers between Thebes and Aswan at the First Cataract. Since the fourth century before the Christian Era Nubian archaeological research designates a larger expanse, which has extended from the Second Cataract in the North to South of the Sixth Cataract at the confluence of the White and Blue Niles in the Sudan.

The most ancient term for Nubia was found in the inscriptions of the ancient Egyptians as "Ta Nehesu "i.e. the "Land of the Blacks". According to Budge "Ta Nehesu" was originally one of the four quarters into which the Egyptians divided the world known to them, the other three being the "Lands of the Thehennu "or Libyans, the "Land of the Aamu", or Asiatics, and the "Land of Men Egyptians". Note the regard the Egyptians have for themselves. In other words the Blacks [Ethiopians, Nubians, or Kushites] occupied the southern quarter of the world; the Asiatics, i.e. the inhabitants of the deserts of the Peninsula of Sinai, Palestine and Syria and the shores of the Red Sea, the eastern quarter; the Libyans, the western quarter; and the Egyptians, who regarded as "men, Par excellence, the lower portion of the Nile Valley, or the northern quarter." [114]

In viewing the general culture of Nubia, it will be based on documentation of material objects found in gravesites as well as textual data because of the lack of other definitive documentation. You will note that at times the material culture of Upper and lower Nubia will differ considerably because of typological difference

NUBIAN NEOLITHIC, 10,000 - 3,000 B.C.

During the Neolithic phase, the Nile Corridor exemplified a number of commonalities between the Lower and Upper Nile. The semi nomadic pastoral evolution accompanies the food producing revolution. Earliest Nubian rock art is associated with the prehistoric Qadan and Abka industries of the final Stone Age and the Neolithic age dated between 7,000 and 4,000 B.C. Pottery making in northeastern Africa seems to have originated in the Sudan in the seventh and sixth millennia and spread to the Northern part of the Nile Valley known as southern Upper

Nubia. it has become apparent that from 7,000 B.C. there was a common material culture throughout Nubia. Besides hunting and fishing, there was a pastoral nomadism and some animal husbandry, which is suggested by the drawings of an array of savanna and game animals.

KHARTOUM NEOLITHIC, 4000 - 3000B.C.

Khartoum Neolithic derived from Khartoum Mesolithic represented as important cultural phase of prehistory. Because the principal site of this cultural phase was located at Ash-Shaheinab, north of Khartoum, is sometimes referred to as the Shaheinhab Culture. Little is known of the cultural adaptations of these people, there is evidence that they lived in settlements and buried their dead. The culture spread along the Nile to the Sixth Cataract. Other known settlements of this culture are distributed over a wide area, in the region of Atbara, Kassala, Wadi Howar in, and Northern Darfur and along the course of the Upper Nile. The inhabitants enjoyed a higher degree of affluence from those inhabitants of similar sites along the Second Cataract.

Pottery was more prolific in the finds, grindstone - mace heads, adzes, ; Amazon stone, beads and carnelian were made into ornaments, as well as bone and shell. In addition, the remains of sites in Lower Nubia indicated a "ruder and more exacting life" than enjoyed by the inhabitants of Shaheinhab. The domestic pots are brown and in more varied shapes with a more advanced decoration as well as motif. The pots are polished and blackened on the inside and around the rim. There is a greater sense of order and symmetry to their patterns with incised wavy lines, round or oval, dot, semicircles, triangles, rectangles and herringbone patterns as well as straight.

The Abkan and Khartoum variant culture are found between Faras and the Second Cataract in southern Nubia. The distinguishing elements in the Abkan culture are the tools and its ceramics. The earliest tool, of course was the fingernail, then fishbone stamps. The Abkan technology for polishing and incising was accomplished with a pebble, thus "Ripple Ware". The Khartoum Variant, used a stone or pottery, rocker- shaped with projections on the side and a form of "Rocker -Stamp" to accomplish the design, generally Abkan ware is undecorated. The Abkan site is located near Wadi Halfa. The Abkan culture is contemporary with the A Horizon in ceramic culture.

NUBIAN A HORIZON, 3,000- 2500 B.C.

According to William Adams, the A Horizon is distinguishable from its Neolithic forebears by four factors: the definite cultivation of grains, the beginning of domestic architecture, and the making of a distinctive black and red pottery and the practice of interring material offerings with the dead.[115]

The A Horizon on Nubian soil also introduced sculpture "in the round." The figurines found suggest a quality beyond what was earlier believed to exist. Found near Wadi Degheim in a burial of a women and child were two small figurines. It has been suggested that these figurines may have been dolls or fetishes to extend the existence of the person represented. According to Ucko (1968), these figures may have originated in Nubia, although the sculpture does appear in Egypt. It must be noted that in examining parallel cultures for originality lies in the fact that originality of invention is construed by use, intent and construction of similar ideas in space and time. Typical of the figurines found, the women are seated and leaning far backward; because heads show no detail with the exception of the beak like noses; arms are stumps or missing; legs taper to a round point and are joined together. The buttocks are emphasized and breasts are de-emphasized. A hippopotamus head and a sunken relief vessel in limestone demonstrate the skill of A Horizon artisans and their originality.

The A Horizon is equivalent in time to the First and Second Dynasties of Egypt. During this period, there was considerable networking with Egypt on a commercial basis. After this period, the records indicate military incursions based on economic reasons and expansion since Nubia held the resources: manpower and gold.

The Nubian C Horizon, 2,500 - 2, 000 B.C.

The C Horizon has been recognized as the most uniquely Nubian of all cultures and a continuation of the A Horizon. The B Group of Reisner's is the only one of his groups that has not found confirmation in the later archaeological work. It is believed that the C Horizon is contemporary with the Egyptian VI Dynasty to the beginning of the New Kingdom. The C Horizon was situated in the same part of Nubia that the A horizon occupied, from Kubbaniya north of Elephantine to the Batn el-Hajar, which formed a natural boundary to the south. It is understood according to Middle Kingdom records that the people of the C Horizon settled in the land of Wawat and the Kerma culture occupied the land of Kush. Wawat was only the northernmost part of Lower Nubia, between the First Cataract and Thomas, bordering directly on Egypt. The districts south of Thomas to the Second Cataract were called Irtjet and Stju, Medju, Kaau and Yam, according to Egyptian texts from the reign of Pepi I, Sixth Dynasty. Further evidence are the seals of the Sixth Dynasty found in the graves and biographies of Uni and Harkuf who made official trips into Nubia to secure the goodwill of the local chiefs. The obvious prosperity of Nubia and the decline in Egyptian influence is noted by her abandonment of their only permanent colonies in Nubia at Buhen and the Diorite quarries.

The parameters that define the uniqueness of this horizon are the continued refinement of the black-topped pottery with the incised geometric designs and the graves with round stone superstructures. Although the Egyptian Fortresses were built during the middle phase of the C Horizon, this was probably to guard against a more formidable enemy further south. By the late C Horizon, there is a fully developed village life with circular houses of one room, and several curvilinear rooms or houses consisting of seven or eight rooms with courtyards. The primary symbol of wealth was the domestic cattle, which was an innovation into the religious and social sphere. The subsistence base was still cereal agriculture supplemented by animal husbandry and fishing.

THE NUBIAN KINGDOM OF KERMA, 2,500 - 1590 B.C.

Kerma is the first Nubian monarchy of extraordinary wealth and extensive holdings to emerge during the third millennium B.C.. Reisner, between 1913-1916, excavated the archaeological site of Kerma, just below the third cataract, which consisted of the gigantic ruins and cemeteries near the village of Kerma. He designated the site Kerma culture and posited that Kerma was an Egyptian trading post and that the Western Deffufa, a prominent mud brick ruin was fortress with adjacent cemetery of prominent Egyptians. Archaeologically we can recognize a culture which may have been the Nubian Kingdom which the Twelfth Dynasty had trade relations and possibly Yam of the days of Harkuf, the trader. We also know now that the culture of Kerma was not limited to the region of Kerma, but was far more extensive as it extended over all of Upper Nubia, from the Second Cataract in the North to just below the Third Cataract at the Island of Argo in the south.

The two large brick ruins, called the Western or lower Deffufa and the large Royal cemetery of over a thousand graves, dominate the archaeological site. The Western Deffufa is one of the most incredible structures in Nubia. It is located one and a half miles from the river on the edge of the Kerma Basin, in the extreme northern end of Dongola reach, the most fertile area in Upper Nubia. Its original construction was a mass of long rectangular mud brick 150 miles long and 75 feet wide. The present structure is over 60 feet high. The top of the mass has been removed by erosion. Traces of a long stairway and room part of the way are remaining. In the irregular cluster of brick rooms around the Deffufa were found raw materials: 130 copper daggers with ivory handles, 565 clay seal impressions which would indicate the site was a former trading post.

The Eastern Deffufa, the second part of the huge complex, was located two miles east across which must have been the eastern branch of the river in ancient times. The Royal cemetery area covers more than a mile long and one half mile wide. The royal dimensions of the culture were extrapolated from the complex, which Reisner had divided into four groups: great tumuli, minor tumuli, subsidiary graves and independent graves. The largest tumuli measured 300 feet in diameter and its interior dimensions were larger than an Egyptian pyramid. They were eight in number, ranging in a line at the southern edge of the cemetery.

Reisner's conclusion that Kerma was a trading post and an administrative center was based on the objects of worth, statues, stelae and articles written Egyptian hieroglyphics. The Boston museum has many artifacts including beads, sculptures of a XII Dynasty official, Hepzefa and his wife Sennuy; ivory inlays, in the form of hyenas, bustard, ostrich chicks, lions, from the footboard of beds; leather caps with sewn mica figures; blacktopped red polished beakers and other luxury pottery items. Fragments, of one funerary bed constructed in blue faience, were found. The legs of the beds were carved to resemble the legs of animals. The frame was rectangular, with crisscrossed leather strips to serve as springs.

In 1964, Hintze presented the view that Kerma was the residence of the "Rulers of Kush" were buried there. He felt that the objects found were either booty from the conquest of Lower Nubia or gifts from the Hyksos kings with whom they traded. Gratien who did a study of the internal chronology of the Kerma culture confirmed Hintze's postulation and further substantiated that all the objects apart from the imports were of Kerma origin.

Gratien's 1978 study also indicates that the first Kerma phase (Early Kerma) followed the A Horizon at the end of the Old Kingdom and can be identified as a transitional period between the A group and the C group. The second phase of (Middle Kingdom) is equated with the beginning of the Egyptian Middle kingdom into the XIIth Dynasty. She places the border of the C Group and the Kerma Group to the south of the Second Cataract. The third phase (Classic Kerma) continued through the XIIIth Dynasty to Dynasty XVII. [116]

The opulence and the magnificence of its existence has been further explored by the Swiss Archaeological Mission of the University of Geneva and Sudan who have spent 25 years of research and excavation up river from the Third Cataract and 15 years at the Kerma site. Many questions were answered during the exhibit "Kerma, Royaume de Nubia "at the Musee d'Art et d' Histoire at Geneva June -November 1990. The Exhibit was for me one of the peaks of the Seventh International Conference for Nubian Studies held at Geneva, September 3-8, 1990.

According to their findings, the history of Kerma began 2500 years before the birth of Christ and ended about 1500 B.C.. These 1000 years of history are divided into three periods called: Kerma Ancient (2500 B.C.), Kerma Moyen (2000 B.C.), and Kerma Classique (1500 B.C.). [117] The Egyptians coveted Nubia, the land of gold, which brought the history of Kerma to an end when it was conquered about 1500. The Egyptians wrote the name of this kingdom in hieroglyphs and called it Kush. Many documents were found, and inscriptions on stelae but the names of the kings have not been discovered. A bronze mirror was found which is dated about 2500 B.C. and the name of the proprietor according to the inscription was a Lady Senetites.

The model of the village of Kerma during the classic period was displayed. The fortifications and the moat protected a village of about 200 houses, some of which were two stories with multiple rooms. The plan is incomplete but it has added to the findings of Reisner and we can expect more in the future as the excavations continue. In certain quarters of the village there were petite circular huts reconstructed in wood and palm leaves. There was also a grand hut for the audience of the king. It is interesting to note that the architecture; "the hall of King Unas is of plaited reeds." The Deffufa has been designated as a principle temple of Kerma. It has also been suggested that the stairs in the interior may have led to the roof where the religious ceremonies were held in celebration of the sun.

Also from the finds, hunting, fishing, viniculture, baking and working with metals were daily pastimes. The materials found were leather, ivory, gold, bronze, mica, fine stone and copperware, linen cloth, beads, fragments of cotton drawers, pillows, sandals, linen cloth, ostrich feathers, bow and worn arrowheads. A tomb of a 17-year-old archer was found. The mummification was 4000 years old. The carpentry of the burial beds was of a Nubian variation with inlaid mica animals, bird and other decorations. The base of the legs of the bed was fashioned in gold from the likeness of an animal; [118] the use of the cattle motif in the furniture and the architecture is in keeping with the complex imagery and elaborate symbolism developed by the Nubians of the C Horizon. Adams states that they have been "the first African people to develop that elaborate complex of social and ritual activities centered around the rearing of cattle, which is so conspicuous in East and Central Africa today." [119]

Although contemporary with the C-horizon, Kerma surpasses it in power and influence. It had direct contact with the Hyksos Kings and traded with the XII Dynasty of Egypt. Their pottery, which Reisner found to be of 17 different varieties, is distinctive and more refined than those of the A and C Horizons. The burial practices differ radically from the peoples of Lower Nubian peoples. Because of the importance of the Kerma Culture as a prototype of the Later Napatan, Meroitic cultures, and later West African culture, I will cite in detail.

Bed burial

In nearly every Kerma grave which has not been plundered beyond recognition. The main burial is found reclining on a native bed (angareeb) of the type still used in Nubia. This custom is only encountered rarely in graves of C-Horizon.

KERMA POTTERY

Trade vessels of the distinctive Kerma blacktopped pottery was occasionally found in non-Kerma graves, and usually occur in large clusters.

DOMED TUMULI

The round tumuli, or grave mound, are a common feature of Upper and Lower Nubian burials. However, the typical C-Group tumulus is cylindrical in shape, built up within a vertical retaining wall of masonry. The Kerma tumulus is dome-shaped, sloping downward from a low crown to the level of the ground in all directions. The ring stones delimiting the tumulus is only a few inches high; it is primarily decorative and perhaps to protect the edges of the mound from erosion. In many Kerma, tumuli are even more variable in size than those of the C Horizon; the largest of them are far greater than anything found in Lower Nubia

HUMAN SACRIFICES

A surprisingly large number of Kerma graves- at least of those dating from the heyday of the kingdom- contain the bodies of one or more sacrificial victims who were buried at the same time as the 'owner' of the grave. The Kerma culture is the beginning of the Dynastic period of Nubian (Kushite) history and the enlargement of trade during her period of weakness. It is quite possible from the evidence of the C Horizon and can be consider - cultural cousins.

NEW KINGDOM DOMINATION, 1,590 - 1,100 B.C.

Although the monarchial beginning of Kerma became more fully expanded, New Kingdom domination was fully inaugurated with the Vice Royalty of Kush. This Dynastic period is considered the second major phase of Nubian development. The Warrior kings of the New Kingdom extended their domination over Nubia up to the Fourth Cataract. The vice regal system initiated by Amenhotep I was to insure peripheral domination through the "King's Sons of Kush." They were the arm of the Pharaoh and governed Nubia and the southern province of Egypt. In reality, their governance included Kush or Upper Nubia, Wawat or Lower Nubia and the region from Aswan to El Kab in Egypt. Some 25 or more viceroys were deputies of the Pharaoh beginning with Thuwwre and ending with the son of Herihor, a Theban priest, about 1050 B.C., the end of Egypt's domain.

The period between the Late New Kingdom and the beginning of the 1st century B.C. is one of mystery shrouded in obscurity and conjecture because of the lack of archaeological evidence and written records. Toward the end of the New Kingdom, the Nubians began to play a more prominent role in the internal affairs of Egypt because of their wealth and their troops. This was no doubt about the result of the Warrior King's domestic policy, which allowed the appointments of foreigners to positions of responsibility at court, in the army, and in temples. The emphasis of foreign expansion and the use of mercenaries drained the local Nubian population and placed an ever-increasing economic burden of Egyptian fellaheen as well as the Nubia farmer. Most of the Nubian farmers lived on the land owned by the local princes or the agents of the Temple complexes throughout the region. Beside the conscription for foreign campaigns, the mining operations caused the loss of population in Lower Nubia.

The shift in the use of land and resources by the Pharaohs caused the development of more intensive agriculture that did not satisfy the court. More of the land was owned by the crown through the Vice regal system and even more by the Temple estates which reduced the economy to that of manorial estate system. Herein, the power of the pharaoh was diminished until it was in the hands of the Theban priests.

By the end of the XXth dynasty, Lower Nubia seemed to have been entirely abandoned, so terminated with the sharp decline in gold prices. The land itself was left with a few military garrisons and it was again, claimed by the eastern desert peoples. Thus 500 years of Egyptian occupation in Lower Nubia was reduced to a 'no man's land'.

THIRD INTERMEDIATE PERIOD

Nubian hiatus, 1100- 900 B.C.

There were many explanation of the disappearance of the Nubians and the C- Group. Williams proposed the most salient explanation:

> "The level of the Nile probably fell during the New Kingdom, and by
> the XIXth Dynasty effective irrigation was possible only in a few
> favored places in Nubia. There was a steady emigration from Lower
> Nubia until in the XXth Dynasty, only a handful of settlers remained,
> and even they were gone by the XXIst Dynasty. Egyptian colonization
> was at an end, but its aftermath was felt for a thousand years. Egyptian
> ized Nubians, perhaps aided by Egyptian émigrés, kept the Pharaonic
> tradition alive in Upper Nubia, laying the ideological foundations for the
> "Successor State of Napata."

THE KINGDOM OF KUSH

NAPATAN PERIOD, 900-300 B.C.

The Kingdom of Kush is also known as the Kingdom of Napata and Meroe. The Classical writers, Assyrian records, as well as Biblical accounts of this kingdom document that the Napatan Kingdom is a continuation of an Ethiopian state. It was known as the Kushite State, which controlled the Nile Valley from at least far north as the Holy Mountain of Jebel Barkal to Thebes and Aswan in the south from 960 B.C. Scholars are now virtually unanimous in recognizing an indigenous development possibly from the great Kerma Culture.

It is difficult to pinpoint the precise origin of the Kingdom of Kush. Historically it is divided into two periods, beginning with the Napatan period, which lasts to the Meroitic period, which begins about 300 B.C. and lasts one thousand years. The cemetery of El Kurru is the earliest source of evidence for the Napatan period. The oldest ruler known to us is Alara, approximately five generations before Kashta, the first Nubian king listed in Reisner's chronology (806-751 B.C.). Kashta was the first Nubian or Kushite king to rule Egypt as Pharaoh of the XXVth Dynasty. His name means Kushite and he was the sixth generation of the Kushite Dynasty according to Reisner's chronology. His chronology lists 67 generations of kings and queens spanning 1200 years.[121]

The first great Nubian of Ethiopian who conquered all of Egypt was Pianhki (Piye) the son of Kashta who died about 751 B.C. One of the major kings of the Napatan period was Taharqa (6900- 664 B.C.) who is referred to in the Bible as the King of Egypt who was characterized as a broken reed. The archeological sources for the history of the Napatan period are the Royal cemeteries and pyramids of Kurru and Nuri not far from Napata, the capital of the Kingdom of Kush. The capital was moved to Meroe the beginning of the fifth century B.C. and thereafter, the Kushite Kings only went to Napata for their coronation journeys and for their burials.

The sack of Thebes and the death of Tanutamon (664-653) brought the heroic age of Nubia and the end of the rule of the XXVth Dynasty in Egypt. The Napatan Kings can be credited with the rejuvenation of the Pharaonic tradition and building activities that were unmatched by any ruler since Rameses IV. Nastasen (335-310 B.C.) was the last Napatan King to be buried at Napata after the burial of twenty other kings. The Napatan period came to a close with a number of decisive moves. One was the transfer of the royal cemetery from its site near Napata to the vicinity of Meroe.

MEROITIC PERIOD, (300 B.C. - 350 A.D.)

Meroe was the capital city of the Kingdom of Kush in its later stage of cultural development. The Napatan period was considered the Heroic Age because of its dominion in Egypt and the Meroitic period was designated the Golden Age.

The Meroitic Age is named after the city of Meroe, as it seemed to be the largest community of ancient Kush. The ancient Greeks knew it as early as the fourth century B.C. It extended 700 miles "as the crow flies' and much longer along the Nile from Dakka in Egyptian Nubia to as far south as Sennar up the Blue Nile. Ptolemaic Egypt was considered provincial expressions of a world civilization whereas Pharaonic Egypt and Napatan Kush were considered parochial civilizations.

The history of Meroitic period of the Kingdom of Kush can be divided into several stages. Hintze cites the following states of the Meroitic Period: a transitional stage (310-270 B.C.) - between the Napatan Period and the Meroitic Period; the Middle Meroitic period (from 90 B.C.) to the threshold of the Christian Era; and the late Meroitic Period 90 B.C.- 350 A.D.).

The Pyramid field is awesome. Hoskins in his travels to Meroe in the 18th century counted 80 pyramids. The 800-year building history of the great Enclosure at Musawwarat es-Sufra is without parallel in the whole Nile valley. The art of the goldsmith and iron production also reached a high level of achievement. The characteristics of the Meroitic period are unsurpassed in language development, the use of elephants for military campaigns, and an extensive reservoir system, all of which speak to a high civilization.

III.

GODSHIP, KINGSHIP,
AND
QUEENSHIP

"All the world's a stage..."
Shakespeare

NORTH PYRAMIDS AT MEROE

JEBEL BARKAL, THE HOLY MOUNTAIN

MUSAWWARET

LION FRIEZE

WARRIOR

QUEEN AMANITERE IN
FULL REGALIA
REAR WALL OF LION
TEMPLE

LION GOD APEDEMAK

STAND OF KING
ATLANERSA

Stand of King Atlanersa

CHAPTER 10.
CONCEPTS OF GODSHIP AND KINGSHIP

<u>BASES OF CIVILIZATION</u>

The dawn of civilization, the very process of developing cultural groups based on kinship, language, stewardship of peoples and land began in the Fertile Crescent and the Nile Valley. It was rooted in the kinship bond, which held groups together and fostered mutual interactions, which evolved into matrilineal societies because they believed that women, the givers of life had divine powers. Therefore, motherhood was the only recognized bond of relationship. "as yet, neither gods nor priests, but only a universal goddess and her priestesses... Fatherhood was not honored, conception being attributed to the wind..."

Early Greek cultures were primarily concerned "with the changing relations between the queen (mother) and her lovers, which begin with their yearly or twice yearly, sacrifices; and end, at a time when the Iliad was composed and kings boasted: ' we are better than our fathers!' with her eclipse by an unlimited male monarchy."

In Mesopotamia, the goddess was supreme because she was viewed as a source of life. There are many African parallels which illustrate these progressive stages of change, several of which are represented by the "matrilineal Koms of the Cameroons, the east African Baganda who still shares the throne with his sister and is dependent for food on the Queen-mother..." In Egypt, according to Budge, she (Isis) was "Being eternal and infinite, the creature and ruling power of heaven, earth and the underworld, and of every creature and thing in them... Godmother, giver of life... All that has been, that is, and that will be. "

These instances indicated that throughout the predynastic ancient world, the concept of Earth Goddess was the source of all life. The goddess symbolically represented the fertility of nature and the periodic seasonal decline represents the loss of the offshoots (children of the Great Mother). If we can recognize in the Great Mother, the Female principle and the First cause and the Fruits of the Earth as her sons, we can see that the male principle is a derivative: the male Principle or god is her son.

Residuals of this concept found in the Dynastic periods were revealed in the ancient title for the Queen of Egypt "she who sees Horus and Seth." The queen is also signified as God's Wife (Pharaoh's Wife). In Nubia, the Queen mother who was the king's wife and royal consort was highly regarded. As King's sister, she also enjoyed favorite stature. Taharqa, Pharaoh of the XV Dynasty, summoned his mother to appear at his coronation. The priests of Amon who chose him from a line of brothers and sons sanctioned his succession. There were several instances of reigning queens during the Kushite monarchy. The title Candace, a corruption of a Meroitic title (Kdke), was thought by the Romans to be held by a hereditary line of female rulers. There is little evidence of this fact although all royal consorts or Queen mothers of Kush held such a title.

The evolution of patriarchy and Kingship came with the devaluation of the Mother-goddess and the development of the dynastic state. At this point, it would be instructive to explore the differing concepts of godship and kingship and their nascence in the Nile Valley and the Fertile Crescent.

Differing expressions of kingship: Egypt and Mesopotamia

In the two centers of civilization, Egypt in the Nile Valley and Mesopotamia in the Fertile Crescent, the concepts of Kingship and godship are very different. Their worldviews both centered on community survival based upon the cyclical occurrences of nature. However, the physiological plains in which their existence took place as well as the cyclical occurrences in the earth tempered each cosmological view. There was an order about the regularity of the inundations of the Nile and the movement of the sun and moon across the skies, which was reflected in the religious festivals. Egyptians seemed to be protected by the richness of the valley and the austerity of the sands of the desert on either side. They believed that they were the beloved of the gods. The Mesopotamians, on the other hand, did not derive this sense of well being and order from their environment because the mountains on the east and the nomads on the west suggested constant peril and conflict in a community without clear boundaries. Their grazing and crops were endangered by rainfall, which was not consistent. The Tigris River, which was known to be eccentric in its turbulence, presenting many dangers to the surrounding inhabitants.

The later Mesopotamian Creation Myth "Enuma Elish" reflects this anger, anxiety, and threat:

Angry, scheming, restless day and night, they are bent on fighting, rage and prowl like lions. Gather in council, they plan the attack. Mother Hubur- creator of all forms- adds irresistible weapons, has born monster serpents, sharp toothed, with fang unsparing; has filled bodies with poison for blood. Fierce dragons she has draped with terror, crowned with flame and made like gods, so that whomever looks upon them shall perish with fear, and they, with bodies raised, will not turn back their breast.

Frankfort asserts that "in the Plain of the Two Rivers the festivals were never free from deep anxiety, and those which we know best show a change from deep gloom to exultation as the aim and the result of the solemnities."

In Egypt, the festivals provided occasion to reaffirm that all was well. For Egypt views the universe as essentially static. It held that a cosmic order was once and for all established at the time of creation. The forces of chaos might occasionally disturb this order but it was merely subdued and never annihilated. The feeling of insecurity, of human frailty, which pervades every manifestation of Mesopotamian culture, is absent in Egypt. For the Mesopotamian, the Festival of the New Year was a rite of atonement, which allowed the people to participate in the change of fortune experienced by certain gods at the change of the year, which culminated in the determination of destiny by the gods. The concept of godship and kingship therefore took a different shape in Egypt and Mesopotamia.

The concept of Kingship in Egypt has primitive antecedents in Africa as rainmaker king with power over the cosmos and culminating in the idea of the Pharaoh as divine in his godship. With the unification of Egypt, the First Dynasty originating in Upper Egypt established the prototype for the rule of all Egyptian men under the Pharaoh who was not considered mortal. Menes, although not the first of his dynasty, declared himself a Horus, who was a god of the sky like a falcon. He also proclaimed himself to be "The Two Ladies; that is, his being incorporated in the beings of the two goddesses who stood, respectively, for Upper and lower Egypt."

The other epithet for the king was that of "The two lords" that had the same symbolism as that of the "Two ladies" but referred to the antagonism of the gods, Horus and Seth, in the religious texts. Horus was the first king of Lower Egypt and Seth was the first king of Upper Egypt. The genius of Menus was to incorporate the manifestations of kingship rooted in the remote prehistory when the universe, its creation and rule was considered supernatural and ruled by a community of gods on earth. The last celestial god to reign over Egypt according to the Turin papyrus was Horus, Son of Isis.

As the first ruler of Egypt, Menus derived his power as god-king from a succession of gods, who were the models for the human dynasties. According to tradition, Menes became one of the Servants of Horus who were theoretically known as gods on earth. The Pharaoh or King in time claimed to be the divine son of the sun god Re, the Supreme God. In this state, the king had absolute authority over the land and its people. A good king does not govern capriciously. He is not only a god but he is the State. It is written, "Authoritative Utterance (hu) in is in thy mouth. Understanding (sea) is in thy heart. Thy speech is the shrine of truth (maat)." These are the attributes of the Sun -god Re and the Goddess Maat.

You will best understand that the ancient mind did not make differences between human and animal, living and dead, human and divine. The very rocks, air, sun, moon, water and sky became personifications. "Re is the sun [who had no divine wife at first]; [who conceived] Shu, the aerial "void" the air, [his mate] Tefnet without cosmic function. Geb, the earth, and Nut, the sky, are their offspring. At first they have no "personal" name, apart from the element or portion of the universe, which they represent. They have no definite shape, until they come to be fused with other deities, whose animal or human form they assume. Nor is their worship peculiar to any town or nome, doubtless because it is common to the whole country. The four last-born are opposed in pairs: Osiris represents the fertilizing Nile and vegetative force and his wife Isis is the fertilized soil in which the seeds grow, while Seth is the dry desert, with Nephthys as the barren consort".

The following four categories of deities will lend a simple guide for understanding the Egyptian pantheon:

1. Local gods, originally animals, later represented with human bodies and animal heads.
2. Osiris and attendant deities. Deities without temples, originally belonging to the Pharaoh only.
3. The Sun and other deities.
4. The council of the gods for the Mesopotamians represented members of a cosmic state.

These gods were those forces of the universe whose powers were viewed with awe and endowed with awesome power. The god of heaven, Anu, was the leader of the assembly of gods. He was the highest god because he was the god of the sky. His son, Enlil, was the second in command as the god of storm and his name meant Lord Storm. The force of the storm was experienced as it roared across the bleak Mesopotamian landscape. These gods together represented authority and force. The next god, who was visible in the universe, was the earth. She was known as Mother Earth, the fertility giver, with the formal name of Ninhursaga. Her male counterpart was En-ki known as the Lord of the Earth because he was the source of the life-giving waters and all of the tributaries, including the sea.

There are many gods representing other entities as in the Egyptian pantheon. The younger god and stronger god, Marduk, emerges as the chosen leader to subdue the forces of Chaos who wrecks havoc on the universe of gods through internecine battles. The concept of kingship was born amidst strife and fear. The form of government for the gods was that of a primitive democracy with certain limitations. This set the pattern for rule on earth that was determined by the gods and accepted by the peoples as divine intervention. The king was not a god but a leader to be chosen by assent when the necessity for leadership arose. This was in contrast to the divine theocracy of the Egyptians where Pharaoh was considered a god.

RELIGION AND STATE: PHARAONIC EMPIRES

For Egypt and Ancient Kush, the whole notion of Pharaonic rule can be traced back to the end of the predynastic Period. There existed a shared material culture from the remote past by the prehistoric inhabitants of the Nile Valley. As Frankfort points out, "they must have shared a common spiritual culture as a correlate to the homogeneous physical and archaeological remains".

The clues that Pharaonic civilization had its genesis in the Northeast African cultural substratum can be found in many of its basic beliefs. The Nile Valley peoples believed in the manifestation of divine power in creatures of the sky, such as birds and falcons, and in creatures from the heavens and earth. The falcon is a symbol for Horus and the Pharaoh is known as Horus. His imagery in Egyptian texts is very compelling. His outstretched wings are the sky; his fierce eyes the sun and the moon.

The cattle cults of modern Africa resemble the ancient attitude of North Africa and the Sub-Saharan stratum. The cattle play an important role in the life of the Nilotes and the Hamites as these people are dependent upon the herds economically and spiritually. The Masai view the grass as sacred because it is food for their cattle and they use the grass symbolically in their rites. One of the Egyptian fertility gods, Min, recognizes the power of the vegetation in his epithet "he who has created the vegetation let the herd live." Among the Barundi, rank, prestige and actual power is derived from the cattle alone. Among the Banyankole, when the king dies, his body is wrapped in the hide of a newly killed cow, after the royal corpse has been washed with milk... and even the cattle are made to participate on the mourning, cows are separate from their calves so that both make melancholy mowing.

The cult of the Goddess Hathor was known and conceived as the Cow Goddess and was very widespread throughout Egypt form the early period. Isis is shown with cow's horns. Other cattle cults are the Cult of Apis in Memphis, Mnervis of Heliopolis, Golden Calf of Canopus of Abydos, to name a few. Early Egyptian texts refer to the king as "a strong bull"; the queen Mother is called "the cow that has borne a bull"; the sun is "the bull of heaven"; the sky is a "Huge Cow" and the snake is called "Bull of the Forelock". You will find in new Kingdom tombs pictures of Nubian princes bringing tribute or taxes in the form of their most prized cattle.

All the kings of the first Dynasty worshipped and identified themselves with Horus as represented by the Narmer palettes and standards represented on monuments. The Narmer-Menes palette shows heads of a goddess with horns and cow's ears and the king on the reverse side hanging from it. The First Dynasty was in the process of consolidation and Menes was given the credit for completing the task of unification begun by an Upper Egyptian of Nubian chieftain. According to our understanding of Nubian Chronology, the A horizon coincided in time with the late Egyptian pre-dynasties and the First and Second Egyptian Dynasties. A major solidification of Egypt's divine monarchy began in the Third Dynasty with the building of the pyramid at Saqqara and reached its zenith with the pyramid built for Snefru and the great pyramids at Giza.

It was during Dynasty Five that the Pyramid Texts which are concerned with the nature of kingship were first inscribed in the pyramid of Unas: The Ka's of Unas are behind him; his Hemsut are under his feet; His gods are over him; his Uraeus-serpents are over his head. The leading snake of Unas is at his forehead, she who perceives the soul (of the enemy), She who excels in force of fire {Pyr.396}

The mythyopoetic speech of the ancient Egyptian is difficult to understand and is thought to be abstract to the modern mind rather than concrete. Ka is interpreted as spirit (soul) or the potency of the king that is derived from the gods. Kas represent the vital forces in nature and Hemsut represents the sustenance of nature or food. Taken collectively the terms express the power emanating from the king and absorbed by the commoner. The relationship of the gods, king and the people is thus understood through these terms. It expresses the involvement of man in nature and the king's role as mediator of the forces of nature.

The Uraeus is the most characteristic symbol of kingship, a rearing cobra worn on the forehead of Nubian and Egyptian pharaohs. The Nubians wore two cobras. The Pyramid Texts suggest that the crowns were placed upon the king's head in the dual shrines of Upper and Lower Egypt. Wedjet, the cobra represents Upper Egypt and Nekhbet, the vulture of Lower Egypt were the titular goddesses of the respective shrines.

It was during the Fourth to Sixth Dynasties or the Old Kingdom that the Pharaonic empress was most absolute. The dogma held that the king was a god and all energies were directed towards his glorification as he lived on earth. The pyramid was his utter deification after death, where it was believed that his life should continue in all of its splendor and glory.

The Ancient Kushite Kingdom of Kerma emerged during this period of absolute Egyptian monarchy. Kerma later became a powerful state ruled by Kushite Kings. Its opulence has already been described in Chapter VII. Although the list of its kings and other texts has not been found at this time, there are clear indications of Pharaonic rule. The Deffufa, the principal temple of Kerma, appears to have religious ceremonies held in celebration of the sun. The Kerma ram of bull sacrifices have great religious implications and represent indications of a cattle cult.

Much later, the Nubian Kings of Napata are credited with the rejuvenation of the Pharaonic tradition. King Shabaka, the Nubian Pharaoh, ordered the Memphite Theology to be copied on a granite block. The texts states: "My majesty copied this book anew in the temple of Ptah-who-is- the - South -of -his -Wall. My majesty has found it as a works of the ancestors. It has been devoured by worms. It was known from beginning to end." The original was apparently written of a leather scroll.

MEMPHITE FOUNDATION.

As noted, the foundation of kingship in the Nile valley had its genesis in early speculations about the purpose of life, organization of realities as they manifested themselves in the daily occurrences in those ancient communities. The Memphite Theology which represents the earliest speculation about the Cosmos and its beginnings was written over two thousands years before the earliest Greek and Hebrew texts. It is difficult to comprehend the vision that it proclaims because of the modern perception of the inability of the early Egyptians or even Nubians to speculate in abstract thought. Yet this document in its mythyopoeic language offers a concept of creation, which reduces its multiplicity of gods, the superhuman and divine, and human to a pantheistic model that is at the same time spiritual and physical in its concept of creation.

The Memphite Theology embodies the theory of kingship from its inception, the religious teaching of Menes and the justification of its new capital, Memphis. The theory for all subsequent capitals is inherent in the theory of kingship. The theory embraces the old and new doctrine rooted in Egyptian and older African traditions which makes it at the same time new, but timeless in its permutations.

The text in its damaged state appears to have six parts that may have been originally joined together. The first section deals with the belief that creation began with the emergence of the Great Land from the waters of Chaos with the appearance of a mound referred to as the Primeval Hill. The Primeval Hill has many analogies in the Egyptian and Nubian belief system. It also alludes to Menes, who unites the land and builds Memphis, the first capital, from the land, which he has reclaimed from the marsh waters.

Section II describes the conflict between the gods Horus and Seth over the sovereignty of Egypt with Geb, the earth-god as arbiter. At first, he divides the land between the two gods but later gives all the land to Horus because he regretted his decision. This lends credence to the idea that the two crowns o Upper and Lower Egypt "grow" form the head of Horus. Menes, as mentioned before is the first human embodiment of Horus, a role which each later king assumed at his coronation as he unites the lands under his single rule.

The duality of kingship expresses the ancient view of the "world in static equilibrium between conflicting forces Horus and Seth, the kingship of Upper and Lower Egypt as the corresponding political form, and withal a ruler ship in the person of a single king. The symbiosis of the united lands is represented by the sedge for Upper Egypt, and papyrus for Lower Egypt was placed at the outer gates of the Temple of Ptah to signify the balance of the two lands and to indicate that Horus and Seth are in harmony.

Section III is very damaged but its statement is repeated in Section VI which is better preserved. Section IV is also badly damaged; however, it deals with the construction of the royal castle at Memphis, its significance as the granary of Egypt because if was the burial place of Osiris, the father of Horus. Continuity is assured mythologically as well as historically, since Memphis is the actual creation of Menes, the human Horus.

Section V is the theological argument for the primacy of Ptah as the sole creator underlying Atun's work of creation through Ptah's Utterance of thought. It was assumed that the organs of creation were the heart and the tongue. The heart stands for the intellect and spirit and for the capacity of understanding. The tongue translates concepts into reality by means of Hu or Authoritative Utterance. Frankfort suggests a true equivalent in St John's "In the beginning was the Word and the word was with God, and the Word was God." This section accounts for the establishment of order in the world for all time. Everything in the phenomenal world including the sanctuaries and cities are a part of this order. The Memphite Text reads: Ptah rested (or was satisfied) after he had made all things and all divine words.

Section VI solidified the importance of Memphis, the connection of the gods and the land and explained the role of the death of Osiris and the recovery of his body in the waters of the Nile. The beneficence of the Nile inundations represented manifestations of the power of Osiris which made the land flourish after floods. The significance of this statement was brought home to me, when in our own time (1988) a Nubian, after an inundation of the Nile that was unusual in its height and staggering in the human devastation, spoke these words about his village that was under water: "there were bodies floating on the water, but this year it will be a better crop." The actual ritual of lifting of a jar of fresh Nile water represents the recovery of the body of Osiris by Isis and Nephythys and the rebirth of the vegetation.

It is remarkable how in the Memphite Theology mythology and reality are commingled. The ancient Egyptians were able to act and think on two levels of thought or consciousness. The gods represented the ancestors of the king, who were gods on earth. In life, each king became in the official rituals a Horus as Menes declared and at death, he became an Osiris. This transformation was reenacted with each coronation by a ritual in the Mystery Play of the Succession where the king acted in person, and the burial of his father was done in effigy. The Sed Festival as the commemoration of the king's accession gives an accurate picture of the nature of kingship.

The divinity of the king is not peculiar to Egypt. Many societies in East Africa believe the chieftain possesses powers closer to nature and the gods than ordinary men. The Rainmaker King is a similar concept. Frankfort insists that this concept of kingship, which is so widespread in East and West Africa, is the basis upon which Menes founded his position. The practical function of kingship was to interpret the will of the gods, to act as an intermediary between the people and the gods and to administer his realm for the benefit of all.

In this capacity, the king was considered the high priest because he knew the secret of how to pray to the gods. As judge and dispenser of Maat (wisdom), he declared what was right or wrong; and as protector, he was the army commander. The king was also owner of all land, which required royal oversight. Over the period of time, these functions were delegated and a vast cult of the Pharaoh as god evolved with priests who carried out his priestly duties. Thus, a vast array of officials with titles appropriate to their functions arose.

On royal occasions, the king wore a red crown of Lower Egypt or the White crown of Upper Egypt or sometimes he wore the double crown with the white one inside the red one. The rook and flail served as the royal insignia and the sickle shaped sword seemed to be a sign of royalty. The Uraeus, the poisonous snake, also was a symbol of royalty, appearing on his dress. In the litany in which the king invokes the power of the crown at his coronation, the crown is referred to as the "Eye of Horus". His power is revealed in the following lines:

> "O red Crown, O Inu, O great One,
>
> O magician, O fiery Snake
>
> Let there be fear of me like the fear of thee.
>
> Let there be awe of me like the awe of thee.
>
> Let there be love of me like the love of thee.
>
> Let me be powerful, a leader of spirits.
>
> Let thy blade be firm against my enemies."

SACRED SITES

PHILAE: CULT OF ISIS

On the ancient border of the Ethiopians and the Egyptians at the First Cataract, the long revered Earth mother, Isis, had her seat of worship. It was on the island of Philae that the sacred site of Isis recreated the primeval world when the sun god Ra ruled on earth. On the opposite island of Biga was one of the many tombs of Osiris, the father of Horus and the brother and husband of Isis. Each of the deities had an island, but Osiris overshadowed Isis in earlier dynastic reigns because of the Osiris myth and the mortuary rites. Isis, although respected and worshipped as a fertility goddess since the beginning of time, did not gain ascendancy until the Greeks in Ptolemaic Egypt. The Romans in time spread her cult as far as the British Isles.

The buildings on the island of Philae date back to Roman and Ptolemaic periods when it became known as the "City of Island or the "Holy Island". The architectural triumph of Philae is the beautiful Temple of Isis and the grandeur of its temple complex that grew with the spiritual power of Isis and the temporal power of her priests. Apuleius, the Roman author, stated the Ethiopians worshipped Isis by her true name Regina Isis, although many other peoples worship her under many other names. Plutarch, the Greek historian, considered Isis as both wise and philosophic. To R.E. Witt: A very important bridge between paganism and Christianity ... the speculative system of the Hellenizing Jew, Philo of Alexandria and in it the cornerstone was "Holy Wisdom" (Hagia Sophia) Mother of the Divine Logos, rightly identified with Isis-Sophia could be thought to produce Harpocrates (Horus) as the Logos."

The regenerative powers of Isis are recounted in the Osirian Myth where she is said to have reincarnated Osiris in the form of Horus. It is through her love that she is able to give back his life. In the Mysteries of Isis, the initiate sought to become Osiris and thus be raised from the dead. With such power Isis is associated with healing, much as the Black Madonna and the Holy Mother of God.

The Ethiopians (Nubians) played an enormous role in the spread of Isiac worship in antiquity. They were the key to Nubian and Egyptian Condominium in the Dodekaschoenos according to W.Y. Adams. "In theory it was the private estate of Isis, and the Nubian and Egyptian monarchs who were consignors of the temples of Nubia... In practice it was a semi-autonomous buffer zone- a feudal principality administered by the priesthood of Isis as nominal vassals both of Egypt and Nubia."[122] This buffer zone was somewhat like the estate of Amon administered by the Theban priests at Karnak.

The status of the Dodekashoenos was clarified by the text of Ergamenes, the king, who formally offered to the goddess Isis twelve Schoenoes of land on each side of the river from Aswan to Takompso. Millet explains that his is the first official statement regarding the land in question. This act of commemoration is repeated in many later temple inscriptions at Philae. During the Ptolemaic and Roman occupation of Egypt, each ruler of Egypt was content to administer the territory with the Meroitic kings.

Under Roman control, it appears that the Romans controlled the roads and military matters and the civil matters were left in the hands of the Meroitic officials. "But it would seem that they were officially at least, felt as co-dedicators of the temples of Nubia... and both as receiving the divine benefits of the "breath of life" from the gods of Nubia in return." The Meroitic great families were devoted to the cult of Isis and their own local gods as well.

Let us consider the opinions of the classical scholar, Frank M. Snowden of Howard University:

> "In their native land Ethiopia, Isis was one of the four deities whom the people in the vicinity of Meroe worshipped because they believed that these particular divinities had been benefactors of the human race. Egyptians, according to one tradition, were colonists sent out by the Ethiopians under the leadership of Osiris, who was worshipped in Ethiopia. Depicted on the wall of a Meroitic pyramid is a seated Negroid king, in the back of whose throne Isis stands; in front, a priest holds a censer of burning incense. Records of obeisance to the goddess at Philae attest to the prominence of Isis in Meroe of the third century A.D. Among those Southerners to leave testimonials of their devotion to Isis at Philae was Pasn, the son of Paese, who when on a mission on behalf of the king, "the beloved son of Isis" left an offering for the goddess and prayed for a safe return to Meroe." "Since

the worship of Isis was highly regarded by Ethiopians, whether in their native land or in Egypt, those who had settled elsewhere could tend to continue their interest in the cult. The head... discovered at Athens, has been interpreted as that of a native priest whom Egyptian metics demanded for their worship." [120]

The cult of Isis became the "supra-national religion" through the temporal power of her priests. Philae became a holy city and attracted pilgrims from all classes and all nationalities in the then known world: Greeks, Romans, Egyptians, Meroites and people from the desert seeking solace.

JEBEL BARKAL: CULT OF AMON

The state cult of Amon at Napata, near the Fourth cataract was of great spiritual and political influence in both Nubia and Egypt. The Amon cult was "originally planted at Jebel Barkal in New Kingdom times, it was to persist for well over a thousand years and to provide the central ideology of the independent Kingdom of Kush. Napata, the capital of the Kingdom of Kush, lay at the foot of Jebel Barkal and Amon reigned in his sanctuary at the foot of the sacred mountain. The Egyptians knew this holy mountain as the Pure Mountain, to the ancient Nubians as the Mountain of Amon and to the present-day Nubians as Jebel Barkal.

This mysterious mountain and the city of Napata, at its feet, remained unknown to the outside world for many centuries. However, the locals tantalized the Europeans with tales of buried kings and unknown treasures. One of the early nineteenth century travelers, Hoskins, wrote that the form of Jebel Barkal was not very unlike that of the Athenian acropolis. He estimated that the height of the mountain was about 350 feet and the total circumference, 5,000 feet. The surrounding royal cemeteries of Jebel Barkal at Nuri and El Kurru represented the pyramid tombs and temples of the Nubian kings.

Many scholars believe that the Amon worship, which is the symbol of Amon both in Nubia and Egypt was well established in Nubia before the cult of Amon arrived from Egypt. The Egyptians characterized Amon as human or simply a ram. The Nubians combined the characteristics and represented Amon as a ram-headed god. To the Egyptians, Amon was the king of all the gods, the creator force identified with the sun and the forces of nature and lastly the father of the Egyptian king and later the Nubians Pharaohs. At Kerma were found statues of ram-headed sphinx and many rams elaborately decorated were found in the burial sites. At ancient Thebes or modern Luxor, Amon was an obscure god who acquired great significance during the Middle Kingdom when he became identified as a solar god and was called Amon- Re by the priests. The Greeks called him Zeus- Amon.

It was during the New Kingdom that the cult of Amon because a state religion and Amon became a State god. As the power of the state increased, so did the power of the priests and the wealth of the Pharaohs, which caused the administrative structure of the priests to expand. What was once the province of a sole priest as spiritual guide to pharaoh became a sacerdotal estate with a great number of priests whose duties and increased power constituted a new social class. To this class was added the High -priest's wife who was named Divine Consort or Concubine of the God Amon. During rituals, she was to lead the singing of the women and rattle the sistrum in honor of the god. Added to her office was the fortune of Amon, which was apart of the temple endowment. Literature and records of the priesthood expanded as records of the pharaohs were transcribed in the tombs. The Book of the dead, Instructions for the priests and the Pyramid Texts were a part of this of this canon. The State god Amon spoke through his statue, which was interpreted by the priests as oracles.

Breasted reminds us that Nubia was a very closely connected with Thebes and the Temple of Amon. As far back as the Nineteenth Dynasty, Nubia was called the "gold country of Amon." The Viceroy of Nubia became the High Priest of Amon at the end of the Twentieth Dynasty and the sacerdotal princesses of Thebes held the same office. It was not long until the Nubian kings ruled Egypt as the Twenty Fifth Dynasty of Pharaohs The control of the fortune of Amon and claim to the throne was achieved by Pianhki when he arranged for the adoption of his sister-wife Amenardis by one of the sacerdotal princesses of Thebes, who was the daughter of Orsokon III at the time. In turn, Taharqa had his sister adopted by Amenardis. This allowed his control of rituals, which are written on the walls of the temples or on papyri that describe the rituals of the priests.

The priest of Amon is one who knows the offerings of the temples, with experience regarding the right moment to bring them; keeping their taboos (but) away, and knowing what their hearts desires (for) each god, in regard to what comes to him; knowing (each god's bread from the (other) offerings; knowing the sacred images of the district- ensigns, and likewise all their estates.

Diodorus wrote that priests taught their sons the sacred form of letters (hieroglyphics) and that which was more suitable to a commonplace type of learning (Demotic), Hieratic, and cursive form, was used for secular writing. They also carry geometry, arithmetic, and astrology to a higher form of perfection. Prescriptions for purges, enemas, emetics, surgical practices as well as magic and incantations are a part of the lore.

The Napatan kings or the XXVth Dynast of pharaohs was distinguished by their piety to Amon. The legitimacy of the Kushite monarchs was sanctioned by the priests of Amon and in return provided their administrative bureaucracy. The exchange reaped huge financial benefits for the temple estates; but the priests could intervene in choice of successors or termination of rule by death. The power of the priest of Amon met its demise when Ergamenes opposed their interventions by putting a number of priests to death. Worship of purely Meroitic gods and some Pharaonic divinities prevailed.

MEROE: CULT OF APEDEMAK

The paramount god of the Meroitic area: the island of Meroe, in the town of Meroe itself, at Basa and throughout the land was the Lion God, Apedemak. He is represented with three heads and four pairs of arms who is indisputably Meroitic although earlier archaeologists wished to ascribe Indian and Persian origin. The god was addressed on terms that would suggest his exalted position in the prayer to Apedemak:

> "Thou art greeted, Apedemak, Lord of Naga; great god, Lord of Musawwarat es-Sufra; splendid god at the head of Nubia, Lion of the south, strong of arm. Great god, the one who comes to those who call him. The one who carries (?) the secret, concealed in his being, who was not seen by any eye. Who is the companion for men and women, who will not be hindered in heaven and earth. Who procures nourishment for all men, in this name 'Perfect Awakener'. The one who hurls his hot breath against the enemy, in this his name 'Great Power.' Who kills the enemy with (lacuna). The one who punishes all who commits crimes against him. Who prepares the place for those who give themselves to him. Who gives to those who call to him. Lord of life, great in his sight."[121]

A local god, Sebewyemeker, is paired with Apedemak. He also has no Egyptian parallels. His name and symbol is the ankh, the sign for life. On a temple wall, Sebewyemeker is represented with a frieze of ankhs, the sign of life at his feet. He appears as a Creator god and Apedemak is represented as the War god with bound prisoners tied to war elephants at his feet.

> "The Creator God said
> I give you everything which comes forth by night,
> I give to you the years of the sun, and the months of the moon with joy
> So speaks Sebewyemeker lord of Musawwarat es-Sufra, who gives life
> like the sun god forever".
> Another place he speaks:
> "I give the lifetime of the sun god in heaven so speaks Sebewyemeker,
> the great god at the head of Nubia."[122]

This great Lion god is shown at a number of other places but the Temple at Naga, which is dedicated to him, seems to be the most significant. On the back of the wall of the temple Apedemak is the only god shown as he receives the adoration from the royal family. At Musawwarat es-Sufra, Apedemak is represented with a line of gods, Horus, Amon, Khonsu and Khnum , all adored by the king, queen and prince. The opposite wall shows him in front of Isis, Mut and the indigenous goddess Hathor and Satis. The accompanying inscriptions are in Meroitic hieroglyphs.

The temple in Umm Usada, a few miles away to the east of Basa, has seven lions and three rams as well as a stela in Meroitic. If only the code of the Meroitic script could be broken as the Rosetta Stone was, much more could be revealed about this great culture. We do know that Umm Usada in Arabic means 'Mother of Lions'. On two outer pylons of the temple a lion is shown aiding the king and queen subduing their enemies. Apedemak is represented with the body of a snake uncoiling from a lotus flower. These representations are most heroic and poetic.

The graffiti and long formal prayers from the walls of a temple at Musawwarat support the importance of the worship of Apedemak. The lion probably roamed the Meroitic plains in abundance and the young lion played a significant role in the rituals. The reliefs in the temple at Musawwarat depict much about the Meroitic cult. The sun god Amon is identical to the Meroitic manifestation of Apedemak as emanating from the sun suggesting that the cult of the lion and the sun are identical. Spatial representations on the wall places Apedemak in first position with Amon following, then Sebewyemeker, Arensnuphis, Horus and Thoth. Arensnuphis originates in Meroe but is also known at Philae. On another wall, Apedemak is seen facing left with the goddess Isis behind him and in front of him is a prince designated as priest of Isis.

Meroitic divinities are diverse emanating from local cults and funerary practices. The Cult of Isis and Osiris is quite evident from the offering tables, with invocation to the respective gods. The inscriptions and the offering tables are Meroitic. There is evidence of the Elephant cult because of the many elephants featured in the architecture at the great Enclosure at Musawwarat.

CHAPTER 11.
GODSHIP: ORIGINS OF THE KINGDOM OF KUSH

The Kingdom of Kush owes much of its heritage to the monarchial leanings of the Kingdom of Kerma. The trappings of Divine Kingship and state-organized trade were a beginning. Adams suggested that" had the culture been left to develop unmolested, stratified society, peasant economy, bureaucratic government, and other 'blessings' of imperial civilization must inevitably have followed in time."[123] However, David 0' Connor makes the following observation: "Whether the Dynasty VI Yamites" are to be equated with the beginning of the earlier Kerma culture is uncertain, but certainly both phases of the Kerma culture may be described as "Kushite" since Upper Nubia was in a general sense, called "Kush," from...the beginning of Dynasty XII on.[124]

A VI Dynasty inscription left by Harkuf, the trader with the Yam, gives a description of careful and scrupulous negotiations needed to trade with the Nubians chiefs. As cited in chapter VII, the Egyptians were strongly acquainted with Kerma from the Old Kingdom contacts. They called the region Kerma, Yam (later Irm). According to Priese (1974), the name became Irame in the Meroitic period and it possibly survives in the modern name Kerma. Amenemhat, called Ameni, the founder of the twelfth dynasty, believed to be a son of a woman from Ta-seti (Nubia) was called upon to pacify the enemies to the south in the twenty-ninth year of his reign. This was the first of a long series of Nubian campaigns to quell the Kushites. A stela found at Buhen documents the triumph of the next king, Senusret I, nine years later, standing before the war god Menthu (Montu) proclaiming, "I have brought for thee all countries which are in Nubia beneath my feet." There is another document that actually refers to the area as Kush. It was found in the tomb of a monarch or feudal prince of Oryx province (Nome) in Upper Egypt.

EXPEDITING AMENI

Here is a more detailed description of the first two expeditions of Senusret's Nubian victory during his eighteenth year and some of the delegated duties of his monarch, Ameni:

FIRST EXPEDITION

"I followed my lord when he sailed southward to overthrow his enemies among the four barbarians. I sailed southward as a son of a count, wearer of the royal seal and commander in chief of the troop of the Oryx Nome, as a man represents his old father, according to his favor in the palace and his love in the court. I passed Kush, traveling southward, I advanced the boundary of the land, I bought all gifts; my praise, it reached heaven. Then his majesty returned in safety, having overthrown his enemies in Kush the vile. I returned with ready face. There was no loss among my soldiers."[125]

SECOND EXPEDITION

"I sailed southward, to bring gold ore for the majesty of the King of Upper and Lower Egypt, Kherkere [Senusret I] living forever and ever. I sailed southward together with the hereditary prince, count, oldest son of the king, of his body Ameni. I sailed southward with a number, 400 of all the choicest of my troops, who returned in safety, having suffered no loss. I brought the gold exacted of me; I was praised for it in the palace. The king's son praised god for me."

AMENI'S ABLE ADMINISTRATION

I was amiable, and greatly loved, a ruler beloved of his city. Now, I passed years as ruler in the Oryx Nome. All the imposts of the king's house passed through my hand. The gang-overseers of the crown possessions of the shepherds of the Oryx Nome gave them to me 3,000 bulls in their yoke. I was praised on account of it in the palace each year of the loan-herds. I carried all the dues to the king's house; there were no arrears against me in any office of his. The entire Oryx Nome labored for me in."

AMENI'S IMPARTIALITY AND BENEVOLENCE

There was no citizen's daughter whom I misused, there was no widow whom I oppressed, there was no peasant whom I repulsed, there was no shepherd whom I repelled, there was no overseer of serf-laborers whose people I took for (unpaid) imposts, there was none wretched my community, there was none hungry in my tie. When the years of famine came I plowed all the fields of the Oryx Nome , as far as its southern and northern boundary, preserving its people alive and furnishing its food so that there was none hungry therein. I gave to the widow as (to) her who had husband; I did not exalt the great above the small in all that I gave. Then came the Niles [floods], possessors of grain and all things, (but) I did not collect the arrears of the field .125

After a series of campaigns, the complete pacification of Nubia was accomplished by Senusret Ill, which won for him the worship in the temples of Nubia as a patron of the deity of Nubia. The Kushite menace was pushed southward to Semna where the southern boundary line was established. The great -grandfather, Senusret I had penetrated to this point and Senusret III was determined to maintain the conquest. The first Semna Stela which Senusret III set up some thirty-seven miles south of the Second cataract marks the boundary line and implies the inherent fear of the Kushites:

"Southern boundary, made in the year 8, under the majesty of the King of Upper and Lower Egypt, Kherkere, [Senusret Ill], who is given life forever and ever: in order to prevent any Negro [Aithiope, Nubian or Kushite] should cross it, by water with a ship, (or) any herds of the Negroes except a Negro who shall come to do trading in Iken [Mirgissa] or with a commission. Every good ting shall be done with them, but without allowing a ship of Negroes to pass by Heb [modern Semna], going downstream forever."

The Nubians were forever in need of chastisement because of the fear of them as enemies. After the Twelfth year of Senusret Ill's reign, he left a meager inscription on a rock in Aswan which included his name and date and what could be read: "His majesty journeyed to overthrow Kush". Disturbances arose again in his sixteenth year which caused the second Semna Stela to be erected, with a duplicate at Uronarti just below Semna. It was on this campaign that the Uronarti fortress was built with a repulsive name 'Repulse-of-the-Troglodytes'.126

Several centuries later, the unique cultures of the C-Group and of Kerma south of Aswan may have been completely assimilated by the conquest of the New Kingdom Warrior kings. However, the traditions of the indigenous populations have been very persistent in spite of the Egyptian civilization of the elite. Excavation and Egyptian sources give us many examples of the practices that emerged in later times with their native customs and practices intact.

The Egyptian cultural influences remained superficial. The most important political cultural and political influence during this time came from the people of the Kerma culture whose power the Egyptians respected. In the Middle Bronze age (Egyptian Middle and Second Intermediate period,) (2040-1540 B.C.) the Kerma Kingdom represented an advanced form of the centralized state. The importance and significance of this early Kushite kingdom and culture is reflected in stelae at Buhen and at Karnak: 'I was a valiant commander of Buhen, and ever had any commander who did what I did. I built the temple of Horus, Lord of Buhen, in the days of the Kings of Kush.' The owner of another (named Ka) also records service with the King of Kush, whose name is given as Nedjeh. Another possible record of mercenary service (not from Buhen) is that of a soldier, Ha-ankhef, who after six years of service in Kush returned to Edfu in Upper Egypt with enough gold to buy himself land'

Kamose, the last king of the Seventeenth dynasty expresses his angst on a pair of stelae which he set up in Karnak, the early stages of the civil war with Thebes and Avaris: 'Give me to understand what this strength of mine is for. A king is in Avaris, another in Kush, and so I sit alongside and Asiatic and a Nubian. Each one has his slice of this Egypt, dividing up the land with me.'

A further indication of power and military acumen of the King of Kush was suggested by a letter, intended for the king of Kush from the Hyksos king intercepted by one of Kamoses' men during an invasion of Hyksos territory: "Come, journey downstream! Fear not! He is here with me, and there is no -one [else] who will stand up against you in that part of Egypt. Behold I will allow him no road until you have arrived. Then shall we divide up the towns..., and our lands will thrive in joy."

The hiatus around 1100 B.C., discussed in Chapter VII, was the result of the depopulation of Nubia, perhaps due to climactic changes. However, the record shows a resurgence of Kushite power in the south near the ancient city of Napata, located near the Fourth Cataract, about the ninth century B.C.

Egypt's attempt at submission and control of Upper and Lower Nubia was the incorporation of the "princes of the south" into to their administrative and political structure through the Viceroyalty of Kush. The Vice Royalty of Kush became powerful agents in Nubia through the operation of Toynbee's law of peripheral domination.

ROYAL SONS OF KUSH: VICE REGAL SYSTEM

The vice regal system apparently had its genesis through the expansion into Wawat and Kush by the New Kingdom pharaohs. The first viceroy was installed, perhaps by Ahmose or most assuredly by Kamose in the Seventeenth dynasty. The expulsion of the Hyksos and the ultimate final control of the Kushites, the allies of the Hyksos, was the military intent of Kamose, the last king of the Seventeenth Dynasty. This Theban dynasty felt the utter humiliation of being crunched by the foreigners to the north of them and the Kushite warriors to the south of them. The anguish of Kamose and his war stance was echoed in this statement that was to become a part of Theban folklore: "No man rest, being wasted through the servitude of the Asiatics. I will grapple with him and rip open his belly, for my desire is to deliver Egypt and to smite the Asiatics."

Not only were the Hyksos driven from the land by a series of campaigns begun by Ahmose and triumphantly ended by Kamose, but also the great fortune of Egypt was to bring many Palestinian and Syrian territories under its control. It was after or during the triumphant Asiatic campaigns that the war machine was turned south. The southern territories of Kush were reconquered and the institution of the vice regal system was initiated. The Fortress of Buhen was reoccupied, a temple built and the first governor of the southern lands was appointed by Ahmose and was given the title King's Son of Kush in the reign of Amenhotep I, (Dynasty XVIII.)

Documentation cites at least thirty viceroys succeeding each other until the reign of Rameses XI, yet , only a few have been discovered by the archaeologists. The viceroy was called the "King's Son of Kush" because of his responsibility for the administration of Wawat and Kush or from Hierakonpolis to Napata. A few of the more prominent viceroys whose names appeared in inscriptions are:

> Thuwre under Amenophis I and Tuthmosis
> Nehi under Hatshepsut and Tuthmosis II
> Mermose under Amenophis III
> Huy-Amenophis under Tutankhamen
> Yuni under Seti and Rameses 11
> Pa-Nehesi under Rameses XI
> Herihor under Rameses XI
> Pianhki under Herihor [128]

The chief responsibilities of the viceroy were to collect and deliver tribute and taxes, to exploit efficiently the gold -bearing regions, and to oversee the civil government of the province. The staff of the Viceroy was limited to the Commander of the Bow- men of Kush, one deputy for Wawat and one for Kush as well as scribes, envoys, and agents.

> The Northern Province was called Wawat and the southern province was called Kush. The administrative seats were in large centers such as Faras, Soleb, Aniba, and Amara. Each town also had a Priesthood to serve the gods as well as mayor to administer the secular and local aspects of government. The Battalion Commander of Kush was responsible for the control of the armed forces, including the commanders and garrisons of the fortresses. As you will see later, the Commander of the Armed Forces and the High priest of the Priesthood of Amon were able to increase their individual powers and domain as the provincial government of Egypt weakened.
>
> When Thuwwre was appointed viceroy, he was in command of the most senior administrative post as Commandant of Buhen. His title and role as Commandant did not follow him. Although the viceroys rarely bore military command with their incumbency and although formal military command was vested in the Battalion-commander of Kush in practice, they could assume direct military

command of the province's forces (e.g. Merymose under Amenhotep ill and Penehasy [Pa-nehesi] under Rameses XI). Moreover, at least a third of the viceroys between the Eighteenth and earlier Twentieth Dynasties were drawn from the royal chariotry or royal stable administration, a fact that preferably reflects their role in the desert campaigning typical of that period.

Lepsius found in the grotto at Ellesiya the following inscription of Nehi, the viceroy of Thutmose III:

"Bringing the tribute of the south countries, consisting of gold, ivory, and ebony, [by] the hereditary prince, count, wearer of the royal seal, sole companion, satisfying the heart of the king at the Horns of the Earth, having access to the king, pleasant to the divine limbs; companion approaching the mighty sovereign, vigilant for the lord of the palace, king's son, governor of the south countries, Nehi."

Another inscription was found containing the name and titles of Nehi on the Island of Sai, one hundred miles above Semna. Nehi was valuable and wise viceroy. He saw to it that the tribute was delivered to Thutmosis In regularly and bountifully. The gold mines and the trade routes were regularly patrolled and the administration of Nubia under Nehi reached its highest level. The tribute in gold, ivory and slaves, and cattle was more impressive which suggests a considerable impoverishment of the provinces. The walls of the tomb of Huy, the viceroy of Tutankhamon, were a veritable codex portraying the intense interaction between the Egyptians and the indigenous cultures of Wawat and Kush. The power of the investiture is displayed in the painted scene and the following text:

Huy is brought before the regaled Tutankhamon by the courtiers. The official, called the Overseer of the White House, greets Huy on behalf of the king with the following words: "This is the seal from the pharaoh, Life, Prosperity, Health, who assigns to thee (the territory) Napata." The distance by the river from Nankeen, the modem El Kab, north of the First Cataract to Dongola province in the Sudan is more than eight hundred miles. The seal of the office is given to Huy, who is addressed as 'King's Son of Kush"; and a further scene depicts Huy 's reception by his family and officials The text above him reads: "The coming forth, favored, from the court, having been appointed in the presence of the Good God to be the King's Son of Kush and governor of the southern countries."

The tribute scenes are very engaging and highly detailed. The first tribute scene shows the two brothers, Huy and Amenhotep presenting the tribute from the North. One scene shows Tutankhamon enthroned at the left under a magnificent kiosk. The brothers present four lines of Asiatics who bring a splendid array of tribute, of gold and silver vessels, costly stones and horses. The Asiatics plead for peace "Give to us thy victories and there shall be no revolters in thy time but every land shall be in peace."

Another scene shows the two viceroys presenting the tribute from the South to Tutankhamon. The array is even more magnificent: chiefly commercial gold and silver, gold and silver vessels, a chariot, shields, and furniture. A second part of the scene shows Huy receiving three lines of Nubians, and a line of Egyptians below. In the top line of Nubians are children of the Kushite chiefs, among them a princess in a chariot drawn by oxen. The chiefs wear Egyptian clothing and they bring similar tribute, and also curiously decorated cattle. Behind all, we see six Nile boats landing.

The inscription over the top line designates. "The chief of Miam, good ruler. The chiefs of Wayet [Wawat] The children of all other countries." Over the middle line the chiefs of Kush say, "Hail to thee 0 king of Egypt, Sun of the Nine Bows! Give to us the breath which thou giveth. Men live by love."

A final scene of the tribute series shows Huy leaning on his staff and accompanied by his family, waiting to embark on a ship which has its sails spread ready to leave for Nubia. A second ship contains his chariot and horses. The boat approaching Huy is filled with four rows of officials under Huy, followed by sailors and women with tambourines.

There are inscriptions over Huy, his family, and his officials that indicate the official visit of Huy with the king and the ceremonies in the temple have come to an end. The inscriptions over the officials designate their rank and position:

Deputy of Kush, Mayor of Khammat (Soleb), Overseer of cattle, deputy of the Fortress called Nekhepprure {the king's throne name), His brother, prophet of the Fortress, Satisfier -of- the-Gods, Mermose, Priest of -, residing in the Fortress: Satisfier-of -the-Gods.

Building or overseeing building operations were also the duties of the Viceroy. Huy contributed his skill and supervision to many of the needed operations. To commemorate the end of the Aton heresy and Tutankhamon's reconciliation with the old religion, Huy built a walled city and a temple at Faras which he called Sehetep-enter, the Conciliation of the Gods.

The King's Sons of Kush, because of their link to Royalty, claimed a unique quasi-divine status that was emphasized by their titles, administrative functions and their origins. They were more powerful than the Levantine princes of the Northern lands were and were considered equal in terms of function. The King's Sons of Kush were directly responsible to the King and were picked for their implicit loyalty. The sons of the chiefs who had either been taken as hostage or tribute to Egypt were brought with the royal family, educated and soon filled the ranks of the bureaucracy and army as sandal bearer, page and possibly viceroy.

In an unprecedented move, Rameses XI was able to restore order in the kingdom, by relinquishing command of his troops to Pa-nehesi and ordering him to take control of Upper Egypt. This action on the part of Rameses XI set a precedent for Herihor who later displaced Pa-nehesi. Pa-nehesi whose name 'the Nubian' maintained his seven year regime in Middle and

Upper Egypt with the use of a large number of Nubian troops. The Theban, Herihor forced Pa-nehesi's retreat into Kush and Pianhki, Herihor's son who was his successor continued to harass Pa-nehesi.

SEED-BED OF MONARCHIAL OR IMPERIAL ASPIRATION

The unprecedented move by Rameses was a reflection of a weakening" of the coercive resources of the kingship" It also reflected the changing relationships between king, the government and the army. The high priest became equal to the king, the individuals were given greater powers and the civil government became less submissive to royal control. The Nubian, Pa-nehesi, was not of elite status, but a commoner, was Viceroy of Kush, an army leader and an overseer of the granaries. Herihor, a Theban, was vizier, High Priest of Amon and generalissimo.

The final disintegration of the traditional government was thus complete with a commoner wielding unprecedented power and the descendants of Herihor, a line of great army commanders in control of Middle and Upper Egypt while at the same time serving as High Priest of Amon at Thebes. The problem faced in the Late New Kingdom and the Third Intermediate period was that of competing forces that were derivatives of some of the same families, and the inability to ward off Assyrian encroachment in the north.

The absorption of the Nubian elite into the administrative ranks completed the large-scale urbanization begun by the warrior king of the XVIIIth Dynasty and the Egyptianization of many of the indigenous Nubians. The economy was transformed into a manorial system through intensive farming, oppressive taxation, and landed interests became another force in the downward spiral of royal control.

POLITICAL AND ECONOMIC ORGANIZATION

The imposed government of Nubia was that of a quasi-divine kingship. The god-king was the most powerful figure in the government. Politically his role as an instrument of the gods was emphasized. The religious texts emphasize the supernatural aspects of government apparent in the rituals and myths. Externally the government was to maintain Egypt's integrity and under the auspices of the gods, extend its frontiers. Internally its functions were more varied. These included maintaining and enhancing the agricultural economy upon which depended Egypt's ability to produce the surplus to support the government superstructure.

Wilbour Papyrus (1143 B.C.) includes in the populace a small group of wealthy and high ranking officials, a larger group of scribes, priests, soldiers, stable masters, citizens, cultivators and herdsmen. Artisans were also included in the populace. Herodotus 700 years later gave priests, warriors, cowherds, swineherds, tradesmen, interpreters and pilot as the principal occupations but omitted cultivators. Only those in the dynasty who were loyal to the king received the most desirable posts. The designated heir or crown prince was appointed 'great army general' who controlled the military in the king's name. The king's chief wife (or eldest daughter) was appointed 'God's Wife of Amon' who controlled a large portion of Amon's temporal possessions.

The next significant group with powerful potential was the government of conquests, which were divided into two groups: Northern lands, which included the Vassal Kings and the Battalion Commanders and the Southern Lands, which included the King's Sons of Kush. The King's Sons of Kush included the Battalion Commander of Kush and the Deputy of Wawat and the Deputy of Kush. Under the Deputies were the Mayors of the Urban centers and the Chiefs of the Indigenous Groups.

The civil government has its components under the Northern and Southern Viziers with occupations and titles to fit the duties, such as Overseers of the Treasury, Overseers of the Granaries for Upper and Lower Egypt, Overseer of the cattle, Village Chiefs, Mayors and Councils including the judiciary and police.

The religious government was quintessentially important as it represents the royal domain before the gods. The most important post was that of the Overseer of the Prophets of (All the Gods) of Upper and Lower Egypt held at various times by Vizier and High Priest of Amon and supported by the Bureaucracy of the Priesthoods.

The Crown Prince, in charge of the Royal Command, is also in charge of the army and navy and the entire military infrastructure including garrisons, military villages, and town and village levies. The King's government was very complex and unwieldy which left room for tyrants as well as the just.

The vice regal system was the interface between the royal and indirect command. Five hundred years of the vice regal system in Nubia gradually resulted in the assimilation of the upper echelon of citizens. The sons of the princes or chiefs were educated in Egypt and became integrated into the bureaucratic structure. The process became the actual seed of the "successor state" of Napata.

The domination of Kush was indirect under the Sons of Kush such as the British during its colonial period. The local princes were left in charge of their areas. The bulk of the Nubians were fellaheen (peasants). The ethnic division of Nubian society had become stratified. Indeed the political and social changes set in motion by the initial colonization of the Nubians by the Warrior Pharaohs was complicated by the Egyptianization of the Nubians themselves, the tension between the Theban priests and the Warrior class.

The power of the priests had grown to the point that the offices of king, viceroy and Chief Priest of Amon had blurred and were finally absorbed into one. They certainly had assumed the reigns of government in Upper Egypt and perhaps in Lower Egypt as well. The military became the main support of the Pharaoh. Later the Viceroys became extremely powerful, both through the control of the gold products and because they commanded a large group of Nubian mercenaries. The landed estate now included more Nubians but most of the estates were in foreign, Royal and Temple hands. The kings gave permanent donations of slaves to the temples and slaves were part of the annual tribute to the viceroys.

An incredible document, found almost intact in 1955 at Thebes has records of the Temple estates that shed light on enormous wealth ascribed to the temples and under control of the priest. This document is known as the Harris papyrus and is located in the British museum. From this document, we are able to estimate the total annual wealth of the great temples in Egypt.

The lists in the papyrus contain six different classes of material: (1) the god's estate; (2) his income; (3) the king's gifts to him; (4) grain for the Old Feasts (5) offerings for the New Feasts founded by Rameses Ill; and (6) Offerings to the Nile God. The lists include such things as cattle, gardens, galleys, workshops, and towns which the Pharaoh gives to the Temple estate as property and annually. Another list gives the number of people and all the serf-laborers of the houses, temples and estates which he gives to them as their yearly dues. A third list indicates the amount of silver and gold that is provided as provisions of the temple from year to year.

The temples own nearly one seventh of all the land space. Thebes ,with 583,313.7 acres , owns the largest amount of the land. The political significance of these lists the question of Amon's [Thebes] share in the land. The estate of the god embraces over ten percent of the lands of Egypt, and at most one and one-half of the population, or perhaps even a little less than one percent. This meant a fortune in the land over five times that of Heliopolis, and over nine times of Memphis, while in the people the disproportion was even greater. Amon's annual income in gold of which the other temples received none, is something less than twenty-six thousand grains. Amon received roughly seventeen times as much silver, twenty-one times as much copper; three times as many garments, two times as much incense, honey and oil; nine times as much shedeh and wine, eight times as many waterfowl, seven times as many ships, as well as all the other temples combined. It is to be noted that these products were from God's land, Syria and Kush.

The drain of the temples on the economy becomes more apparent with the analysis of the papyrus lists. The king was responsible for the large funded temple building but the state commandeered the labor force and collected the food and building supplies required. The Wilbour Papyrus and other documents indicate that secular officials had responsibility and power over the temple lands only to a degree. The land was divided into large estates and smaller farms. The institution (temple) rented out the estates to investors, wealthy officials and priests, for half their annual yield and paid a tax on the income. The investors expected a profit from their half even though it had to be divided between the agents and cultivators who supervised and worked the land.

The small farms were let to two groups: (1) priests, scribes, herdsmen, cultivators and (rarely) artisans who worked for the temple institution and (2) those persons such as the military personnel who were unconnected with the institution, but were settled on temple land. The normal farm was about six acres and could maintain a family of eight or so. The military had less land because they had family elsewhere.

Inflation was a very big problem during the later Twentieth dynasty. Manufactured material did not rise, however grains and other produce increased in value. There might have been administrative abuses as in today's economy. During the Twenty- First Dynasty, the documentation indicated abuses in the collection and distribution of food and artisan strikes because of arrears. The Theban area was plagued with robbery of the royal tombs and private tombs at the time and the integrity of the administration was in question. The beginning of the decline of dynastic power and godship was immanent.

The subordination of the king was complete when Herihor usurped the throne of the king. The evidence for his rise as High Priest of Amon, until his usurpation of the kingship can be found in the inscriptions and the reliefs in the temple of Khunsu at Karnak. The temple of Khonsu was actually the only monument where we can trace the fall of the last Rammeside and the succession of the High Priest Herihor. The dedications of Rameses XII appear to give the usual powers to the king, but if one looks at the base of the wall in the same hall, there is hardly a reference to the king. It is Herihor who receives full billing:

"High Priest of Amon-Re, king of the gods, commander in chief of the armies of the South and North, leader, Herihor, triumphant; he made it at a moment of 'House of Khunsu-in-Thebes-Beautiful Rest;' making him a temple for the first tie in the likeness of the horizon of heaven, extending his temple as an eternal work, enlarging his monument (more than) before. He increased the daily offerings, he doubled that which was before, while the gods of Thebes are possessed of joy and the great house is in festival. That which the son of Re, Rameses XII, beloved of Khunsu, made for him."

CHAPTER 12.
GODSHIP: THE ETHIOPIAN DYNASTY

CONQUEST OF EGYPT (785-760 B.C.)

Egypt's decline in power eventually gave rise to the Ethiopian Dynasty known as Egypt's Twenty -fifth Dynasty of Pharaohs. They were known, at the time by the Asiatics and King Hezekiah of Judah, as the Kingdom of Kush.

The Kingdom of Kush, remarkable for its dynastic durability for a span of twelve hundred years, has been divided into two cultural periods: the Napatan period and the Meroitic period, notwithstanding its several centuries of intermittent dark ages. Although the information is still spotty, we have the following evidence for its division based on changes in socio-economic and political structure of the kingdom:

1. Transfer of the royal cemetery from the region of Napata, near the Fourth Cataract, to Meroe, above the Atbara estuary.
2. Replacement of the Egyptian language as the only written language by the Meroitic.
3. Immanent advance of their indigenous cultural traditions reached a high degree of expression through their own perceptions of art found in the tombs, cemeteries and temples.

The Godship and Kingship of the Kushite monarchy is reflected in its remarkable endurance in the Nile Valley between the Second Cataract and the Sixth Cataract. The most recent exhibit of the culture of the Sudan, *Sudan: Ancient Cultures of the Nile* (1998) reflects the current assessment of the research in the Sudan and the glories of the ancient Kingdoms of Kush. It invites the modern mind to undergo an intellectual transformation , learning for example , of the 223 ancient pyramids found in our land , of the ancient capitals of Kerma, Napata, and Meroe and their empires.

At the present state of archaeological finds, we know that the ruling class in the Kingdom of Kush was not made up of Egyptians or Libyan immigrants, as was frequently assumed in the past. The custom of matrilineal succession and the development of royal tomb installations reveal that the social and cultural traditions of the ruling class were derived not from the Egyptians but from the peoples of the Upper Nile Valley.

The importance of the Kingdom of Kush was not lost on the ancient Syro-Palestinian world. The prophet Isaiah protested too loudly in his curse against the Kushite nation:

> Disaster! Land of the whirring locust
> beyond the rivers of Kush,

who send the ambassadors by sea,

in little reed-boats across the waters!

Go, swift messengers

To a nation tall and bronzed,

To a people feared far and near,

a mighty and masterful nation

whose country is criss-crossed with rivers.

For this is what Yahweh has told me.

For, before the harvest,

once the flowering is over

and blossom turns into the ripening grape,

the branches will be cut off with pruning knives,

and the shoots taken off, cut away

Through the consolidation of priestly power with military acumen of his Nubian troops, the Egyptian Herihor brought the Rammeside to the end of their power in 1086 B.C. The Kingdom of Napata arose, during the Twentieth dynasty, out of the ashes of Egypt's decline at the end of the New Kingdom. The decline prepared for the ascendancy of the princely families and chiefs and the dependency of the priests of Amon for their protection and control. Their great religious center was at the foot of the Holy Mountain Jebel Barkal. Several centuries later, Kush conquered Egypt through a reversal of fortunes.

Although the Theban priests had apparent independence during the period of the Twenty-first to the Twenty-third dynasties, they were obliged at times to pay tribute to one or another of the powerful dynasts in the north. Thus, the stage was set for the curtain-raising of the Napatan Empire. In the background on the political stage were the northern warring factions in the Delta between the Libyans and declining monarchs while the ever-present Nile was at its lowest ebb. During this period, the kings of Assyria were recipients of Upper Nubian products from the pharaohs as evidenced by Assyrian texts. One can deduce that Egypt had resumed trade relations with the south. In this context, according to Timothy Kendall "from the tenth century onward one or more dominant chiefdoms had emerged in Nubia again, as in the case of Kerma centuries before, beginning a process of material, cultural, and political enrichment through commerce with Egypt." [129]

KASHTA: FIRST RECOGNIZABLE KING

The Kushite monarchy was hereditary from its inception. The genealogy of the Ancient Kings of Kush, (according to Torok (1995a table II) places the name Alara, the first prince of Kurru, in

125

his chronology before Kashta who was the fifth generation in the Twenty-fifth dynasty. Alara is the name that is first known to us. He is first mentioned on the stela of Queen Tabiry who was the daughter of Kasaqa and wife of Piye (Pianhki). He is also considered as the founder of the dynasty and brother of Taharqa's grandmother on a Kawa IV stela. It is apparent that Alara was the brother of Kashta who succeeded him (-760). The two Kawa Stelae give significant information about the relationships of the royal family. As a matter of fact, Arkell states that brother-sister marriage within the family was prescribed, and the inscriptions on the stelae mention the piety of Alara several times. Alara's prayer preserved in the Kawa VI relief reflects his piety and his belief in the providence of the God Amun:

> O beneficent god, swift, who calls upon him, look
>
> Upon my sister for me, a women born with me in one womb.
>
> Act for her (even) as you have acted for him [Alara] that acted
>
> For you , as a wonder, unpremeditated, and not disregarded by reflective people. For
>
> you put a stop to him that plotted evil against me after you set me up as king

A stela from Kawa, now located in the Ny Carlsberg Glypotek in Copenhagen, shows Alara making offerings to the god. The temple B at Kawa depicts the earliest post new Kingdom temple and affirms that Alara was the first significant restorer of the Nubian Amun cult. The first surviving sculptures of the dynasty are a series of ram sphinxes of heavy cut stone placed by Kashta by its pylon when he enlarged the mud-brick temple of Alara (B800) at Jebel Barkal. Alara rose from the prince of Kurru to king and it was fitting for his successors to be known as the Kingdom of Kush. He was buried in 747 B.C. at Kurru in a pyramid tomb (Ku) contained a Nubian bed burial.

Kashta's legitimacy as king was established through the installation of Alara's sister as princess of Amun, which created the justification for royal succession and facilitated the shared concepts of traditional Kushite practice with Egyptian concepts of kingship. Kashta's peaceful takeover of power is clearly indicated by the joint activity and double-dating of the Divine Adoratrice Shepenwepet I, daughter of Osorkon III, and the God's Wife of Amun Elect Amerdis I, daughter of Kashta during the course of the third quarter of the 8th century B.C." This was a practical arrangement as it assured the legitimacy of the father's successor.

Kashta's Throne name, The -Possessor-of truth/Equity-is Re, suggests his divine kingship and restorer of Justice. According to A.H. Sayce that Kashta means Kushite. The personal name indicates Kashta's origins. However, the throne name appears on a fragment of a dedication stela of Kashta from Elephantine dated before 747 B.C.:

> "The king-of Upper-and-Lower- Egypt, "he -who belongs -to-Re's-order'
>
> Son of Re, Lord of Two-lands, Ka-sht,
>
> Beloved, living forever,

Kashta was married to his sister Pebtatma indicated by her Abydos stela. Her roles are also given as Sistrum-player of Amen Re, King of the Gods, King's sister, king's daughter, mother of the Divine Adoratrice (Amenerdis I). Kashta was affirmed king by the priests of Amun when he arrived in Thebes. Adams posits that there was no suggestion of military activity connected with this visit. To the Egyptian priests threatened as they were from the north and long accustomed to rely on Nubian troops for their protection, the rise of a new and effective commander may well have appeared as a deliverance. They hastened to recognize him and to claim his protection... Kashta's assumption of power at Thebes set the stage for a brief, meteoric appearance of Kush as a world power.

There was an increased in building as mentioned above. Kashta also built the first mud-brick palace (B1200) at Jebel Barkal. There are all indications that he was the first of the dynasty to reside at Napata permanently. Kashta's pyramid tomb at Kurru was larger than the previous ones. With his death about 751 B.C., a most remarkable son succeeded him and his legacy is the most astonishing chronicle of arms and administration at that time.

PIANHKI (PIYE): CONQUEROR AND DELIVERER

It was Pianhki, the son of Kashta, who completed the submission of Egypt. The Sandstone Stela of Piye (747 B.C.) records that Pianhki was appointed by Amun as lord of the Thrones of the Two Lands. Pianhki's mother was Pebatma; sister was "Sistrum-player of Amun Re, King of the Gods and Mother of the Divine Adoratrice (Amenerdis I). Pianhki married Tabiry, sister of Kashta. Pianhki's daughter was Shepenwepet II whom he installed when he became king, as God' Wife of Amun Elect. His other daughters were Tabekenamun, Naparaye and Arty. His brother, Prince Pakartror, was buried at Abydos with the Kushite Royal wives of Kashta and Pianhki. Pianhki also had three sons: Khaluit, Taharqa and Piye-Har.

Pianhki's genius as titular King of Egypt, liturgical wizard in the synthesis of Egyptian and Kushite concepts of order as priest, and military might as general is captured in his Great Triumphal Stela from the Gebel Barkal Temple of Amun in the year 727 B.C. which is now in Cairo. The more recent contributions to the translations and understanding of the text by such scholars as Jean Yoyotte, Karl-Heinz Priese and Nicholas -Christophe Grimal are very compelling experiences. I can now read it with the passion that kept me enthralled with Virgil's Aeneid and the exploits of Memnon the King of Ethiopia.

James Breasted in 1906 wrote in *Ancient Records of Egypt* that this stela is the most instructive in respect of the internal political condition of Egypt at the time when no strong central power and no aggressive monarch controlled the whole country. He further asserts that the Kushite kingdom was already a dominant power. Richard Holton Pierce gives us his impression of this great work:

"Pianhki's stela is a work of great and varied artistry.

Its dramatic movement flows along three parallel lines in that it records at one and the same time a royal progress through the course of the inundation of the Nile, a cultic pilgrimage, and an expedition of conquest.

It weaves together a variety of genre, from encomiastic (eulogistic) poetry to terse military records, into the most operatic performance. Subtly differing styles of language bring out contrasts, as between Tefnakht's cajoling speech to his forces in Memphis before he abandons them and Pianhki's incisive discourse as he employs his bold plan..."

Be that as it may, we will have those that see Pianhki as bombastic or a great tactician. His love of horses and the scorn he heaps on the king that maltreats them and his purity when it comes to diet and women is seen as extreme piousness or a ploy to imitate other Kings of Egypt. The following lines from the stela will give you some inkling of his character:

"And they did not enter the house of the king, because they were uncircumcised, and they were eaters of fish, which is held in abomination in the royal house."

"Then his majesty (Piye) set out to go to the palace of the king Nemereth. he made them bring to him the queens and princesses. but his majesty did not permit his face to turn towards them."

"And his majesty went into the palace where the horses were kept, and into the stalls of the foals and he perceived that they had been suffering from hunger, and he said, "I swear by my own life, and the love I have for Ra... .that to my mind, to have allowed my horses to suffer hunger, is the worst violence of all the evil things which thou has done in the violence of thy heart."

It has been noted in recent studies of horse skeletons from el Kurru by Bokonyi (1993) and the textual evidence of use of horses in Kushite warfare indicates that the finest horses used in contemporary Egypt and Assyria were bred and exported from Nubia.

This splendid large stela of pink granite with a rounded top has a lunette relief which gives a pictorial summary of the event in the text that describes his wars fought under the protection of Amun bringing him the victory he envisioned. At the left of the lunette is Amun sitting on the throne with Mut the goddess standing behind Amun and Pianhki standing before him. King Namlot, of Hermopolis, is leading a horse in front of Pianhki shaking a sistrum in order to pacify him. Namlot's queen is raising her hand in adoration. In the lower register the three kings Osorkon IV, Iuput II and Peeftjauawybast, are kissing the ground in front of Pianhki. In two other registers, the hereditary prince Peteese and the chiefs of the Libyan Ma Patjenfy, Pemui,

Akanosh and Djedamenejankh are in prostrate positions kissing the ground behind Pianhki and the deities.

The text, on the stela, describes the process of submission by the king's foes, two major military actions, the capture of Hermopolis and Memphis. The cultic procession from the south at New Year, restoring order, taking in possession and "giving life" to the land at the same time satisfies the gods in accordance with the Inundation and in recognition of his rule in Egypt. Upon his return to Napata after the celebration of the Festival of the New Year and confirmation of royal power, the Opet Festival and the Sed Festival were celebrated three months later at Thebes, after which he continued the siege of war.

Pianhki after his return to Napata was content to receive tribute from the vassal princes of the Delta as king of the two lands, Kush and Upper Egypt. He erected his Great Stela and concentrated on his role as restorer of order and justice of the two lands to Amun and building activities to honor himself and the gods.

I will summarize the sequences of Pianhki's war activities as carefully staged dramatic scenarios and significant text that can be explored through the literary and ancient records: There is then report of Tefnackht's aggression ,. The princes, counts and generals who were in their towns who were not Piye's subjects, ask Piye every day to intervene. Piye hesitates but decides to act after learning of Namlot's defection. Then his majesty made soldiers march into Egypt, and gave them strict command saying: "Ye shall not [pass] the night in pleasure, but as soon as you see he has set the troops in marching order, do battle with him. If any man shall tell you that he is with his forces in another town, and let the dukes whom he hath brought to help him be gathered together, [and] let the Thehennu (Libyans), [and] as many soldiers as he pleaseth muster [where they will] and let them do battle according to ancient custom...

> "Then fight in battle boldly, for we know that it is the god Amen who hath sent us forth. And when we arrive at the sanctuary of Usast go ye into the water, and cleanse yourselves in the waters of the stream. Undress yourselves at the head of the lake, unstring your bows, lay aside your arrows and let not any chief imagine himself to be the equal of the lord of two-fold strength, for the strength of no mighty man shall prevail without help. He who is feeble of arm he maketh strong of arm; if the enemy be many, he maketh them to flee before the land of the impotent man, and he maketh one man to lead to lead captive a thousand. Wet yourselves in the water from his altars, and smell ye the earth before him, and say unto him; 'O make thou a way for us, and let us fight under the shadow of thy sword, for a child, if he be sent by thee, shall overcome him that hath overcome multitudes."

Pianhki in the tradition of the pharaohs donated his tribute of war to the god

Amun which was vast:

> "a mass of copper or turquoise as large as yourself, finest horses, gold, silver, lapis-lazuli, property of all kinds, suits of apparel made of byssus of every quality, and couches and coverlets of linen, and anti perfume, vases of unguent, metal vessels or gold ornaments for the neck, crowns for your head, gold vases for ceremonies of purification, precious inlaid stones…"

At Kawa, Pianhki added a colonnaded forecourt where his stelae could be erected and pylons to the temple of Amun and built a paved processional road. On the walls of the temple, the ancient thirty-year Sed festival is depicted showing the king restoring his powers. At Kurru, he is entombed in a pyramid with subterranean chamber accessed by a stairway, and his wife Tabiry is buried nearby. The horses that he loved were buried as well at Kurru with elaborate trappings of silver and gold. The reign of the conqueror lasted 30 years.

Pianhki is also remembered from the Sandstone Stela by his speech:

> 'The Son of Re, lord of Diadems, "beloved of Amun,
>
> Pi(anh)ki says:
>
> Amun of Napata has granted me to be ruler of every foreign country.
>
> He to whom I say, you are chief, he is to be chief.
>
> He to whom I say 'You are not king !' he is not King .
>
> Amun in Dominion (Thebes) has granted me to be ruler of Black-land.
>
> …Gods make a king, men make a king,
>
> But it is Amun who has made me

The earliest throne name of Pianhki, as Lord of Two Lands was indicative of his godship and kingship. The new Horus names, assumed after the campaign of year 21, have political implications: "Strong Bull Appearing in Thebes" and "Bull of Two Lands". His other name Creator of Crafts (Yoyotte, 1989) establishes him with Ptah as founder of temples and creator of sanctuaries and sacred images while his Golden Horus name "Multiplier of Gallant Warriors" is his greatest legacy as conqueror.

SHABAKA AND SHABATAKA: SHADOWY KINGS

Shabaka, the brother of Pianhki, and Shabataka, the son of Shabaka, inherited the triumphs and gigantic tasks of Pianhki, the Conqueror, and Builder of the Ethiopian or Kushite pharaohs of the XXV Dynasty of Egypt. They stood in the shadow of historical events and caused through intrigue and tenuous ambition the scorn of the Assyrian envoys as they assailed Hezekiah, the King of Judah: 'Now behold, thou trustest upon the staff of this broken read, even upon Egypt, where on, if a man lean, it will go into his hand and pierce it; so is the Pharaoh, king of Egypt, unto all that trust on him.'

Shabaka, "He- who-blesses "two -lands" was married to Kalhata (of unknown parentage). During his 15 years reign, the capital of the Kushite Egyptian was moved from Napata to Thebes and had he his daughter adopted by Amenirdis as Adoratrice. Prior to his reign, during the period from 750-700 B.C., battles were being waged in Iraq, Iran and the Hittite country and elsewhere which left Assyria the dominant power in western Asia. The Book of Kings and the Chronicles record the King of Judah temporizing between his submission to Assyria and cooperation with Egypt under the Kushites. Shabaka's ambition caused him to become involved through intrigue and chicanery with Palestine and Judah against Assyria .The Assyrian emperor, Sennacherib, eventually led an army against Egypt to put and end to the these provocations. Shabaka engaged his nephew Taharqa in the fray instead of taking command himself. The Assyrian army did not reach Egyptian shores because it was besieged with a deadly plague which caused the evacuation of Palestine. This was the third time that Providence prevailed as Pianhki had been engaged in campaigns against the Assyrians and the formidable swamps kept the Assyrian armies from Egypt's shores.

The Commemorative scarab of Shabaka with a historical text records "the out come of the conflict in the Delta in Year 2. The defeat of the Sand-dwellers may refer to the restoration of border security in the Sinai. The donation stelae from Years 2 (from Pharbaitos erected by Chief of Ma Patjenky), 3 (from Bubastis), 6 (from Buto) are evidence of Shabaka's successful control of the former domain of Tefnakht and Bakenranef [whom he supposedly burned to death]; and his victories are also commemorated in the dedicatory text on the Fourth Pylon of the great Amun Temple in Karnak in which he states that the victories were "decreed" for him by his father Amun."

Shabaka is credited with the preservation of the Memphite Theology found on a worm eaten papyrus discussed in detail in chapter eight. The last years of the reign of Shabaka seemed to have been without conflict and when his end came, he too was buried at Kurru as well as his horses. The tomb of Shabaka was twenty yards north of Pianhki.

Shabataka assumed the reign of the Kingdom of Kush and Egypt, following the death of his father. His attested wife was Arty, a daughter of Pianhki. Shabataka was enthroned at Thebes in the great temple of Amun. His titulary included "Whose appearances -endure, Beloved of Ptah and Beloved of Amun.

This 'shadowy king' falls through the cracks of history as so little has been found to affirm his reign. The Karnak Nile level record, year three of Shabataka, records that he arrived at Thebes, the compound of Amun on the fifth day of the first month of summer in his third regal year. Here again an association with the Inundation in the Pianhki stela, legitimized his reign.

If Shabataka had his moment of greatness, it was recorded on Tarharqa's Kawa inscription, which described that he was confronted, early in his reign, with an Assyrian threat that had not been resolved with his father and he sent an army to Palestine, headed by Taharqa, as an aggressive strategy. There was a series of maneuvers ending in defeat. Shabataka died without a male heir and was buried at the ancestral cemetery at Kurru after a reign of 12 or so years.

TAHARQA (TIRHAKA): THE BUILDER

From the curse of Isaiah to the tribute paid by the land of Khor in Palestine lies a tale not only of 'arms and men' but of the formidable task Taharqa assigned to himself as the successor of Shabataka: his great program of commemorative temple building, He not only surpassed the total building of the previous Kushite Pharaohs in the Napatan phase of their culture but set a standard for the Meroitic phase to follow. The Kushite kingdom extended from Khor in Palestine, the Phoenician shore where the cedars of Lebanon were prized for building, to deep in the Sudan, possibly as far as the Sudd. "And the excavation sites at Zankor and Sofyan in Kordofan may one day show that it extended three hundred miles or so west of the Nile."

Taharqa, the son of Pianhki and Abar, was loved by Shabataka "more than all his brethren" was written on his stela. His wives are listed as his sisters, Atakhebasken, Tabekenamun, Naparaye, and Takahtamani whose parentage is not known. The sons are Atlanersa whose mother is Salka and Nes-Anhuret, Nes-shuTefnut whose mothers are unknown. The daughters, Amenerdis II, Yeturow, and Kahlese were each God's wife of Amun elect.

From the accounts of the various Kawa inscriptions, we learn that Taharqa, as a youth of twenty, left his beloved mother and Nubia, at the summons of Shabaka, to aid in his military exploits in western Asia. Taharqa received military training and knowledge of state affairs under his tutelage. Hebrew and Assyrian annals record his military encounters with Esarhaddon, who continued the campaigns of Sennacherib, the antagonist of Taharqa's father. At the age of 32, Taharqa ascended to power, not fully prepared for the ensuing wrath of the Assyrians. From all accounts, Taharqa, early in his reign, was constantly menaced by the Assyrians, as they prepared assault after assault to bring the Kushite-Egyptian regime to the dust. In the first decade, he was able to achieve some victories over the Libyan people and the people of the western oasis and maintained parts of the coasts of Phoenicia in Phillistia. He was able to repulse the Assyrians in several campaigns until they attempted a massive invasion in the latter years of his regime.

These inherited military problems did not hinder Taharqa's remarkable resolve to restore order and justice (maat) within his own borders, which he accomplished in his beautification and edification of monuments to glorify Amun and the stabilization the Two Lands. The only stela of a military nature ascribed to Taharqa is that on the race of his soldiers, from Dashur road. (Dated about 685 B.C.). Taharqa actually ordered this stela to be to be placed at the back of the western desert to the west of the Residence to honor the troops of Taharqa that they may live forever. On the stela is recorded that he commanded his five platoons' troops to run every day and reviewed his running troops at on horseback. He praised and rewarded them for their splendid condition and let them eat and drink. "For you see, His Majesty liked the work of battle that was given to him."

The titulary of Taharqa mirrors his building covenant with Amun: Taharqa, Son of Re, "Whose-appearances -are lofty", "Protector of Two Lands" and "Nerfertum-is Protector of Re" or Nefertum -and Re- protect(me)". There are 26 building inscriptions credited to Taharqa. The first building inscription was found in the Mut temple at Gebel Barkal/ Napata dated after 690 B.C.:

> "...What he made as his monument for his mother Mut of Napata: he rebuilt for her a temple-compound of beautiful, fine white sandstone.
>
> Now His majesty found this temple-compound built from stone by the ancestors (but) in humble workmanship, then he had this temple-compound built in excellent, enduring workmanship. (that he might be) given life and dominion like re."

The second building inscription addresses his mother Mut as Mistress of Heaven and states that he built her house and enlarged her temple -compound, renewed in fine white - sandstone in order for her to give him all life from her, all stability from her and all dominion from her.

This Mut temple, often referred to as the rock -temple of Amun, was built on the southern slope of the sacred mountain of Amun at Napata to the south of the great Amun temple B 500. The reliefs of the inner rooms (sanctuary room and side rooms) of the temple B 303 are carved in the rock of Gebel Barkal with a similar orientation to the Amun temple was analyzed recently by Robisek in 1989.

> "On the west wall of B 303 the King offers Maat to Amun Re of Thebes and Mut. He is followed by his mother Abar, who is shaking the sistrum , whose titles are "Great of Praises, Mother of the King, Sister of the King, Lady of the South and North, Noblewomen". On the opposite east wall, the King, followed by his wife Takahatamai, offers wine to the ram-headed Amun of Napata. She bears the title" Noble Women, great of Praises, Lady of All Women, Sister of the King, Wife of the King Whom He loves". Abar is associated with Taharqa's rule over Egypt and Takahatamai is connected with Kush."

The importance of the inundation with the legitimization of the king and his mother's visit to Memphis is captured quite poetically in the Stela of Taharqa on the high Nile in Year 6 from Kawa (Kawa VI) 685 B.C.:

"His majesty had been praying for an inundation from his father Amen-Re, lord of the Thrones of Two-Lands,

In order to prevent dearth appearing in his time."

When the time for the rising of the inundation came,

it continued rising greatly each day and it passed many days rising at the rate of one cubit every day....

It rose to a height of 21 cubits, one palm, and 2 1/2 digits at the harbor of Thebes.

...

Every man of Bow-land was inundated with an abundance of everything.

Black-(land) Egypt was in beautiful festival.

His Majesty's heart was happier than anything. ...

causing endowments to be presented to all gods,

his heart being joyful at what his father did for him,

The inundation came like a cattle -thief, and flooded this whole land,

'It made the entire countryside good,

it killed off the vermin and snakes that were in it (the country side) it kept the devouring locust from it (the countryside), and it prevented the (scorching) south winds from stealing (the harvest so I was able to reap a harvest into the granaries, the size of which was incalculable."

Taharqa had not seen his mother since he was recruited twenty years ago in his youth. He sent for her to be at his side at his coronation:

"She found me on the throne of Horus, after I had received the diadem of Re, and

wearing the Uraeus on my head, all the gods being the protection of my body."

She was exceedingly joyful after seeing the beauty of His Majesty, (just) as Isis saw her son Horus appearing on the throne of his father Osiris the south and the North and every foreign country were bowing to the ground for this king's mother they being in great festival, both great and small' as they acclaimed this king's mother, saying,

"Isis- when Horus received her-was like the king's mother

after she had (re)joined her son."

Professor Adams suggested that the temples of Kawa and Gebel Barkal are the great religious centers of the Kushite monarchy. Taharqa also built small temples in Semna, Buhen and Qasr Ibrim. The sites of ruins of Second Cataract forts and XVIII Dynasty temples were used to build Taharqa's own temples. This was an intentional act on his part because of his awareness of their symbolic value indicative of Pharaonic power and they remain the only datable signs of human activity of the last millennium B.C..

One of the fine columns of the temple of Karnak erected by Taharqa, remains today. Around 674 B.C. Taharqa built four colonnades approaching the temple of Amun there are inscriptions in the peristyle court north of Pylon VI of this Amun Temple.

The inscription at the far western part of the wall seems to convey that Taharqa, the beloved of Re, was beginning to doubt himself and is faced with reversals and is beseeching Amun for aid or succor:

> "O Amun, what I did in the Land of Nubia grant. ...
>
> let me do it with your tribute from the land of Khor,
>
> which is turned away from you.
>
> O Amun, ... my wives. Let my children live
>
> Turn death away from them for me. Preserve me from...."

Finally, in 669 B.C., Esarhaddon forced Taharqa, to withdraw to Napata, after losing his army, his capital, his treasure, and his chief wife and sons to the enemy. Taharqa with this ignominy died within five years. He was laid to rest in his pyramid that was larger than any built in the Sudan, his own monument as the builder of Commemorative sites to Amun

Tanutamon: The final dynast

Tanutamon, the son of Shabaka, who had only two known titular names,was destined to live as king to live as king for only a few years (664-656BC) because of the chain of political and military events that preceded him. He possessed the same cupidity and ambition as Shabaka and Shabataka . Shabataka was his older brother. He married his sisters Piankharty and Istemkheb. There were no children recorded.

According to his dream stela, Tenutamon went to Thebes of the thousand gates, then returned to Memphis, as an invader, to eliminate the Asyrrian vassal Necho, reconquering Lower Egypt in 663 B.C. Although the Delta chiefs recognized him as king , Tenutamon sas not so accorded by the Assyrrians . A year later Assurbanipal recaptured Memphis and Tenutamon fled wit his wives to Kush. Thebes was sacked , which was still remembered fifty years later by the prophet Nahum:

> "Art thou better than Ne-Amen [Thebes] that was situated among
>
> the canals, and that had a nile round about it for a rampart and a
>
> wall? Kush and Egypt were her strength... Yet was she carried
>
> away, she went into captivity; her young children were dashed
>
> in pieces at the top of all the streets; and they cast their lots for
>
> her honorable men, and all her great men were bound in chains."

CHAPTER 13.
KINGSHIP: MEROITIC PHASE - THE LONG DENOUEMENT

MEROE (650 B.C.-320 A.D.)

The utter destruction of "Thebes of a thousand gates" and the withdrawal of Tenutamon, the last Nubian Pharaoh, to Napata began a kingdom in exile. It is difficult to determine the effect of these events on the priests of Amon whose spiritual might flowed from Thebes and the political power of the Nubian- Egyptian Pharaohs. The exile was more spatially apparent than real as the Kushite dynasty had apparently maintained two capitals or power points. One was at Napata and the other at Meroe indicated by the location of the Royal cemeteries at Napata and Meroe as well as the palaces and towns when the Kushites were the pharaohs of two lands, Memphis in the Delta to Meroe in the South.

Several centuries of political stagnation and cultural decline passed while Egypt contended with her Saiite aggressors in the north while the Napatans secured their dominance in the South. The Heroic Age of the Napatan Pharaohs came some centuries later when they moved from Napata south to Meroe located at the foot of the Holy Mountain Jebel Barkal.

A very powerful statue of last dynast of the XXVth dynasty of Ethiopian Pharaohs" of Egypt was brought to the Boston Museum of Fine Arts in 1916 by the Harvard MFA expedition in Nubia. A statue cache was excavated north of the first pylon of the Great Amun Temple at Gebel Barkal. This headless statue of Tenutamon was found in several broken sections. It was identified by the hieroglyphic inscription at its base and back pillar which reads Tanutamon, "beloved of Amun of Napata.'

According to the Hintze chronology, there were charted sixty -seven kings and queens in the Kushite Kingdom that endured politically, culturally and spiritually for well over one thousand years. Nastasen was the twenty-sixth generation of pharaohs buried at the royal cemetery at Napata (Nuri). The approximate date of the dynastic move to Meroe can be placed between Nastasen's burial and that of Arkakamani in the South cemetery at Meroe. Shinnie maintains that "there is little archaeological fact on which to assume a date for this move. It is certain that a town existed at Meroe from early in the sixth century if not earlier. The names of Aspelta, Amtalqa, and Malenaqen, all of whom were buried at Nuri, have been found at Meroe and there were even earlier graves in the South cemetery. From the existence of these graves, Reisner argued that from as early as the reign of Pianhki a branch of the royal family had come to Meroe to hold the southern area for the king."[130]

LATER NAPATAN KINGS: TAHARQA'S PROGENY

Atlanersa (653-643 B.C.) was the successor of King Tanutamami and probably the son of Queen Asalka. She appears in a pylon scene in Temple B700 at Gebel Barkal as Queen Mother dated about the latter half of the second century. Atlanersa's titulary includes, "protected -by the Ka-of Re.", "Who-establishes the laws" and "beloved of Ma'at" and "Founder -of the Two Lands" He was married to his sister Yeturow, who had the titles of "wife of the king, daughter of the king, sister of the kings, mistress of Egypt" and married to another of his sisters, Kahlese, who was known as noble woman, lady of the im? t, singer, great daughter of the king and as a member of the female line of succession was destined to become mother of the crown prince. Maloyaral usurped the role and function of Kahlese, as the third wife of Atlanersa. She became Queen Mother and mother of Atlanersa's heir and successor. Her shawabti figures and a heart scarab were found in her grave at Nuri cemetery.

Atlanersa built Temple B700, which was completed by his successor Senkamanisken. There are foundation deposits of this temple at the National Museum of Khartoum and the Museum of Fine Arts in Boston. The Louvre in Paris has a New Year seal in its collection, (possibly from Thebes) inscribed for Malotaral as Mistress of Kush. Little is known of the military and political activities of Atlanersa at this time. Yet his titulary suggests that he was a restorer of order and controlled through legislation. He was the second ruler to be buried in the Nuri cemetery opened by Taharqa.

Senkamanisken (643-623 B.C.) "Pacifier' of Two -lands "Who-appears -in- Ma'at" "Whose -strength -is mighty" is ascribed as the son of Atlanersa and his successor. Queen Nasals, his wife, produced two sons Anlamani and Aspelta. A very powerful statue of Senkamanisken from the Great Temple of Amun B500 stands in the Nubian Gallery of the Boston Museum of Fine Arts. It was unearthed in the cache at the same time as was that of Tenutamon. The description in *Sudan: Ancient Kingdoms of the Nile* is very fresh and compelling:

> "With the retreat of the Kushite kings from Egypt, the art of the Napatan gains a new dimension. Its characteristic fashion of representing the human form and face were already visible in the works of the Twenty-fifth Dynasty. But they were toned down through direct contact with the tradition -bound art of Egypt, failing to come to full fruition. Once freed, however, from the restrictions of the Pharaonic legacy, a style developed in the Napatan dynasty that brings the more "African" components to fore. The forceful striding legs become more massive, the feet larger The arms end in balled fists that bespeak raw power, the musculature is strongly emphasized The head rests on the short neck, thickest

in profile view. The southern profile is characterized by the full lips, broad nose, the widely spaced, slightly bulging eyes, and the low brow. The double Uraeus at the forehead is completely preserved in Napatan homeland the statues were spared the persecutions wrought by the succeeding dynasty in Egypt. The Kushite cap closely conforms to the round skull. Around the neck hangs the cord with three ram's heads. Surface areas left rough for gilding or silver plating include the jewelry bands on the upper arms, wrists, and ankles, the sandal straps, the tripartite royal kilt, and the cap."

In Temple 700B started by Atlanersa and completed by Senkamanisken was found a fragment of his obelisk dated about the second half of the 7th century, presently in the Boston Museum of Fine Arts recorded by Dunham in 1970. Reisner found this small black granite obelisk in the "court"(room702) of the temple in the disturbed debris at the entrance to the pronaos in 1918.The four columns of inscription were arranged in opposite faces: two concerning Amun of Napata and the other two columns giving complete names of the king, his divine son ship and predestination contained in the statement concerning the womb:

> The Two Ladies: "Appearing on behalf of Ma'at"
> Golden-Horus: "Whose-strength -is mighty",
> the King -of Upper-and-Lower-Egypt: Sekheperenre"
> the Son -[of-Re:] Senkamenisken.
> Amun of Napata [who resides in] ...the great seat of
> the Son -[of Re;] Senkamanisken,
> I knew him in the womb before he was (even born.
> I gave to him the scimitar on [this] day...

Senkamanisken was buried at Nuri in grave no three .It is interesting to note that his shabtis (Shawabtis) exceeded in number that of his grandfather Taharqa, which will be discussed in a later chapter.

Anlamani (643-623BC) "Strong Bull, Appearing -in Truth", "Nourisher-of-the-Hearts-of-two-lands" was the son of Queen Nasalsa and King Senkamanisken and elder brother of Aspelta. He had several wives, a sister Madiken, Asata, Artaha and Maqmalo. The parentage of the later three is unknown. Anlamani also had a daughter, Kheb, but no sons have been found.

Anlamani came to power fifty years after his great -grandfather, Taharqa. Documentation of the reign of Anlamani can be found on his Enthronement stela from Kawa VIII, fragments of a red granite naos from Sanam and two monumental statues from the Amun Temple B 500 in Napata (Museum of Fine Arts, Boston, and Khartoum). On the partially damaged double-scened lunette, King Atlamani and the Queen mother, Nasalsa, are represented making offerings to the ram-headed Amen-re of Kawa. The text of 28 lines, included dating which was partially destroyed, the king's titulary, a dialogue between Anlamani and his entourage, his journey to Kawa, campaign against the Blemmyes, a brief accounting of the restoration of the Golden Age, and the mystical encounter of Anlamani with Amun Re of Kawa.

Lines 22 to 28 are of special significance as they include the titles of the Queen Mother Nasalsa and the record of the appointment of the four royal sisters to priestly offices and their role of sistrum players:

> "Now the king's mother Nasalsa, may she live forever, was in the midst of the kings sisters, (she) the mother of the king, sweet of love, mistress of all women, so His Majesty had "friend" go to fetch her....
>
> His Majesty gave his sisters, four women, to the gods, to be sistrum players: One to Amun of Napata
>
> One to Amen-re of "Finding-(the)-Aton" (Kawa)
>
> One to Amun of Pnubs,
>
> And one to Amen-re, bull of the Bow-land (Nubia)"

Anlamani gave the priests and prophets in each of the temple compounds he visited great stability, dominion and happiness. Each district rejoiced when they saw him and his court. It was during the second month of winter that he made his journey northward, giving a third prophet to god of Aton at Kawa. Appearing in the First Festival of Amun, he gave a festival of beer and bread, bulls and birds and wine..."servants ...making festival by day and night for seven days of the appearance of the god...."

The "Son of Re", "Lion over the south country", "Lord of the Thrones of Two lands", caused his army to invade the land of the Beja, in the Middle Nile region. Remaining in his palace, Anlamani issued orders: "a great blood bath was made among them, the number therefore (of the dead) being unknown. They seized four soldiers as living captives and gained control of all their women, all their children, all their cattle and all their property. He appointed them to be man- and maidservants of all the gods.. So this land was joyful in his time." Anlamani was the first Napatan king of the long denouement or the twilight of the heroic age... "The enemies were no longer the Assyrians and the Egyptians, but obscure tribal peoples of obscure origins." Anlamani was buried in grave no six at Nuri.

Aspelta (593-568 B.C.) came to the throne at the death of his brother King Anlamani. He was married to his niece Kheb, a daughter of Anlamani and Queen Madiken. He had three other wives, Asata, Maqmalo and Artaha.

Judging from the surviving inscriptions, the quantity of monuments and the richness of the grave goods, Aspelta's reign was very prosperous. In the lunette scene on the stela, the enthroned ram-headed Amun of Napata accompanied by the goddess Mut' Lady of heaven, the king and the Queen Mother are shown. Amun Re wears tall plumes and one Uraeus, Mut, the Double Crown, the king the Kushite skullcap with the double Uraeus at his brow and he carries the crook and flail in his right hand and ankh in his left hand. The Queen Mother is wearing a skullcap with a diadem of streamers and one Uraeus which appears to have a crown like Mut.[this passage needs revision]

The king kneels before Amun Re who extends his hand over the head of the king as he is presented to the gods. The Queen Mother shakes the sistrum as priestess and points toward titles of Theban God's wives. The scene is reminiscent of the enthronement of kings, queens and bishops through the ages, with variations.

The main text of the stela records:

> "Son of Re, lord of crowns: [Aspelta}
>
> Beloved of Amen Re, lord of the two lands,
>
> Who is upon Pure Mountain (Gebel Barkal)
>
> the god in which is Dedwen,
>
> the foremost of Bow-land (Nubia)
>
> -he is the God of Kush
>
> after the falcon settled upon his throne".

In the second year of Aspelta's reign, an internal conflict occurred when a family of priests was expelled from the Temple of Amun because they intended to bring about the death of an innocent man. They were burnt by fire as a warning according to line 8 of a text from the Cairo sarcophagus: "He slaughtered them to cause every prophet and every priest to be afraid when they enter bearing this noble god."

The adoption stela from year 3, from Sanam about the end of the 7th century B.C. seems to be a legal document, in which a legal council of six overseers of the treasury and five other high officials proposed the investiture of Kheb into the office of sistrum player and Gods wife of Amun and income to be conferred for maintenance of the temple.

The appropriation was listed as follows:

> "Nasalsa... placing a libation bucket of silver in her right hand,
>
> placing a sistrum in her left hand , to propitiate the god ,
>
> while giving her a maintenance in this temple compound:

daily , bia bread:	10
bread:	10
monthly beer (jars):	15
yearly oxen:	3
every festival; beer: (jug)	2

> Give it (from now on) to the king's sister and king' s daughter .."

The Stela on the mortuary cult foundation of Prince Khaluit was erected in a prominent place in front of the south tower of the pylon of the great Amun temple B500 at Gebel Barkal. Aspelta erected it around the end the 7th century B.C. Its uniqueness lies in the fact that Prince Khaluit, mayor of Kanad, was the son of Pianhki who died decades before Aspelta's birth. The stela commemorates Aspelta's donations for the funerary cult of Khaluit. The text glorifies the just kingship of Aspelta and loyalty to an ancestor

Aspelta's prosperous reign was apparently fraught with a military incursion. It appears from broken statues of Aspelta and several of his predecessors and graffiti left by Greek and Carian mercenaries in the Egyptian army of Psammtik II that a border conflict had occurred. Aspelta does not mention it in his annals, however. The effect of the Nubian campaign seemed negligible and had no lasting effect on Egyptian-Nubian relations as the two powers, became occupied with local affairs with Egypt decidedly in the North and Nubia in the South.

Although Aspelta was buried at Nuri, he was the first Nubian king whose name was found in the ruins of Meroe.

Amani-Nete-Yerike (Irike-Amanote) (431-405 B.C.) Was Twenty-First Ruler Of The Kushite dynasty. There are ten kings between Aspelta and Amani-nete-yerike including Aspelta's son, Aratelqo, and successor, Amani-nete-yerike was the son of King Malewiebamani. Amani-Neke-Yerike became king after the death of Takahtamani, who was probably the younger brother of Malewiebamani. Little else is known of his family.

The Kawa IX inscription records the complete titulary of Amani-Nete-Yerike:

Horus: "Strong Bull" "Appearing -in- Dominion (Thebes)"

Two-Ladies: "Seizer -of -every-land" "Subdoer of every-land"

King-of-Upper-and Lower-Egypt: "Re is one whose heart is beautiful"

Son-of Re: Irike-Amanote, may he live forever

The aggressive tone of the titulary upon Amani-Nete-Yerike's ascent to throne may have been adopted because of the knowledge of the internal struggles going on in Egypt between the Persian rulers and the revolt led by Amyrtaeus in 404 B.C.

The Kawa IX inscription of Amani-Nete-Yerike reflects some of the cultural changes during this period. His inscription was put up in his honor on the wall of Taharqa's old temple at Kawa. Shinnie records:

> "It is interesting linguistically and historically, the language in which it is written is Egyptian, but it shows that knowledge of that language is fading and it was probably no longer spoken....The great inscription of Amani-nete-yerike (Kawa No. IX) is of fundamental importance for the history of this period, since it contains the first mention of Meroe, and tells us that a king resided there. Inscribed when he was forty-one years old, it first describes a campaign against

the Rehrehs, who seem to have been occupying the north-end of the Island of Meroe. After defeating them, he went to Napata to be accepted as king by the priesthood of Amun, and took part in a ceremony in the Barkal temple where he was recognized in the traditional way by the god. From Napata, he sailed downstream to an unidentified place called Krtn, probably on the right bank, where he fought the Meded, a people described as 'desert dwellers' he went on a seventeen-day journey from Napata to Kawa and to Pnubs(Argo), where he gave land to the temple. He then returned to Kawa, where he cleared the approach to Taharqa's temple and ordered repairs to be carried out to a number of buildings."

The Kawa IX inscription was found in the Temple T of Amun of Kawa, by the Oxford expedition in 1930-31 under the direction by F. Ll. Griffith. The text filled 126 columns, in 12 sections, on the south half of the East wall of the Hypostyle hall (1.10 x722m) and covered almost the entire surface from floor to relief line from the Pronaos Door to the corner of the Hypostyle, under the relief showing Taharqa inaugurating the Temple of Kawa. The columns were written from left to right starting from the Pronaos Door.

Section 7, columns 49-55, describes the enthronement of Amani-Neke-Yerike in the temple of Amun at Kawa. It cites for the first time, the presentation of the bow and arrows as an insignia of dominion and universal rule. This feature is uniquely Nubian (Kushite). It emphasizes the divine kingship of Amani-Neke-Yerike as Son of Amun -and the Kushite legendary prowess with the bow. Amani-nete-yerike is granted kingship and given the bow and arrows as. Amun-re utters these words:

"I have given to you every land, South, North, West, and East."

Then there was given to him a bow together with its arrows of bronze "This bow is given to you to be with you to every place to where you go."

In section 9 (cols 63-81) of the inscription, the king and his entourage return to Kawa for a festival of Amun; bountiful donations are given to the temple and repairs begun. One is filled with a great sense of a united community as they beautify and beatify the temple complex.

"Then His majesty found the road of the god after the sand had taken it in regal year 42, without this god having gone upon this road and this nome. Then His majesty brought a 'multitude of hands',

To wit , men and women as well as royal children and chiefs.

To carry away the sand; and His Majesty was carrying sand with his hand(s) himself, at the fore front of the multitude for many days, staying on the 'stairway' of this god doing work before him even after he had opened up the road of this god.

Second month of inundation, last day. He caused the noble god to appear in a procession by night.

All the soldiers and all the people went with torches in their hands

As soon as this god came out and as soon as this god went around the city, then the noble god rejoiced very greatly in the midst of the multitude."

The Kawa IX inscription records the first and second regal years of the king, which included all of the events summarized by Shinnie. Three other Kawa inscriptions were inscribed as graffiti on the face of the doorjambs between the First court and the Hypostyle hall of the Temple of Amen. They were basically lists of donations and sacrifices to the god. Kawa XII indicated a reign of more than twenty-five years.

King Amani-Neke-Yerike was buried at Nuri, although his ancestral home and residence was at Meroe.

Nastasen (335-310 B.C.), the twenty-sixth generation of kings, was buried at Nuri, the Napatan cemetery. King Harsiotef (404-369 B.C.) was the twenty-third generation to be buried at Nuri. Both Nastasen and Harsiotef, who also resided at Meroe, left inscriptions at Jebel Barkal. The granite stela (JE48864) or Annals of King Harsiotef year 35 was first discovered in the First or Outer Court of the Amun temple at Gebel Barkal and removed in 1862. A beautifully carved granite stela (2268) of Nastasen was found in 1853 at New Dongola by Count W. Von Schlieffen. It is now in the Statliche Museen, Agyptiches Museum. It probably comes from the Temple of Amun at Gebel Barkal. These two documents are especially significant as they" represent a rather homogeneous and special unit within the continuum of Kushite Royal monuments." "... as documents of a new imperial era of prosperity and territorial expansion."

It is from these stelae and classical texts that we find that Harsiotef and Nastasen inherited the political problems of Amani-Neke-Yerike. Yet, Harsiotef, in his thirty-fifth year, rebuilt the temple complex of Amun at Napata with extensive grounds, palm groves, gilded the statues that were fashioned from acacia from Arkure in the land of Punt.

The increase in prosperity of the Kushites is indicated by the following passage from the annals of Harsiotef's year 35:

"When, however, I saw the temple, the Karnak of Amun,

Without any gold on it

I put on the Temple, Karnak,

Specification,' Total gold, deben -weight 40; making gold, thin sheets 5120.

When they spoke to me, saying,

"It lacks a shrine of gold.

I bought the acacia wood of Arkure"

Furthermore, I had it brought to Napata.

I had gold put on its two faces: gold, deben-weight 20

I had put gold in the treasury, deben-weight 20,

making gold, deben-weight 100"

Section 7 of the annals cites wars with the rebels north of the Nome and the surrounding desert dwellers: beginning in year 2 in the N. Butana (5 campaigns);year 3 and 5 in the E. Desert; year 11 in Mirgissa ; year16 and 35 in Lower Nubia and in years 16 and 23 at Meroe city. The conflicts spread as far as the Second Cataract and the territory between the First and Second Cataracts near Aswan. The wars at the City of Meroe are reminiscent of the pacification of Amani-Nete-Yerike before he could start his coronation journey to Napata.

The stela of Nastasen was dedicated to the Amun of Napata and Amun of Thebes It measures 1.63meters high, 1.27 meters wide, and 0.298.meters thick and. contains hieroglyphic text engraved in 26 lines on the front and 42 lines engraved on the back. At the top of the rounded stela is a winged sun disk, under which is the king's cartouche is placed, and the human-headed Amun of Thebes and the ram-headed Amun of Napata stand back to back. Each god is offered a necklace and a pectoral. Nastasen is accompanied by "the king's sister, and king's mother, the ruler of Kush", Pelkha, on the left side of the lunette. Both wear the Kushite cap with diadem. Pelkha holds in her left hand a sistrum, while pouring a libation with her right. Nastasen is followed by his wife, Seckmakh, on the right side of the lunette.

The main text begins: Nastasen ,Mighty bull, Beloved-of -the-Ennead, Appearing in Napata,. acknowledged as The Horus, the bull who tramples those who rebel against him under his sandals, the great-devouring lion who establishes every land, son of Amun.

Karl -Heinz -Priese encapsulates the text succinctly:

> "...the text begins with a description of his appointment to the throne" When I was 'the good son (i.e. crown prince?) in Meroe, Amun of Napata, my good father called to me , saying 'Come!" Nastasen heeds the call of Amun to Napata, where the city's inhabitants receive him. "He has laid the rule of Nubia at your feet, Amun of Napata, your good father". During a "dialogue" with the god in the temple, Nastasen receives from his hand the "kingship of Nubia, the royal cap of King Harsiotef, and the power of King Piy-Alara." A coronation journey to Kawa and Pnubs then follows. After a listing of gifts for Amun, the text continues with a description of several campaigns, in which the identity of both opponents and the battle locations remains mostly anonymous. The conclusion of the text contains the king's confession to Amun: "O Amun of Napata, my good father! The matter which you 'silence' does not happen (Kairos). And when your pronouncement is absent, they do not have by which people gain sustenance under the sky."

FORTY GENERATIONS OF MEROITIC KINGS AND QUEENS

After the reign of Nastasen, the last king to be buried at Napata, the Kingdom of Kush reached its Meroitic phase of cultural -political development. For the next millennium, impelled by the their activities on the world stage with Egyptian, Roman, Greek and Asian competitors, the Kushite Kingdom reached a high stage of civilization, evidenced by the greatest amount of preserved monuments on the continent. ."But within this context, a clearly original development may be observed. Earlier research of nineteenth and twentieth centuries wanted only to see here elements the elements of increasing isolation, alienation, and gradual decline. In reality, the culture of the Kushite kingdom had only sporadically lost contact with contemporary Egypt. It was constantly receiving new impulses.   On the other hand, many characteristics of the millennial-old cultural traditions of the Middle Nile region gradually came once again into their own, features we are now able to appreciate thanks to intensive investigations. In fact, the culture of the kingdom of Kush stands with equal importance next to that of contemporary Egypt.

The basic Kushite royal titularies from Kashta to the Meroitic kings included five parts :
1. Horus-name,
2. Nebty or Two-Ladies-,
3. Golden Horus-name,
4. Throne -name
5. Son of Re-name (nomen or birth-name).

The last two names were usually encircled by the rings or cartouches which appeared as the most important title used on inscriptions, buildings, and other objects associated with the king or queen. However, with the introduction of the Meroitic language and script, the five-part titulary was gradually abandoned.

According to the Hintze Chronology of Napatan and Meroitic rulers, forty generations of Meroitic rulers were found at the royal cemetery of Meroe. Two kings, Arkakamani (295 B.C.) and Amanislo (275-260 B.C.) and Queen Bartare (260-250) are buried in the South Cemetery at Meroe. The rest are buried in the North Cemetery.

KING ERGAMENES (ARKAMANI): THE ICONOCLAST

Ergamenes (218 -200 B.C.), "The heart -of Re-rejoices" is one of the earliest kings buried at Meroe. His titulary was found on cartouches inscribed in his mortuary cult temple and on an offering table that is presently at Khartoum. There is nothing known of his family or relations. He had some knowledge of Greek and studied philosophy as well. However, in the literature, Ergamanes is known as the "heretic" king. This epithet, was ascribed to Argatharchides, a fourth century B.C. historian, and preserved by Diodorus Siculus in his History of Egypt. Ergamenes used violent tactics to break the power of the priests of Amun over the Kushites kings by slaying them at Jebel Barkal. Before that time, it was within the power of the priests to have a king slain or order his death by suicide if they did not approve of him. With this coup and an eye on the activities of the Ptolemies in the south, Ergamenes became more aggressive with his building in the region.

Ergamenes added a small entrance hall to the temple of Ptolemy IV at Pselchis and inscribed his own royal cartouches. He also built a new temple at Philae. With an air of *noblesse oblige*, Ptolemy IV added an entrance hall to it. This would suggest that each acknowledged the rights of the other as the temples and the inscriptions were allowed to stand unmolested yet during a later period when hostility broke out, the cartouches of Ergamenes was erased by Ptolemy V.

King Ergamenes was the last King to have his inscriptions in Egyptian hieroglyphs and will always be remembered as the first Kushite king to establish formal relations with the Ptolemaic rulers in the south.

QUEEN SHANAKDAKHETE: THE FIRST RULING QUEEN

Queen Shanakdakhete (170-160 B.C.) was the earliest royal name preserved in Egyptian Meroitic hieroglyphs. Her name was inscribed on the doorjambs of the altar niche of Temple F, Naga:

> "The royal-waab-priest of the Son of Re: Shanakdakhheto given life every day 'beloved of Ma'at' like... ,
> The son of Re, Lord of the Two-lands (Egypt):Shankakdakheto."
> Her family relations and filiation remain unknown. All three of the representations of Queen Shanadakhete clearly depict her wearing crowns associated with the ruling kings. She is represented, wearing the three-part royal costume in the company of a non-ruling man with a simple diadem crown on his head. The steamers on the Queen's crown are touched by the man with his right hand, indicating her legitimization as ruler.
> The decorations of her mortuary chapel, Beg.11, "with their innovative iconography and artistic quality as well as the architecture indicate a remarkable intellectual milieu."

QUEEN AMANIRENAS (20/21 B.C.): ONE-EYED CANDACE

Queen Amanirenas "Amnirense qore li Amanirenas" "ruler, Candace" (Meroitic cursive) was probably the wife of King Teriteqas as a non-ruling partner. She achieved ruling status upon his death. According to Strabo, her son Akinidad was her co-regent. .The Great Stela of Amanirenas and her son is known as The Hamadab Stela of Amanirenas and Akinidad. It was found at Hamadab by John Garstang (1914-16), in an unexcavated settlement south of the center of Meroe city. It is the longest and best known of those 1ˢᵗ and 2ⁿᵈ century B.C. royal inscriptions engraved in Meroitic text found in the temples of Napata and Meroe.

The four inscriptions that identify Amanirenas as queen, Candace, and ruler are the Dakka graffito, the Teriteqas Stela from Meroe city, the inscription on a bronze naos from temple T at Kawa and in the text of the Hamadab Stela. The latter Stela is a record of military campaigns. In both the scenes represented on the lunette, the queens stand before Amun on the left half and the goddess Mut on the right half. On the frieze below these scenes, the queen is depicted in triumphal stance as ten bound enemies are prostrated before her.

Strabo identifies Amanirenas as the one eyed Candace who opposed the Roman prefect, Petronius in the war between Rome and Meroe between 25 and 21/20 B.C.

QUEEN AMANISHAKHETO

Queen Amanishakheto (Amanishakheto) (41-12 B.C.) has many attestations of her reign:

1) her cartouches on two blocks from Temple K at Kawa;

2) a granite stela discovered in the forecourt of the late Amun temple at Meroe city

3) her cartouches from the palace at Wad ban Naga ;

4) an unpublished stela from Qasr Ibrim now in the British Museum;

5) her cartouche on the pylon of (Beg.N6); her presumed funerary offering table from (Beg.6.) The queen was the first ruler to use Meroitic hieroglyphs and cursive script in her titulary.

Queen Amanishakheto's name occurs in the following forms:

    Mnishte (in Meroitic hieroglyphs)

    Am(ni)sheto qor kd(key) (in Meroitic cursive)

    (Am)nishhete (in Meroitic cursive)

    Amnsheto qo mol wi,,,

    Amnsheto qore.

The term *kd (ke)* refers to Candace and the term *qore* refers to ruler (male or female).These terms were used in the Greek literature of the Hellenistic period before the first female ruler, Amanishakheto. "The interpretation "[king's] sister" or "[royal] sister"" should be preferred to the generally accepted interpretation of "Candace" as "Queen Mother" or" Mother of the [reigning] King." "If the derivation of "Candace" from the Meroitic word for "sister" is correct, this term also emerged, as a Meroitic variant of the Egyptian term(s) designating the *snt nswt*, "Sister of the king", a common title of royal wives in Egypt from the Eighteenth Dynasty as well as the consorts of the Twenty-Fifth Dynasty and Napatan rulers."

Queen Amanishakheto was thought to be the daughter of King Amanikhable. She appears to have been married to King Teriteqas and became the successor of Amanirenas as ruler of Meroe. The extreme prosperity of her reign was indicative of her building activity in Kawa and Wad Ban Naga, sumptuous in its expanse.

The relief fragments from the pylon tower of the offering chapel depict the Queen's power and triumph. "On both sides of the chapel entrance the queen stands holding a group of prisoners, striking their shoulders with her lance. A wide diadem supports as attached, ram-headed shield ring at the brow, and then runs around the close-cropped, curled locks. A vulture pelt sits atop her head, probably to be understood as a diadem fashioned from gold foil. A narrow band extends from the neck to the chin, bearing two Uraeus cobras at the cheek.

Today when one speaks of Queen Amanishakheto, one speaks of "The Treasure of Amanishakheto" or the Gold of Meroe. However, the earlier literature referred to "Ferlini's Jewels" because of his discovery of the jewels in 1837. These exceptionally fine pieces will be described in the chapter 15. Dietrich Wildung states that "the quality of craftsmanship cannot be compared with the work of the Hellenistic goldsmiths .The unique significance of the find lies in the combination of Egyptian, Meroitic, and isolated Hellenistic elements into an original composition." [131]

QUEEN NAWIDEMAK (EARLY 1ST CENTURY B.C.)

Queen Nawidemak "Nwidemak qore" represents the 47th generation of the Kushite Dynasties. Her titulary is representative of the new protocol for royal Meroitic inscriptions. The personal name is given and qore designates her as ruler. Queen Nawidemak follows three ruling queens during the golden age of Meroitic glory and her iconography is similar wearing the insignia and costumes associated with the male rulers: the royal coat, the sash and the tasseled cord. The gold statuette in Khartoum and the reliefs in her funerary cult chapel represent her wearing those royal elements. However, the N. wall relief of her pyramid burial tomb Bar.6 shows the Queen wearing a long haltered skirt leaving her pendulous bosom bare," which emphasizes her fertility as a ruler and, probably, as mother of a ruler." King Amanikabale is regarded as her successor and son. Judging from the number of his inscribed monuments, he accomplished many donations; built and restored temples in the area.

The golden statuette and fragments of an incomplete offering table survive the reign of Queen Nawedemak.

KING NATAKAMANI AND QUEEN AMANITORE (12BC-12AD)

King Natakamani and Queen Amanitore were co- regents in the most prosperous time in Kushite-Meroitic history. Their throne and Son of Rre names appear in both Egyptian/and Meroitic hieroglyphs. In all royal inscriptions, they appear as equals. Natakamani: "Re -is-One whose-ka-is come into -being", "Ntkmni, ruler" and Amanitore, "Re-is One whose-ka-is-loved", "Mnitore/Imn'ryt", "Candace" also appear on their monuments in the company of their three princes Arikhankharor, Arkhatani, and Sherakarer.

Sherkarer later became king and his brothers, who successively became crown princes, predeceased the co-regents. A rock drawing of King Sherkarer incised into the cliff at Gebel Qeili is astonishingly skillful in its representation of the victory of the king over his enemies .who appear to be falling off a cliff. Their bodies seem so life like as their limbs are distorted in the fall. It shows the king with regalia and weapons not depicted before and a god with a full head of hair surrounded by halo and nimbus. The god has a string of enemies in hand and is apparently helping the king to conquer his enemies.

King Natakamani and Queen Amanitore are to be remembered for the sheer quantity and sumptuous splendor of their buildings and the great growth of the Naga, Wad ban Naga and Napata. The list of buildings includes:

1. Temples of Amun erected by them at Naga.
2. Late temple of Amun erected at Meroe City.
3. The Great sanctuary of Amun at Gebel Barkal was restored and enlarged.
4. They built and dedicated a temple to Isis at Wad ban Naga.
5. An Apedemak sanctuary was erected at Naga
6. A large palace was built at Gebel Barkal

The pylon of the Apedemak temple at Naga shows on the right side, King Natakamani slaying his hand -grasped enemies with upraised lance and Queen Amanitore holds her enemies as she slays them. Her tremendous body exudes power. A snake with a lion's head represents the god, Apedemak.

It is interesting to note that the burials of the two regents were built at the two opposite ends of the plateau of Begarawiya North. Queen Amanitore was buried at Beg 1 in a stepped- pyramid which was built in two stages and looks like a steep pyramid placed on top of a truncated pyramid. (Dunham 1957) King Natakamani was buried in of similar style.

QUEEN AMANIPILADE (MIDDLE 4ᵀᴴ CENTURY A.D.): LAST KUSHITE DYNAST

Queen Amanipilade is the last recorded ruler of the Kushite kingdom. She represents Generation 74. Her royal name Mnipilde, Amanipilade was found on an offering table in a secondary position at Beg. W104 by Dunham in 1963. The inscription is completely preserved and includes Queen Amanipalade's mother's name, Mkehnye and father's name Tehye.

The S wall of the mortuary chapel (Beg. N. 25), shows a female ruler seated on a lion throne with legs resting on the figures of bound captives. The Queen, under the protection of a winged-goddess, wears a skullcap with the streamers and Uraeus; and is dressed in the three part royal costume. There is no text and there is nothing to suggest by the iconography that the kingdom of Kush is in a state of dissolution.

Karl Priese states, "It remains unclear when and how the Meroitic kingdom met its end. Around A.D. 300, it was still in full possession of its power, even over Lower Nubia; the last royal tombs of Meroe are dated to about A.D. 350, and a tomb in a cemetery of the royal family dates to the second half of the fourth century. One of the unanswered questions is if and how directly attacks by the kingdom of Axum resulted in the fall of Meroe."

CHAPTER 14.
ROYAL TOMBS, CEMETERIES, AND CITIES

The royal tombs and cemeteries of the Kushite civilization have been documented by the archaeological adventurers and excavators of the nineteenth and twentieth centuries beginning with awe and sometimes with disbelief. The Harvard-Boston Expedition was the first to excavate the five royal cemeteries almost in their entirety. There were nearly 400 individual tombs, including those of at least seventy-two rulers, their royal wives and dependents. The royal cemeteries are Kurru, Nuri, Jebel Barkal located in the Napata region, and the Northern and Southern cemeteries located north of the town of Meroe. Although Reisner was responsible for the first relative chronology of the Napa tan and Meroitic rulers, one has to admit that a more comprehensive record of the thousands of objects discovered is lacking. "However, we have to deplore the unrecorded destruction of many offering chapels and the displacement of pyramid and chapel blocks throughout the site, which caused an irreparable loss of information about the reliefs and architecture, subjects which were obviously of little interest to that expedition. The clearing of the site during 1903 and 1921-22 amounts to an extraordinary estimated volume of debris and stone at 10,000 cbm."[140]

When Hoskins traveled in Ethiopia and published in 1835 ninety illustrations of the temples and pyramids of Nuri, Meroe, Jebel Barkal, and Soleb with accompanying maps, he studied carefully the previous visits of Burckhardt and. Cailliaud and compared the ancient calculations and observations of Aristophanes, Artimidorus, the accounts of the centurions of Ptolemy with his own observations and measurements. So equipped, Hoskins was the first to document his perceptions of the peoples and details of the royal monuments and cemeteries of Kush. He wrote, "Never were my feelings more ardently excited than in approaching, after so tedious journey, to this magnificent necropolis," "The appearance of the Pyramids, in the distance, announced their importance, but I was grateful beyond my expectations, when I found myself in the midst of them. "As every stone in these plates is drawn with a camera Lucida, the reader will have an opportunity of studying their construction, and I may also add , of appreciating their picturesque appearance" … "There are the remains and traces of eighty of these pyramids , they consist chiefly in three groups."[133]

One hundred and fifty years later the necropolis was the scene of massive stabilization and restoration of the pyramids under the direction of Friedrich Hinkel, Director of the Works .in the necropolis of Meroe between 1976 and 1988. In his summation of Meroitic architecture, both secular and religious, Hinkel drew the conclusions: "That the overview of various aspects of Meroitic architecture has shown that original forms mixed with external influences, utilized both traditional and foreign elements and practices to create new and impressive forms of expression. These are fascinating developments that we are just beginning to discover, discern and to understand." [132] A new perception of the necropolis has emerged with the work of Hinkel, and represents a new benchmark in the evolution of Nubiology and Meroe.

NAPATAN REGION

The Napatan region in its broadest geographical sense refers to the area, which includes all of the earliest Kushite monuments and cemeteries: Kurru, Nuri, and Jebel Barkal. The place or city of Napata was first mentioned when Amenhotep II sacrificed seven rebellious Asiatic princes found in the district of Tikhsi (Ty-h-sy). They were placed head-down on the prow of his majesty's barge. "One hanged the six men of those fallen ones, before the wall of Thebes... Then the other fallen one was taken up river to Nubia and hanged [on] the wall of Napata, in order to be manifest the victories of his majesty.".

The cemeteries in the Napa tan region string geographically along fifteen miles immediately downstream from the Fourth Cataract of the Nile in the region of modern Kareima. Napata was on the west bank of the Nile. Floating down stream from Napata, Hoskins found the pyramid fields of Kurru and upstream the pyramid fields of Nuri on the east bank of the Nile. These royal cemeteries are the monumental glories of Napata's heroic age.

The first six Napatan Pharaohs of the Twenty-fifth Dynasty of Egyptian Pharaohs, called the Ethiopian Dynasty, were buried at Kurru with the exception of Taharqa who was buried at Nuri, on the left bank of the Nile, a little upstream from Jebel Barkal. Tarharqa's pyramid was much larger than those built at Kurru and more visible. Its original size at the base, 28.5m square, was encased by a grander, more imposing structure totaling 51.75m at the base with steeper sides and twice as high with a stepped appearance. Taharqa's pyramid became the norm at Nuri as well as a number of the pyramids found at Jebel Barkal and Meroe.

Pyramids of Kurru and Nuri are the earliest known royal monuments of the Kingdom of Kush, which consisted of thirty-six royal tombs within the two necropoli. Here lay all of the Nubian kings that ruled Egypt and their consorts, five or six of its kings, sixteen of their queens and five generations of their ancestors. Arkell gives a very good description the development of the cemetery:

At Kurru the main cemetery with the tombs of the first four kings is a sandstone plateau between two wadis, beyond which on either side are the tombs of the queens of those kings. The best site was occupied by a small grave of tumulus type; and the next fifteen places in the point of desirability were filled with a succession of tombs of increasing size and excellence of construction. Then came the four royal tombs in the four worst sites in the cemetery, obviously the latest burials in the cemetery, which had been in continuous use since about 800 B.C. There is a gradual development in tomb form - first, the simple pit grave under a tumulus with the corpse buried on the right side with the knees slightly bent, head north, face west; then an improved tumulus with a casing of sandstone masonry, a mud brick chapel, and a horseshoe-shaped enclosing wall; then a roughly square masonry mastaba over a pit tomb with masonry chapel, the whole surrounded by a rectangular enclosing wall; and then a later type of mastaba under which the burial pits were oriented east-west, the orientation of all the later royal tombs. Next in point of time came the graves of six queens of Pianhki, in which the burial pits were roofed with corbel vaults of masonry. The tomb of King Pianhki himself was situated in front of a row of mastabas, lower down the slope towards the river; and in it, in order that the vault could be built before the funeral, a small stairway was cut into the rock and opened into the eastern end of the pit through a rock-cut doorway.

Nuri was the royal site for the burials of at least twenty generations of kings and queens from Atlanersa to Nastasen, the last of the dynasts to be buried at Nuri. Their tombs were large, elaborate under ground chambers covered with pyramids at ground level. At the Kurru cemetery were simpler, tumulus graves which seemed to antedate the royal cemeteries. According to Reisner, they were used by the families of princes or chiefs of the formative Nubian or Napatan dynasty before they conquered Egypt, which accounted for the sixth or seventh generation that began with Kashta, before 750 B.C.

According to Hinkel, the early Napatan mortuary superstructures developed from tumuli over square mastaba like the ones at Kurru into the pyramids of Nuri. The earliest tomb in the east cemetery was developed after the last tomb of the preceding cemetery. The earliest Nubian royal tombs were essentially pyramids from the time of Pianhki, built of solid stone blocks.

Beneath the pyramid, the royal tomb generally consisted of a connected series of two or three small chambers, of which the innermost contained the burial. These were hewn from solid rock, though in a few of the Kurru tombs it was necessary to provide them with masonry because of the overlying strata. The main burial chamber was directly beneath the pyramid, while the subsidiary chambers and the approach ramp eastwards from it. Access to the underground chambers, except in the very earliest and the latest tombs, was a long flight of descending steps. After the royal interment had been made, the doorway between the steps and the easternmost chamber was blocked with masonry or rubble, and the approach ramp was filled with earth every Kushite royal tomb has been broken into and plundered in antiquity, As a result, the archaeologist is left to reconstruct the details of burial practice from the scanty remains overlooked or disdained by the robbers.

Hoskins gives us a tourist's-eye view of the pyramids of Nuri in his *Travels in Ethiopia. (1835)*:

"April 1. This afternoon we spent three hours in sailing eight miles to the pyramids of Nouri. They are situated in a slightly elevated part of the desert, a full half hour's walk from the river. There are traces of thirty-five pyramids, of which about fifteen only are in any kind of preservation.

These are not very interesting, except as tombs, and from their imposing appearance, not being ornamented with porticoes or hieroglyphic inscriptions. The pyramids are all at right angles and their direction are generally the same. Their size varies from a 110 feet square to 20. There are eight above 80 feet square, and four more above 70 feet square; their height is generally about the same as their diameter."[133]

The Nuri cemetery is much larger than that of Kurru. According to Reisner, it was twice Kurru's size. It contained tombs of nineteen kings and fifty- three queens. In the center of the necropolis is the largest pyramid, belonging to Taharqa. The pyramids of the later kings range in two lines southeast of Taharqa's pyramid. The queens are buried in much smaller tombs, tightly packed on the opposite side.

The awe and mystery attached to the glorious past of the royal pyramids because of their legendary material wealth and grandeur will never cease. The plundering of the tombs has continued to the twenty-first century. On April 10 it was reported that Sudan's chief archaeologist, Hassan Hussein Idries, told AFP (Agence France Press) that a well preserved mummy was found three months ago in a grave of the royal cemetery of Napatan Kingdom in the Nile river town of Nuri. The independent Akbar Al-Youm daily reported from Nuri that tourism police, acting on a tip, captured four thieves making a deal to antiquities smugglers for 800 million Sudanese pounds (more than three million dollars).

Idries said the thieves partially unearthed the mummy, and "our men took over and unearthed it scientifically." The mummy, with hair, nails and black skin still distinct was "one of our ancient kings of the 25th dynasty buried in the royal cemetery of Napata's King Taharqa." Idries and the tourism minister flew the mummy to Khartoum and it was placed it in a laboratory of the Archaeology Administration for treatment before it is taken for display in the National Museum.

A most compelling feature of the Kurru cemetery, especially to most Kentuckians, are the graves of twenty-four horses plus two small circular graves a short distance from the main tombs. In one of the small circular graves was found a dog. The graves have all been plundered, but there have been found remains of such trappings as silver collar and headbands, miscellaneous ball beads of hollow gold and faience, and gold plume-carriers. There were four rows of graves. Two rows had six horses in them and two with eight. The horses were buried standing with their heads towards the south. These horses were attributed to Pianhki and Tenutamon [Tanutamami] as the second and third rows had amulets in them that were attributed to Shabaka and Shabataka. [Shabitku] undoubtedly these were the teams of horses from the royal chariots.

The Nineveh Horse Reports, cited by Torok, mention that chariot horses said to be Kusayya (Kushite) validate trade contacts with Assyria in the early period of the Twenty -Fifth Dynasty. The citation can be dated to 681-669BC during the early reign of Sennecherib's successor Esarhaddon. The annals of Sennacherib written on a hexagonal clay tablet, describe in detail eight of his military campaigns which agree with the biblical account of the King of Judah's trust in Pharaoh to come to his aid against the King of Assyria.(II Kings18:21). Sennecherib, King of Assyria would not countenance the rebellion of the Judean king and sent Rabshakeh from Lachish to Jerusalem with a great army. He sent a messenger to Hezekiah to bargain for his fealty, saying:

"Now therefore give pledges, I pray thee, to my master the King of Assyria and I will give thee two thousand horses, if thou be able on thy part to set riders upon them. How then wilt thou turn away the face of one captain of the least of my master's servants and put thy trust on Egypt for chariots and for horsemen?"(Isa. 36:8-9) Rabshakeh returned to his own land and rejoined the king of Assyria in battle against Libnah. The king left Lachish when he heard that Tirhakah, (Taharqa) king of Kush, was coming to make war on Assyria. (Isa. 37: 9).

Chapters 36-39 in Isaiah form a historical appendix, reproducing the story of Isaiah given in 2 Kings 18:13, 17-20:19. The biblical text makes no further reference to Taharqa, although he is known to history for his opposition to the Assyrians. However, the biblical text is explicit about the aftermath of Sennecherib's invasion of Israel and the prayer of the prophet Isaiah to Yahweh, the God of Israel, on behalf of the King of Judah. That same night the angel of Yahweh went out and struck down a hundred and eighty-five thousand men in the Assyrian camp. In the early morning when it came time to get up, there they lay, so many corpses. Sennecherib struck camp and left; he returned home and stayed in Nineveh. One day when he was worshipping in the temple to his god Nisroch, his sons Adrammelech and Sharezer struck him down with the sword and escaped into the territory of Ararat. His son Esarhaddon succeeded him."

JEBEL BARKAL

Beside the mountain of Jebel Barkal are two groups of about 25 pyramids, one group dating from the beginning of the 3rd century and the other dating from the first century B.C. The pyramids at Gebel Barkal are the best preserved in the Napatan region. According to the latest listing or assignments of burials, during the period of 515-270 B.C., five rulers were buried at Barkal: Artisans, Aryamani Kashmerij Imen, Irike-Piye-qo, and Sabrakamani. Aktisanes was probably the earliest to be buried at Gebel Barkal and is suspected to have built one of the anonymous pyramid tombs in the southern part of the cemetery (Dunham 1957 and Hoffman 1978). Arymani has been assigned the largest pyramid in the southern section of the necropolis by Wenig (1967) and Hoffman (1978). During the period of 90-50 B.C., an unknown king and queen were buried as well as Queen Nawidemak, representing the 45th to 47th generation of rulers.

Gebel Barkal's significance is more than a burial site for the Kushite royalty. It is a source of magical powers and the symbol of Godship and Kingship not only to the Kushites but also to the Egyptians who believed that the god Amun dwelt inside of Gebel Barkal... This conspicuous table mountain, known as the Pure Mountain or Holy Mountain, stands seventy meters high directly behind the ancient town site of Napata, about one and one half kilometers from the right bank of the Nile. The ruins of the temples, tombs, and palaces, swept with sand, lie in mute testimony before the sheer cliff as sanctuaries. The eighty-meter, freestanding pinnacle, on the south side of its cliff has been conceptualized as a huge Uraeus. (sacred cobra) "The god was believed to dwell behind the "Uraeus", seated on the throne inside the mountain.

Meroe region

Three hundred miles south of Gebel Barkal is Meroe, the ancient capital of Kush. A short mile east of the city lays the Sun temple in the direction of three of the royal cemeteries of Meroe. One is unable to view the cemeteries from the banks of the river as the pyramids blend into the higher desert hills which rise just beyond them. As one approaches the pyramid field more closely, they jut out perhaps a 100 feet above the rocky ridge from the surrounding desert plain. Seen from the summit of the ridge are other and smaller pyramids lodged along the eastern flank like gigantic sentinels. This group of tombs comprises the Northern Cemetery of Meroe, containing the remains of 38 pyramids. Burials in this group continued from 250 B.C. to 350 A.D., (Dunham 1957).

The Southern Cemetery is seen at the top of another stony ridge, some 250 yards away. The destruction is more apparent in this cemetery. However, out of the 220 burials about 24 pyramids are recorded, which include the pyramids of the first two kings to be buried at Meroe during the period of the first half of the third century B.C.

The Western Cemetery lies between the two pyramid groups and the remains of the town the latter of which are not conspicuous because of the denuded surface remains. Of the more than 800 graves, there are about 80 superstructures built in the style of the pyramids for the royal family. They date from the 2nd century B.C. to the 4th century A.D. (Dunham 1963)

Although the three cemeteries are physically separated, they are developmentally one burial complex viewed in a social context. The South Cemetery " is unique among the royal cemeteries of Kush in that it comprises only a few royal monuments surrounded by a much larger number of humbler tombs-nearly 200 in all... The North Cemetery is the most exclusively royal of all the

Kushite cemeteries. Retainers and lesser nobility , even the queens consort were relegated to the west Cemetery, situated in the gravel plain below the royal pyramids... The common people of Meroe were buried in a series of cemeteries immediately beyond the outskirts of the city...

The royal pyramids in the Sudan are distinct in structure from those of Egypt because of the addition of the chapels before their structure. The added element was a small one- room temple at the pyramid's east side which had a pylon and often a small portico and a small surrounding wall.

Hinkel reminds us that the interior walls of the chapels were often decorated with funerary scenes in relief. Ancient graffiti written in Meroitic and later in Greek, Old Nubian and even Ge'ez are found occasionally on the pyramid walls and tell us about early visitors who came to the site and carved their names, monograms, prayers and thanksgivings on the surface of the sandstone blocks. Hinkel also clarifies for us the story of "Ferlini's Jewels" (discussed in Chapter 3 which we now know belonged to the famous Kushite Queen Amanishakheto. (C 15-1 B.C.) "During the first years of the last century, the three visits to the Meroe pyramids by E.A.W. Budge of the British museum in 1899, 1903, and 1905 (Budge 1907) and the photographic survey of J. Breasted (1908,5-14) of Chicago University and Nina Davies (Nov.1906) are among the most important. It was left to Budge to find out, -after destructive trials what casual remarks by Ferlini and Lepsius had already signaled, i.e. that the burial chambers were not constructed inside the pyramids but in the subterranean chambers beneath them. As early as 1834, this understanding led Guiseppe Ferlini to the discovery of the famous 'Gold of Meroe' treasure hidden in the burial chambers beneath the pyramid of Queen Amanishakheto. However, perhaps to mislead future treasure hunters, his account describes the location of his discovery as being a room under the top of the pyramid itself. We have already have already mentioned the evidence from Cailliaud's and Ruppell's panoramic drawings of the pyramid field which show that the southern part of the top of this pyramid was missing some years before Ferlini's arrival. The sequence for the construction of the substructure and the superstructure, the use of the *shaduf* in the construction of the pyramid proper, and a number of golden objects later found left in the burial chambers by G. Reisner which were similar to those left by Ferlini are further evidence against Ferlini's story (Hinkel 1985, Markowitz and Lacovara 1996)

The Sudan Antiquities Service has been engaged in the protection and restoration of the monuments in the pyramid field from 1976. One of the overall goals of the restoration project is to restore the offering chapels and relief walls and to provide them with roofs and doors "The overall idea should be to harmonize and treat the area between Meroe town and her necropolises as a historical landscape. When the restoration is completed generations will experience the awe of Hoskins, as well as the stunning views of others through the ages. The site for a museum selected in 1986. The selection of the site will allow a visual connection between the museum and. view of the sun temple and the place where Meroe town is hidden under acacia trees on the Nile. Standing in the center of the sacred landscape reaching from the Nile and the town site to the pyramid fields and stone quarries in the east- a landscape over more than 1000 years of Kushite history.

ROYAL CITIES

The civilization of Kush and the ancient site of Meroe have been known since the early dawn of Greek literature In the *Iliad*, Zeus and the other gods went each year to feast for twelve days among the 'blameless Ethiopians'. In spite of the early travelers and explorers, it is to John Garstang and the Liverpool team of excavators between 1909 and 1914, that we are indebted for the present knowledge of the ancient site of Meroe, since known as the Royal City. The city of Meroe was a natural outlet on the Nile to the Red sea and the northern prehistoric trade route. From the east to the north of it are the sandstone hills that contained the massive quarries that provided the stones for the extensive building in the area. An hieroglyphic inscription found on the Lion Temple gives the name of the city as Mer (port) and in the Meroitic cursive texts it is spelled m-r-u and the hieroglyphic inscription gives it as M-r-<-(wa-a).

When the team arrived, the only visible masonry on the site was a length of stone walling, standing three to four yards in height, and running north and south over a distance of a hundred yards. The spot is about half a mile from the river, on the east bank, in a partial clearing of the trees which surrounds the small villages of Keyek (north) and Begerewiyeh (south)... About a hundred and fifty yards, eastwards from the wall were seen two pairs of stone rams, lying prone in the sand which partially covered them.

Within the walled city was a complex labyrinth of buildings. In the center of the compound were two very large buildings that appeared as palaces. The other buildings were postulated as magazines, audience chambers and buildings for the royal staff. The town, for the most part, consisted in many mounds covered with red brick which remain to be excavated. In the examined area were found the temple of Amon, a walled section containing palaces, and a royal bath. Cleared also was the Lion Temple, the Temple of Isis, the Shrine of Apis, the Sun Temple, east of he town, and some non royal cemeteries.

An unusual building was found indicative of the Mediterranean life style of the period... It was referred to as the 'Roman Bath'. It consists of a large brick-lined tank with an elaborate system of water channels leading into it from a well nearby. A ledge running around the upper part of the tank was decorated with plaster figures and medallions, as well as water -spouts in the form of lion heads.

A small temple within the Royal City is of special interest because of the head of Augustus found in front of the temple, partially buried in the sand. Some believe that it was a gift from the emperor and others believe that it was part of the loot from the Nubian raid on the Temple of Philae. The description of the interior painted stucco walls within the temple contains references to scenes of the King and Queen of Ethiopia, their gods, officials and captives of foreign races.

The unexcavated areas, according to Shinnie, contain mounds of slag from the iron workings of Meroe for which it is famous.

THE TEMPLE OF AMON

On the eastern side of the Royal City is the Temple of Amon, the largest building excavated, 450 feet in length. It was approached through a small shrine. On either side of the walk are flanks of four stone rams. The temple was constructed of brick with columns, pylons and doorways faced with dressed bricks of sandstone. There was an outer hall and a middle hall containing a small shrine, with the names of Queen Amanitore and King Natakamani inscribed on the walls. To the west of it was a stone dais with steps engraved with scenes of bound and kneeling prisoners. A series of smaller courts led to a sanctuary decorated with religious scenes.

Placed at the foot of the altar on its eastern side were found two small votive tables, and an inscribed stone lay on the table of Horus -on-the crocodile. This tablet is described by Professor Newberry as 'the lower half of a cypphus or tablet, representing the Child Horus standing upon two crocodiles, holding in his right hand a scorpion and hare, and in his left hand a lion and snakes. In the same sanctuary was a very high altar with reliefs, a spinning whorl of baked clay, part of a pottery bowl decorated with an Ankh pattern near the rim and miscellaneous fragments of faience, pottery, glass and metal.

THE SUN TEMPLE

The Sun Temple is religious in nature as it is dedicated to the sun. Garstang identifies this temple with the account of "The Table of the Sun" by Herodotus. Fragments of a stela, ascribed to Aspelta, were found in the outer courtyard. The temple, like the Amon temple, was surrounded by a wall of red brick with stone-faced doorways. A ramp led to a platform with a colonnade enclosing the sanctuary.

On the eastern wall, there was a series of figures of prisoners represented by cartouches indicating the names of conquered peoples from other countries. The south wall shows Meroitic soldiers with prisoners and the north wall shows the scenes of a seated king before a long line of women. The west wall of the corridor portrays another victory with reliefs of bound soldiers under the foot of the king, dancing figures, cattle and a chariot with four horses. The approach to the sanctuary was a flight of stone steps with its walls and floors covered with blue glazed tiles.

The Lion Temple

This temple was built on top of the slagheap where the railroad now runs. One wonders how much of the area was destroyed with the construction of the railroad. The building itself was of the Meroitic style, covering the top of a mound, and approached from the desert to the east by a slope and a flight of steps. The mound itself was one of a kind which freely abounds in the locality, being largely composed; it would seem, of the refuse and products of iron-working and similar industries. The surface of such mounds is freely covered with black stone-like slag left from a very imperfect refining of ore and the great quantity of such slag strewn about is evidence of very extensive workings through the centuries

One gained access to the chambers up a flight of steps, guarded on each side by a seated lion carved in soft stone. There were two columned chambers fronted by a pylon of red brick. The temple was apparently for the worship of the Lion God as there was found other lions within the enclosure, as well as an inscribed plaque dedicated to the lion god.

Garstang notes that the sculpture in the round of two representations of bound prisoners is of considerable skill and proportion. He further describes three smaller objects that attest to the skill and style of Meroitic work. One object is a "fine laminated stone like red slate, carved in delicate false relief after the Egyptian tradition, and inscribed with several small panels of Meroitic writing incised in the cursive style." On the face of the stone the king in a 'complex crown', is wearing a decorated robe. Garstang states that upon close examination, one could note that the piece is of Meroitic portraiture, while yielding to Egyptian convention. The other side of the plaque is the lion god wearing a crown similar to the king. He is robed in a short skirt with a broad ornamented waistband and a collar of beads and jewels similar, no doubt, to one originally to be seen upon its counterpart. He carries a scepter, upon the top of which there may be noted the emblem of the seated lion. The second object is the king carved in dark stone with such freedom of expression that it suggests knowledge of anatomy and the disregard of rigid convention resulting in a quiet dignity of royal dimensions. The third object was curious to Garstang because it was the pylon of a temple carved in hard wood. It was in this temple that the best Meroitic inscriptions were found; these will be discussed in a later chapter.

The Temple of Isis

The Temple of Isis, known to the natives as El Keniseh, is also a purely Meroitic structure. The Sun temple was an earlier prototype. The building was outside of the town proper and a little north of the village of El-Deragab. The main part of the building was found on the mound and the entrance was accessible through a sloping causeway or a flight of stairs. Upon excavation, two superimposed structures were examined, one of which was reused in Christian times. The upper structure and its extensions were known as the keniseh, which was translated as church by the natives. The substructure was soundly Meroitic but could not be excavated completely without endangering the upper structure. The dating of the structures was pre-Christian, with later use about sixth century A.D.

The upper structure was columned, leading to a shrine with standing altar on blue and black tiles, triangular in design. Other tiles in the chamber were of a lighter blue hue. Fallen from the walls were broken pieces of the lighter tiles of considerable quantity with figures and emblems embossed. A stela of King Teriteqas found in the upper building was evidence of the first century B.C. provenance.

Sayce describes this stela as small and made of granite, found lying on the floor of the keniseh. Its importance lay in the short demotic inscriptions behind each figure and the four lines of cursive below the scene. The top of the stela is rounded and on one side are engraved a scene of the king before Isis and the inscriptions. The king wears a Uraeus diadem on his head, and is crowned with plumes and disk; on his feet are large sandals; his dress is a short tunic with two large pendants and tassels from the girdle, while over the right shoulder and under his left arm is a broad band of Ureai. In the left hand, he holds a scepter with its hawk's head, while his right hand is raised in adoration of the goddess .

Isis, crowned with vulture disk and horns, is standing, holding a palm branch, the leaves which form a series of ankhs, the terminal one curving to the nose of the king. In front of her is a bowl on a stand with dippers hung from the rim. Below the scene in the inscription is the name of King Teriteqas followed by his title; and at the end is Isis again.

The lower structure contained an altar and two large sculptured statues of a king or a god. Two statues of Isis and Horus seated on her knees found on ground level of the mound led to the speculation that the temple was dedicated to Isis. One statue was in bronze and the other was in carved stone. Small pottery fragments were found along with minor objects. A bronze cupid with other bronze fittings was also found, thought to be of Roman influence. There was also found a complete water trough or tank with a lions head at each end.

THE SHRINE OF APIS

The Shrine of Apis lay about a mile and a half from the Royal City near the modern village of Hamdab. The dedication of the shrine to Apis, ascribed by Sayce, is obscure because he does not give a reason. The shrine is important in itself because two large stelae were found inscribed in Meroitic cursive. One stela was removed to the main site where it still remains .The other stela is now in the British museum which contains the names of Queen Amanirenas and King Akinidad. It is thought to give a version of the war with the Romans in 23 B.C.

NAQA

Naqa, a city of immense importance and magnitude, is between forty or fifty miles from the Royal City. It lies on an open plain in the Wadi Awateib about 20 miles from where the Wadi drops into the Nile beside Wad ben Naga. The seven or so stone temples mark Naqa as a great religious center. The most famous of the temples is the Lion Temple, built by King Natakamani and Queen Amanitore better known because of their exterior reliefs. Lepsius named the temple the Lion-god, because it seemed to have been dedicated to Apedemak the local deity. Apedemak is represented as a coiled snake with a lion's head; the famous scene of the king and queen capturing their enemies is captured on the two pylons at the entrance of the temple. The temple walls, both inside and out, portray the King Natakamani and Queen Amanitore with Prince Arikhankharor worshipping the various gods.

The royal trio is seen on the back wall, with the prince represented twice, standing before the Lion-god who is uniquely cast with three heads and four arms. The details in dress, jewelry, and attitude are carefully addressed, even to the wrinkles in the neck, a highly regarded sign of beauty in Africa today.

Another temple contemporary with the Lion Temple and much larger but less well preserved has the name of Amanitore and Natakamani on the lintel of the main entrance. However, a different prince, Arkhatani forms the trio. Lying east of all the other temples is a temple that bears the name of Queen Shanakdakhete. The inscription is bilingual: the cartouche is in Egyptian and the royal name is in Meroitic hieroglyphs, giving it the distinction of the first Meroitic inscription to which a date can be given. In addition to the town site strewn with stone blocks, column drums and fragments of red brick are two cemeteries with stone covered mound graves. The one cemetery, which was opened, belonged to the post-Meroitic age.

MUSAWWARET ES-SUFRA

Of all the royal cities, Musawwarat remained an enigma as to its origin and its purpose until recent excavations by the German expedition shed some light on the mystery of the "Great Enclosure". Mussawwarat lies some ten miles to the Northeast of Naga and is surrounded by hills on all sides. Like Naga, it lies at the upper reaches of the Butana wadi system and at the foot of the raised sandstone plateau where the main region feeds the area with rainwater. Both Naga and Mussawwarat are a day's journey by camel or donkey from the river. Shinnie's suggestions are that the importance of both sites lay in the fact that they are at staging points on trade routes to the east and that they have great agricultural potential, since located in a flood plain. Within this plain are only monumental stone buildings, no cemeteries or evidence of a town.

Of all of the cities, Musawwarat is the most dramatic and spectacular. The Great Enclosure is the largest of the stone monuments which Shinnie describes: "The main feature consists of a number of buildings and walled enclosures surrounding a temple built on a platform, rather similar in lay-out to the Sun Temple at Meroe. On stylistic grounds, this central temple appears to belong to the first century A.D. or a little earlier; but there are no inscriptions other than secondary graffiti, which is plentiful. This temple is surrounded by a colonnade, some of whose columns have interesting reliefs. Outside the colonnaded temple is a series of corridors and ramps which connect the various parts of the complex, and which are not known from any other Meroitic site. The number of representations of elephants in the sculptures suggests that this animal played an important part at Musawwarat es-Sufra; the large enclosures may have been designed to herd them in, the ramps being for their convenience since they could more easily negotiate them than they could the steps. It may be that here was a center for the training of elephants for military and ceremonial purposes. The remarkable wall terminating in the figure of an elephant is unique and is further evidence of the importance of this animal.

It is also evident that the function of the great enclosure was religious in nature by the number of temples incorporated in the area. Also there is a walled area known as the 'Little Enclosure ' that is only for ordinary dwelling rooms.

Another unique feature at Musawwarat is the remains of a huge hafir, a man made structure, to catch and hold the run off of waters from the Wadi es-Sufra. These hafirs are the only source of water during the nine-month rainless season that still exists today. There are many hafirs throughout the Butana region; however, the Great Hafir at Musawwarat is the largest known. It could provide water perhaps for a herd of elephants. It measures over 1,000 feet across and 20 feet deep. The sides of the structures are built up above the ground level with material excavated from the bottom, and partially reinforced with stone.

WADI BEN NAQA

Wad ben Naqa is the last of the known cities in the Central Sudan. It is forty miles upstream from Meroe, on the east side of the Nile. By virtue of the fact that Wadi ben Naqa lies at the mouth of a wadi coming down from the inland city, it is sometimes identified as the 'river-port' for the city of Naqa. The ruins of Wadi ben Naqa include two small temples, an enormous round structure of brick resembling a huge silo; its purpose is unknown. Recently a palace resembling the royal palaces at Meroe has been uncovered. It is a huge square building almost 200 feet per side and at least two stories high. The outside walls were faced with burned brick and plastered over with white stucco.

IV.

FINALE:
VESTIGES OF GREATNESS

"the moving finger having writ, moves on"
Khayyam

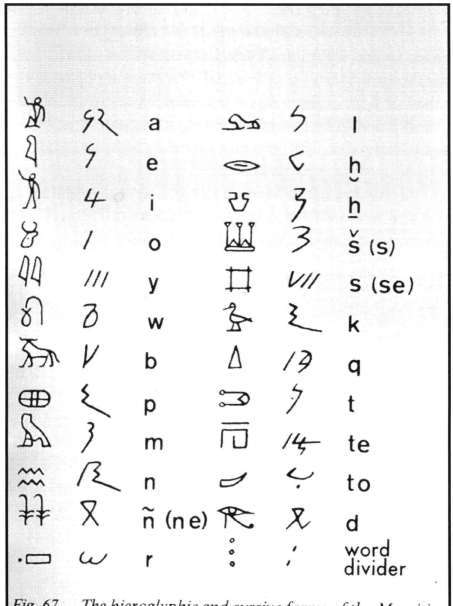

Fig. 67.   The hieroglyphic and cursive forms of the Meroitic script with their phonetic values.

MEROITIC SCRIPT WITH PHONETIC VALUES

166

KERMA POTTERY

ROPED JUG

SILVER MIRRORS OF
KING NASTASEN

BEADED NECKLACE

Treasure of Queen Amanishaketo

GOLD ARM BRACELET

CHAPTER 15.
THE RESTORATION OF PHARAONIC GREATNESS

The Pharaonic tradition of kingship and queenship reaches back into predynastic times when the population of the Nile Valley was as homogeneous, both physically and culturally as such a large group can ever be. We know that the physique of the inhabitants of this valley from the Delta deep into Nubia remained much the same from predynastic to late historic times. They also shared a common material culture in predynastic times. It seems that the Pharaonic civilization arose upon this Northeast African Hamitic substratum. In any case, the prehistoric inhabitants of the Nile Valley must have possessed a common spiritual culture as a correlate to the homogeneous physical and archaeological remains. It has been argued that the change in the cultural dynamics in the Nile Valley came about with the invention of writing in the north while the south continued an oral tradition. The North was accorded a sense of superiority and the South was referred to as a backwater. You will note that the Meroitic language was written in a form that has yet to be thoroughly deciphered.

When the Napatan Pharaohs seized the Egyptian throne and established the XXVth Dynasty of Egyptian Pharaohs, the splendor of Egypt had been on the wane since the XXth Dynasty. The diminished level of the Nile and steady immigration of the population from Lower Nubia left few settlers remaining by the XXth dynasty. The stratification of Nubian society, and the emergence of a peasant economy during New Kingdom dominance of Nubia politicized the superficially Egyptianized Nubians who had filled the ranks of the elite. With Nubia's enormous gold resources, military prowess, her meteoric climb to kingship was inevitable. Thebes was no longer the Pharaonic seat of power. The seat of power was changed to Napata in Upper Nubia and the Pharaonic tradition was intentionally continued by the Napatan Pharaohs and later the Meroitic kings when the seat of power was moved deeper into the Sudan, at Meroe. The intentionality is reflected in the Egyptian elements of Pharaonic Egypt that were absorbed into the Kushite culture and transformed into continued Pharaonic greatness long after Egypt has lost its luster and power.

The chess game between Egypt and the Kushite states, as early as Kerma was critically checkmated by the political and military collapse of Egypt through a series of foreign occupations by several empires: Assyrian, Persian, Macedonian, and Roman, notwithstanding the erstwhile Kushites.

AGRARIAN TRADITION

The main source of subsistence of the kingdom of Kush at the time of its Napatan Kingdom, the Twenty fifth Dynasty, was animal husbandry and agriculture. Animal husbandry had attained a millennial tradition, perhaps beginning with the kingdom of Kerma, 2400 B.C. Kerma is the first African kingdom to develop an elaborate system of rituals and cultural artifacts around the cult of cattle. The wealth of the kings and temple priests was measured in cattle. Fishing and hunting were among the daily activities of the commoners.

The climate and the types of arable land influenced the development of agriculture, throughout the history of Napata and Meroe, seluka, saqia and shaduf, named after farming systems introduced to supply water, mentioned in chapter VI. The main cereals were barley, wheat, sorghum, or durra of local origin, lentils, cucumbers, melons, and gourds. Cotton, unknown in ancient Egypt, was first developed in the Kingdom of Kush before the beginning of the Christian era. Evidence from earlier times is scanty, but about the fourth century the cultivation of cotton and the knowledge of its spinning and weaving in Meroe reached a very high level. It is even maintained that the export of textiles was one of the sources of wealth of Meroe. An important branch of agriculture was the cultivation of fruit in orchards and grapes in vineyards; many of these belonged to temples.

TRADE AND COMMERCE

It seemed apparent that the subsistence base agriculture and animal husbandry did not account totally for emergence of Kush and the diminution-of Egypt on the world stage. However, it did preserve its pastoral and agricultural modes, while gradually establishing extensive trade contacts. There is scant evidence of the Nubian economy because of lack of surviving texts and limited archaeological evidence. "The earliest evidence of internal trade and power was suggested by Dunham. The economic basis of power lay in the control of the trade along the river highway to-Egypt, the traffic in gold from the mines to the Eastern Desert, the trade in cattle, hides, slaves, ostrich feathers, ebony, and the many other products from the south which Egypt imported from the Sudan. In the Napatan district itself, agriculture, while adequate for local needs could hardly have formed the basis for the extensive and profitable export trade, for the region lies north of the rain belt, and land cultivable by irrigation from the Nile was limited."[136]

POLITICS AND WAR

The Twenty-fifth dynasty of Napatan pharaohs was celebrated as Warrior Kings. The Louvre Stela C100 attributed to Pianhki [Piye] by J. V. Beckerath indicated two alterations on his stele (that is, if correct.) The titulary is recorded: 1 "Uniter of Two-lands", 2 "creator-of crafts", 3 Multiplier of gallant warriors", 4 "Enduring-are-the- manifestations of- Re" Reference to gallant warriors is a political metaphor praising his valiant warriors and praising also his greatest tribute as conqueror and restorer to order.[137]

The Pianhki's titulary that appears on the inner court of the Amun temple 500 B reinforces his power for all to see and hear: "Nebty name "whose-kingship-endures -like Re's - in -Heaven and the Golden Horus Name Whose Appearances are holy, Whose might is powerful" in an unaltered form, the Horus name "Strong-Bull appearing [Crowned]- in- Thebes" of the New kingdom model was changed into "Strong Bull, Appearing [Crowned] -in- Napata" in order to announce a momentous reversal in history. As the title powerfully manifests, the place of Thebes, where the Egyptian conqueror of Kush had been crowned, was now taken by Napata, where the Kushite ruler of Egypt is crowned."[138]

The surviving part of the Sandstone Stela leaves no doubt about Pianhki's Imperialistic notions and his awareness of his divine origins and his territorial duties:

> "Amun of Napata has granted me to be ruler of every foreign country. He to whom I say, "You are chief' He is to be chief. He to whom I say "You are not chief." You are not chief. Amun of Thebes has granted me to be rulers of Black-land (Egypt).
>
> He to whom I say, "Make (your formal) appearance (as king)"; he shall make first appearance... Whoever of these princes does not pay tribute to me..."[139]

Pianhki consolidated his two kingdoms at the same time as his military successes during his incursions with Tefnakht in the north in the first 15 years. He also managed to maintain trade with Asia during this period. The temples of Amun begun during Kasha's reign were expanded and acted as governmental, economic and religious centers of Nubia.

It was during Pianhki's accession that he improved his war machine, which reflected on his military successes with Tefnakht and his allies of Lower Egypt. He developed cavalry tactics and insisted on ritual purity of his men as he refined his methods of siege warfare. On the field of battle appeared better types of shields, larger and better breeds of horses and, heavier chariots with three men to each chariot. One must not forget the greatest concentration of the army machine was the famed Kushite archers. Over time from the predynastic age to the dynastic age, Nubian or Kushite archers were utilized by the Egyptians, Romans, and Greeks as mercenaries.

Pianhki accomplished the supreme political act or event of the Napatan Pharaohs during his coronation when Shepenwepet, God's Wife of Amun, and daughter of Orsorkon Ill adopted his sister Amenirdis. This assured that upon Shepenwepet's death, the supreme authority invested in her in a divine religious sense and secular sense as mediator between the Amun priesthood and the pharaoh in Lower Egypt would past to the family of Pianhki and his descendants.

Politically the role of the queen mother was not clear in the earliest Napatan period. We know of the reverence Taharqa-had for his mother and her role in his coronation. Anlamani also mentions his mother at the election and coronation ceremonies. The queen mother had influence and devotion early on. She exercised a special influence through the system of adoption, which was quite complicated. The queen mother designated as the Mistress of Kush adopted the wife of her son.

In later periods the queens as mothers or wives began to assume political power and proclaimed themselves sovereigns. Meroe was ruled by a line of Candaces, (kandakes) or queens regnant, during Graeco-Roman times. The title is derived from the Meroitic Ktke or Kdke meaning queen mother. The title *qere* did not appear until Meroitic script was used. The four queens, Amanirenas, Amanishakhete, Nawidemak and Maleqereabar were by definition Candaces. Shanakdehete was the first attested reigning queen.[140]

Timothy Kendall asserts that, "if they have traditionally been portrayed by modem historians as 'foreigners' in Egypt, they surely did not perceive themselves as such,..." In their minds, Egypt and Kush were northern and southern halves of an ancient domain of Amun. These two lands, they believed, had been united again in historical time only by the greatest pharaohs. As "sons of Amun, the Napatan monarchs saw themselves as heirs of those pharaohs who thus became their ancestors. Like them, they had received their authority to rule from the great god in both his northern and southern aspects. Their kingship was thus a return to that "of the time of Ra," which was symbolized by the wearing of the two Uraei on their crowns."[141] Taharqa, another warrior -king and descendant of Pianhki was the-Conqueror and Deliverer discussed in Chapter X. Taharqa installed his daughter Amenerdis II as God's Wife of Amun elect early in his reign (around 69 (BC) and while the office-of the-High.

Priest of Amun was occupied by Haremakhet, Shabaka's son, Taharqa appointed as Second Prophet of Amun his own son, Nesi-Shu- TefnutTaharqa accomplished during his reign the amalgamation of the central features of the Theban Amun Theology, and the expansion of the Amun temples .The trend politically has been termed "archaism" based on the intellectual and political traditions that developed before and during the Twenty -Fifth Dynasty period. We might be looking at cosmic (mythic) time as well as historical time when referring to the process of archaism.

ART AND ARCHITECTURE

The art forms of the kingdom of Kush, viewed developmentally, spans approximately three millennia, from ancient Kerma, in 2500 B.C. to the fall of Meroe in 300 A.D. The earliest forms were pottery, wrought by hand and later by wheel for domestic use. The black topped red polished ware found in early Nubian cultures were exceptionally fine in form and fabrication, which was peculiar to Kerma. The art objects beside pottery included bronze swords, daggers, jewelry, amulets, scarabs and seals. The coffins, beds, and other forms of furniture exhibited a refinement and artistic departure from the Egyptian models that were available to the artisans at the time. The tradition of using a gold cattle hoof for the leg of a bed in Kerma has been cited. Centuries later, a bronze leg from a funerary bed was found in the-tomb of a minor queen of King Shabataka of the-Twenty Fifth Dynasty.

The upper portion of the bed leg grows out of the-back of a goose; which nestles down on the box support. Its feathers were finely chased after the form was cast. The head and pointed beck are examples of particularly fine artistic and technical workmanship.

"The significance of the motif lays in one of the god Amun's many divine forms in Egypt from the new Kingdom on; he is represented as-a goose. Furthermore in the Pyramid texts of the Old Kingdom, the deceased utters the desire to ascend to heaven as a goose; and in New Kingdom royal tombs, wooden figures of geese are found among the images of the deities buried with the deceased in order to accompany him to the next world."[143]

Sculpture was a profuse art form for the Kushites from statues of kings and queens, sculpture in the round, sculpture relief and Shawabtis. The Shawabtis, servants in the service of the king in-his after-life, took the form of small figurines or small sculptures a few as tall as sixty centimeters. Tarharqa's shawabti were transformed into first-rate sculptured art with each individually carved face. In his tomb were 1,070 stone Shawabtis stacked in neat rows. Not far from his grandfather Taharqa's pyramid, Senkamanisken placed 1,277figures in his tomb. He might have exceeded him in number but not in style. However the faces of the kings are typically Kushite in depiction.

When I ascended the ramp in the British Museum in the Northern Sculpture Gallery, I was awe stricken by the-two pieces of sculpture that claim the most attention, according to the Egyptologist T.G.H James. Both of the statues are of Kushite origin. The sphinx of different colored granites from Kawa; incorporates the image of Taharqa with a striking force called barbaric power by some and massive grandeur in-repose by others. The double Uraeus on his brow signifies Kushite kingship and godship. The statue is 42 cm. high. The large seated ram is represented with a small figure of Taharqa placed between the flexed legs of the ram in a protective mode.

The reliefs in the temples are formulaic in design with representation of the classical Egyptian canon infused with Kushitic elements and-traits in form and substance.

The skill of the-goldsmiths is without parallel. There was a heavy gold knife found in the tomb of the queen of Senkamanisken. It has been suggested that the knife was used for the opening of the mouth ritual during the funeral

Cylinder sheaths of precious metals were found in nine royal tombs. Their function has not been determined. Fifteen sheaths were found in Aspelta's tomb, and two gold tweezers. Also were found gold finger and toe sheaths in Aspelta's wife's tomb. "The cylinder sheaths are assembled from two pieces: a lower cylinder, sealed at the base with a round disk, and a shorter open cylinder placed over the internal sleeve on the lower piece. On the gilded silver sheet there is sometimes additional decoration in applied gilded silver; or gold-wire, or granulated gold bands; inlays in semi-precious stones." [144]

The wealth in materials, artistry and artisans is astounding. It makes one pause and reflect over what the losses of the Kushite civilization have incurred since the adventurers and archaeologists and discoverers of the past uncovered the treasures of dark Africa. The treasure of Amanishakhete, known for centuries as Ferlini's Gold, can now claim its place in historical time and become a cosmic message of things unsung. The quality and craftsmanship of the Sudanese-goldsmiths is beyond the mere comparison of the Hellenistic goldsmiths. The uniqueness of the treasure that is now known as the Gold of Meroe is without parallel in the Mediterranean-Nile Valley-Red Sea cultures. Dietrich Wildung, Curator of the 1997-98 European exhibition, *Sudan: Ancient Kingdoms of the Niles* summarizes quite succinctly the significance of the treasure :

"The quality of craftsmanship of the jewelry cannot be compared with the work of Hellenistic goldsmiths. The unique significance of the find lies in the combination of Egyptian, Meroitic, and isolated Hellenistic elements into an original composition. The rich iconography of the shield and seal rings, [ear studs] armlets and necklaces significantly expands the repertoire of reliefs from Meroitic temples and the offering chapels of Meroitic pyramids. They also provide the original evidence of royal costume as represented in the reliefs. Stylistically noteworthy is the typically Meroitic reinterpretation of Egyptian motifs from the corpulent form of the goddesses to the anhk ("life"} signs and wedjet eyes. Their proportions replace the refined elegance of the Egyptian representations with a fresh originality."[145]

The power, divinity and queenship are represented in the sandstone Relief of Queen Amanishakhete in the Berlin Museum. The queen stands on both sides of the chapel entrance, holding a group of prisoners, striking their shoulders with her lance. Attached to the wide diadem at her brow is a ram-headed shield ring with cropped locks appearing under the diadem. Her cartouche bears her name in Meroitic hieroglyphs. The shield-ring attached to the queen's brow is very exquisite.

"The elaborate piece of jewelry places the three dimensional ram's head in the center of a tripartite facade of a chapel with round gold side posts. In the center of both the doorway and each of the two cavetto cornices appears a sun disk, the lower one is fashioned from a carnelian bead. A frieze of Uraei surmounts the entire architectural structure. The ram's head wears a spherical sun disk with a band of Uraei around its lower section. A necklace of a gold ball beads over an inlaid green band is suspended from the ram's neck. A miniature gold pendant, containing at the very bottom a minute, probably leonine, divine figure with a sun disk, is part of the bead necklace. The broad collar itself displays alternating bands of bead and lozenges, separated by bands of gold wire. A horizontal band of abstract Uraeus cobras terminates the decoration at the top. Despite the miniscule scale, the shield-ring possesses an obvious monumentality achieved by the balance of its composition."[146]

Six other shield rings of equal craftsmanship-were included- in the exhibit representing other motifs: wedjet eye, goddess Mut, a-lion's head and the god Sebuimeker.

Two broad collars in the Egyptian Museum of Berlin have been reconstructed from the beads found with the treasure of Amanishakhete. The broad collar is worn not only by kings and queens but the gods also. "The most popular amuletic forms are represented in the broad collar reconstructed from the elements [in stone, carnelian, glass, and faience} of the treasure of Amanishakhete: life (anhk) signs, djed pillars, wedjet eyes, and scarabs along with fish and various blossom and plant motifs."[147]

There were thirteen gold signet rings also in the treasure. They seem to represent the various stations of the queen's royal life, including election by the gods, sacred marriage, birth of a child, and the ring that shows Amun of Napata within the sacred mountain (silhouetted with Uraeus). The scarab necklace was very interesting. It showed the scarab back, made from chased, repousse gold sheet, soldered onto a gold base plate. The legs are made of gold wire and-the eyes-are inlaid with blue glass. The bases of the larger scarabs in the necklace are decorated with hieroglyphic signs that were indecipherable. A necklace featuring Hathor heads show the frontal female faces with cows' ears and curled hair enclosed with two Uraeus serpents. The negative spaces are filled with-turquoise and blue-colored enamels.

A painted gold stucco relief from the Wad ben Naga palace shows her sumptuous jewelry adorning her arms and her neck. Also found at Wad ben Naqa was an extremely unusual leg from the funerary bed of Queen Amanishakhete fashioned-in wood. "A papyrus umbel extends as a capital from the rounded shaft, surmounted by a head of the goddess Hathor with stylized horns and naos, the standard form of a sistrum (musical rattle)."[148]

The armlets displayed seemed so very modem to the eye and erased time momentarily. The descriptions of two oft he armlets attest to their timelessness.

"One armlet is 4.6 cm high and the width of each peace is 85 cm. wide. The other is 3 cm. high and the width of each piece is 9.2 cm. wide. The armlet did not extend completely around the arm as it was fastened by an element of leather or linen. "Circular and lozenge shaped gold -wire cloisons are set on a sheet -gold base and decorated with fused glass in varying colors. Rows of granulated balls run around the upper and lower edges, and also frame the rectangular "window" area in each of the two halves. Within the "windows" are the repousse busts of the female *deity,* while the zones between these images are decorated with an enamel feather pattern. Over the hinge is a separately worked figure of a four-winged goddess standing on a papyrus umbel. On top of her vulture diadem she wears the Double Crown, and is thus to be identified as the goddess Mut, consort of Amun."[149]

The other necklace is even more elaborate with a ram's head of Amun within the sun disk, inside a chapel façade much like the broad collar of the shield -ring described above. "The entire composition is soldered together from tiny individual elements. A larger piece of blue glass with a floral pattern forms the lower portion of the hinge; perhaps this represents the pool surrounded by plants. Framed at the top and bottom by decorative gold wires, the horizontal bands consist of a Uraeus frieze, pendant drops, lozenges, applied rosettes and two more rows of lozenges. All the gold elements are soldered onto the gold sheet base and filled with blue enamel and red glass inlays "[150] It would be a clear omission not to mention that the grave goods in the other Royal cemeteries were of equal splendor. Fittings from horse trappings were also found in several burial chambers in the northern cemetery at Meroe. There was a silver gilded lion head, which-sat at the intersection of horizontal and vertical straps on the headstall, representing the warlike god Apedemak. Another trapping represented an ankh sign and two flanking "was-scepters" appearing on a tall rectangular silver plaque affixed to the leather strap of the trapping. The charging lion fastened to a horizontally running leather strap was quite compelling as the reflected early battle scenes with the lion running aside the king into battle.[154]

Kushite architecture has been discussed in Chapter XII as the royal lambs, cemeteries and cities were described. They fall into the following 11 forms based on the recognition of at least 15 types of Meroitic architecture, a third of which are represented by only one example:

1. Temples
2. Funerary Monuments
3. Palaces4. 'Castle"
5. Fortifications, Enclosure walls
6. Enigmatic monumental structures,
7. Commercial storehouses
8. Taverns
9. Wine presses

10. Baths

11. Domestic architecture.[155]

According to Adams, "the so-called "castle" at Karanog, was before flooding, a unique example of Meroitic architectural design." It was mud brick, with walls approximately 120 cm. thick and rooms covered by barrel vaults. The ground floor was divided into small, square chambers, each interconnected. From the height of the walls there appeared to be a third story. There were stairways to the upper floors located in the northwest and southwest corner rooms, with numerous windows on the ground and upper floors and windows opening onto the center light well in the middle of the building. From the floor plan and other affinities, one could compare it with the palaces at Wad ben Naqa and Meroe." [151]

The Fortifications and the walled enclosures appear to be clear examples of Meroitic defensive architecture found at Qasr Ibrim, Gebel Adda, and Faras. The fortification at Gebel Adda is a "massive wall of mud brick about 2m. thick, with reinforcing bastions every 10 or 12 meters. As first published by Millet, who excavated the area, there was wide gate in the middle of the eastern wall and stairways to the top of the battlements on either side.

The Kushite fortification wall at Qasr Ibrim originally had a relatively simple gateway, secured by a pivoting door and sliding bolt, at the southern extremity of the citadel. This was later blocked and was replaced by the door (nametag), fortified gateway that remained in use down to the time of its inundation in 1965.

Griffith in 1926, found the walled area at Faras to be roughly 300m.longand 200 m. wide, which was about the same size as the Royal City at Meroe. The wall was about 12m high, with square towers arising from the exterior of the wall at regular intervals of about 50 m. The enclosure also was entered through an ornamental defensive gateway in the middle of the south wall.

Enigmatic monumental structures would include the Great enclosure at Musawwarat, the massive brick circle at Wad ben Naga, the southern Bastion tower at Qasr Ibrim, and possibly at Gebel Adda.

Meroitic domestic architecture for the most part was mainly known from Lower Nubia. One of the better - preserved, houses was found at Ash-Shaukan. The house described by Klassens was a type of three- room house with walls heavy enough to support the leaning mud brick vaults and slit -windows high up under the vaults. The walls were plastered white and sometimes painted. One entered the house through a monumental stone entrance. Another variant of Meroitic domestic architecture was that of one or two and three rooms in a congested area. At Abu Geili, in the far south area, was a clustered type house with more than 80 small rooms. The same kind of arrangement was discovered at the Second Cataract sites of Garnierite and Meili Island.

At the town site of Kawa was a tight cluster of small, irregular rooms. In the houses at Gaminarti and Abu Geili were left large pottery bases that served as small fireplaces as they were filled with fine ash. The houses at Gebel Adda and Qasr Ibrim were built with stone rather than brick.

Deluxe houses, ringed by flimsier structures represented, congested town development at Wadi- el- Arab-, Arminna, and Meinarti. There was always space between the deluxe houses, which were strongly built as square and rectangular models. The deluxe houses had as many as three or four rooms there is nearly always a lengthwise interior partition which divides the dwelling into more or less equal halves; there may or may not also be cross-partitions so as to form one longer and one shorter chamber on either side of the central partition. These houses perhaps belonged to or were made available for the administrators and the more flimsy type houses for the retainers.

DOMESTIC ARTS: POTTERY, WEAVING, AND IRON.

Of the domestic Kushite arts, pottery is the best known. Ceramic art, was not only basically utilitarian, it was highly developed artistically. Nubian ceramics have been placed on the same par, with the goldsmith's art by Deitrich Wildung. As an Art historian, he posits that the finds from Kadero, el Kadada from the late fifth and early fourth millennia B.C. are unequal in technical and artistic standard in the Egyptian Nile Valley and credits Kerma with an unsurpassed perfection in the creation of ceramics.

The twenty-year personal odyssey of William Y. Adams, in the field of ceramic analysis has resulted in a chronology of ancient and medieval Nubian pottery wares. The chronology is based on the systematic description, classification, and illustration of the materials found during ten archaeological campaigns and his own excavations. In his memoirs, Professor Adams states that he has inspected perhaps 600 complete vessels and over one million potsherds.[152] Hans-Ake Nordstrom, Scandinavian Joint Expedition, has also contributed to our greater understanding of Sudanese Ceramics.

"The indigenous pottery industry of Nubia really came on its own in the A-group period beginning around 3500 B.C. A-group pottery is derived in considerable part &from the earlier local tradition &from the Khartoum and Abkan Neolithic..."[153] The Neolithic, A group, C-group, Kerma potters all created their wares by hand. Although wheel-made pottery was adopted during the New Kingdom period, both modes coexisted without rivalry. A possible explanation of this may have been that mass-produced pottery was in the province of men and their innovative impulses concomitant with trade and commerce. However, women remained true to handmade ware and the same traditions that had evolved from prehistoric times. This deep- rooted African style is still made today in the same style not only in Nubia but also in other parts of Africa.

Weaving was another important domestic industry of the Meroitic period. It did not become industrialized, as it remained home industry monopolized by women. It has been suggested that much of the cotton cloths were exported which added to the wealth of the period. And much of the cotton and linen textiles were perhaps used to decorate the temples and the raiments' of the kings and queens. Over fifty mud-weights were found in one room in Meili Island and many were found in other home sites. Evidence indicates that the Meroites used warp-weighted looms on which the weaving is done from the top downwards. More recent knowledge of the industry was obtained at the Qasr Ibrim excavation site. The textiles produced were usually white cotton decorated with embroidery and macramé. The garments were usually white with green and blue embroidery. Cotton garments were also found at the cemeteries in Karanog and Meroe. According to Pliny, Meroe or the Sudan was the first to produce cotton about the first century A.D. Egypt first produced linen fabrics.

In 1986 an undiscovered mud-brick temple was discovered. Of special interest were the textile curtains and the fabric containers found dating back to Meroitic and X-group levels at Qasr Ibrim. The temple had survived for more than a millennium from Napatan times. Preliminary evidence suggests" a swift and violent death perhaps as one of the official acts or demands of a newly Christianized government in the 6th century A.D. One curtain had been torn into pieces but showed no sign of wear. It was of plain cotton weave dyed blue after weaving. It was reassembled from 15 pieces: Another curtain was like the first, assembled from 23 fragments but of a much lighter blue. The third specimen was of finer yarn with more open weave and more delicate than the others. The decorative border at the end and a selvedge edge is found commonly in Meroe, Karanog, Gebel Adda, and Qustul. One fabric container was "constructed of two cylindrical basketry structures covered by plain blue cotton cloth and joined together side by side. Another was a long narrow bag very deteriorated from long handling and possibly from being rolled or folded down. It was made from a single piece of cloth, folded and stitched along one side and across the bottom. Decoration was rendered in bands of blue and dark blue on an undyed ground. The last problematic fabric container is a linen-lined leather fragment. One long edge appears to be finished; the other edges are ragged and incomplete. The lining was composed of three layers of plain-weave undyed linen, attached to the leather by bold decorated stitching in flax thread... It might have been a bag or a case to hold a sacred or precious item." [154]

It is apparent that weavers prepared linen and cotton for various use sand tanners processed the hides and leather.

The Kingdom of Kush was recognized in antiquity as one of the richest countries in the known world. The mineral wealth of her borders and within her country was responsible for this fame. "The Gold of Meroe" is not a misnomer. Kush was one of the main gold producing countries dominated at times by Egypt. Excavations at Meroe and Mussawwarat es-Sufra revealed temples with walls and statutes covered with gold leaf. It was the gold of Kush that attracted the Egyptian incursions from the north and influenced foreign relations as far as Israel, Persia, Greece and Rome. "It was computed that during antiquity, Kush produced about 1,600,000 kilograms of pure gold. [155]

Even though the mines were not all controlled by the Meroitic Kingdom, the minerals in the eastern desert which were abundant (amethyst, carbuncle, hyacinth, beryl and others) were channeled through their trade routes. It was not these minerals that caused Sayce to call Meroe the "Birmingham of ancient Africa." The many large slag heaps found near Meroe and other places in the Butana prompted this speculation, regarding iron working within the Meroitic economy. According to Shinnie there were six large mounds of slag found in Meroe and near the cemeteries. The sites have not been excavated and it would be difficult to discuss the origin, importance and dispersion to other parts of Africa. The fortunate occurrence of the two basic requirements for iron production-the ore and the fuel- in one place was of great advantage to Meroe, and it was certainly due to the production of this metal that Meroitic power was maintained so long and that such wealth built up.

CHAPTER 16.
THE LEGACY OF THE KINGDOMS OF KUSH

INTERNATIONAL TRADE: GOODS AND IDEAS

The legacy of the Kingdoms of Kush to civilization was brought into my consciousness early in my own mind as a student at Wayne State University in 1937. Yet scholars at the time accepted uncritically the statement by Toynbee "*The Black races alone have not contributed too positively to any civilization-as yet.*"[156] This mind-set is no longer tenable in the twenty-first century as attested by the current research in Nubian, Meroitic and Sudan Studies. The longevity of the Kingdoms of Kush and its centrality on the African continent places it among the most ancient civilizations of the world, Egyptian, Greek, and Roman. Herodotus, the father of history, Homer, the Greek poet, Virgil, his Latin counterpart, Strabo, the geographer, the early biblical writers as well as early Babylonian and Assyrian kings mentioned the Kushites in their records. Memnon, the King of Ethiopia (Kush) was first mentioned as protagonist during the Trojan War. Derek A. Welsby who has been excavating in the Sudan since 1982 for the British Museum suggests that to place Kushites along with the other giants of the ancient world such as the Greeks, Romans, and Egyptians is justifiable for no other reason than the longevity of Kush. . He points out "At the time when Rome was a small village on the banks of the Tiber and the Greek city states held sway over minuscule territories, the Kushites ruled an empire stretching from the central Sudan to the borders of Palestine. The Kingdom of Kush outlived the Greeks city-states and the period of Macedonian hegemony over vast tracts of the ancient world, and co-existed with the rise, heyday and much of the period of decline of the Roman Empire.

To determine the legacy of the Kingdoms of Kush, one must consider the pre-Kerma culture, the Kingdom of Kerma, the Kingdom of Napata and the Kingdom of Meroe. The recent settlement, called pre- Kerma, excavated by Charles Bonnet as a result of his studies at Kerma and Kadruka (1995), upstream from the Third Cataract, revealed that people lived there about 3000 B.C. He is suggesting that the settlement may have been an important center, which has to be proved. However, it may be considered a buffer zone whose development may have been the result of participation in a trading chain for materials important to the Egyptians who were always raiding in the south for gold, ivory incense, and skins of wild animals. The settlement in the early stages of the research suggest later connections with Kerma and the rise of its kingdom, which replaced pre-Kerma culture about 2500 or 2400 B.C.

The Kingdom of Kerma, probably the first African 'empire' known to history to achieved a high degree of civilization, which enabled it to exert a profound influence on countries situated to its south, along the upper Nile and in Central Africa. Kerma had direct contact with the Asiatic Hyksos as the Hyksos king proposed a military alliance against their common enemy Egypt when the Hyksos ruled Egypt in the north. It was during this period (-1650 to -1580) that Kerma increased profitably their trading alliances with the Hyksos while Egypt was trying to drive them out of their territories.

Close trade and diplomatic relations existed between the princes of the Kingdom of Kerma and the Hyksos of the Middle East during their domination of Egypt during the Second Intermediate Period. These Alliances also led to alliances against the Theban princes. The power, which was derived from these relationships, has not been fully explored. However, Hintze suggested that it was possible that the Kerman princes exploited the apparent weakness of Egypt and were also able to bring Lower Egypt under Kerman power and possibly moved the capital from Kerma to Buhen.

The stela of Kamose reveals the content of the letter he intercepted, written by Apophis, the King of the Hyksos to the King of Kush:

"Aaweese-se, son of Re, Apophis, greets the King of Kush, "why have you not informed me that you have become the ruler of Kush? Have you not seen what Egypt has done to me? Its ruler Kamose has attacked me on my own territory. I have not attacked him as he did you."

He intends harming both our lands... Come North without fear, see, he is with me; no one will offer you resistance in Egypt and I will keep him until you have arrived. Then we will divide the towns of Egypt between us and both our lands will live in joy. We need only emphasize that this kingdom may have greatly influenced neighboring cultures through its techniques, especially in metallurgy, and that of political strength.

Bonnet, proving that some of the bronze items were manufactured on the spot, found a bronze-smith's kiln in the main temple. The bronze techniques were extended to the fine pottery, which featured a metallic band running below the black mouth of the cups and beakers, highly unique in presentation. Some of the items found in abundance were daggers, swords, knives, axes, razors, tweezers and mirrors. The highly complex diversified craftsmanship is attested to by the stone or bone tools and mica used in ornaments, leatherwork, ivory inlays and wickerwork. Trade, a great factor in facilitating the transmission of ideas and language whether oral or written, was also a great transmitter of ideas. The geographical location in itself assured a privileged role in the trade chain that reached north and south via the routes from Darfur and east and west from the Red Sea via Kassala.

The Kingdoms of Kush are recognized in the two phases of the Kingdom of Napata and the Kingdom of Meroe. The Kingdom of Napata is included in the famed Twenty-fifth Dynasty of Pharaohs who ruled Egypt from 750 B.C. to about 160 B.C. followed by the Kingdom of Meroe who ruled in the Sudan from Meroe for until 350 A.D. The culture of the Kingdom of Kush is better appreciated after a number of investigations, especially in the last thirty years. Karl-Heinz Priese states in fact that the culture of the Kingdom of Kush stands with equal importance next to that of contemporary Egypt, its wealth and power notwithstanding. The control of the desert mines by the Nubians is reflected in the grandeur of their temples and the proverbial "Gold of Meroe". The genius of the Nubian pharaohs restored the philosophical and religious trappings of Godship and Kingship during the reign of Shabaka with his restoration of the Memphite Theology. The significance of Nubia was its bridge on the crossroads of Africa and its link to the civilizations north and south, east and west, as it became a link between the Mediterranean and Central Africa. The Kushite or Nubian wells are still in use today for irrigation. Hafirs associated with Kushite influence and occupation are still being constructed and in use today in the Sahel region of the Sudan. Temples speak to a glorious African civilization that has past but remains as mute testimony of the Africa about which Toynbee knew nothing.

The Meroitic period was considered the golden age of the Dynastic Kushite civilization. Its greatest achievement during this period was the territorial expansion surpassing that of the Napatan period made possible by the development of overland caravan trade routes into the interior of Africa. The old caravan routes up the Nile were not the only alternative to the ever-present barrier of the Fourth Cataract. The rapid colonization of the steppe-lands above the Fifth Cataract extended the influence of Meroe to Sennar on the Blue Nile, which was the farthest extent of Meroe, this of course until modern time. This of course contributed to the political and economic decline of the Napatan Pharaohs on the throne of Egypt.

The introduction of the ox-drawn waterwheel afforded dual trade options as the tropical agricultural products found their way to the Red Sea and into the local neighboring markets of the Roman colonies in the Dodekaschoenos. Thus, the center of gravity of the political and commercial base of trade shifted from the north to the south and remained so until the middle ages. The intellectual thrust and the ideological base remained essentially true to the ancient Kushite tradition with few exceptions.

The cultural landscape changed drastically as the wealthy middle class emerged entrenched between the Royal class and the fellaheen of the land. The growth of urban centers and settlements went hand in hand with local manufactured goods and the influx of luxury items from Hellenized Egypt and the products flowing in from the Alexandrine maritime trade as the result of Alexander's conquest in the south. The prosperity of Meroe was greater than it had ever been before. Meroe continued its unbridled building and rebuilding temples and tombs while new towns arose with land expansion. It even earned the name of 'the Birmingham of ancient Africa' from A.H. Sayce; as he described the conspicuous slag heaps, which had accumulated over time. By the private merchant agricultural families attempted to match the grandeur of the nobility with their own versions of tomb, tumuli, and houses to be found in the urban centers as well as the provincial towns of Lower Nubia.

Consonant with the 600-year long building period of the great Enclosure at Musawwarat es-Sufra, beginning about 300 B.C., were the periodic pilgrimages for the festivals for the local gods, especially to the lion-headed Apedemak and to the human headed Sebuimeker. At the start of this period, it is believed that the Meroitic script began to emerge. The pilgrims, ambassadors, and other elite travelers left graffiti. Meroitic script differs fundamentally from that of the Greek, although it has been suggested that the Greek model was used for its invention. The Meroitic characters have been read without difficulty, since first deciphered in 1911 by F.L.I. Griffith. However, the meaning is not understood with the exception of a few words and phrases. With the help of computer decipherment in the future, the breakthrough in its understanding well unlock the mysteries held within its symbols just as in the Rosetta stone before its decipherment. Hopefully, this will be one of the contributions of Kush to the linguistic canons of the African continent.

The legacies of Kush have been obscured by intellectual arrogance and scholarship beset with omissions and oversights that continues to plague the critical assessment of the Kushite contributions to the world and especially to Egyptian culture. It was the Kushite Pharaohs of the Twenty-Fifth Dynasty who contributed to Egyptian culture art, architecture and statecraft that was thought to purely Egyptian.

Even though Pharaonic traditions persisted for a long time in Lower Nubia, we gradually see another cultural shift from the concern for monarchial leanings to that of more popular governance by local officials who were not as concerned with the traditional symbols and ideology of Kingship. In assessing the Meroitic remains, royal authority and state authority become less apparent. If the Meroitic north had any state religion, it was the cult of Isis at Philae, this was not, however, a proprietary cult of the ruling family and the imperial bureaucracy; it was a supranational religion whose sanction was claimed alike by Meroitic kings, Roman prefects, and Bedouin chiefs. In this emerging separation between church and state, as in the nascent feudalism of Meroitic Nubia, we can recognize the beginnings of two of the most profoundly important themes of medieval civilization, which were soon to reform not only Nubia but also most of the Western world.

The Kushite Kings, at the beginning of their dynasty, came to the rescue of Jerusalem in 701 B.C. as the Assyrian armies devastated their cities and towns; just as the fabled Memnon, the King of Ethiopia, came to the aid of the Trojan King against the marauding armies of the Greeks as they scaled the walls of Troy during the Battle of Troy and left us with the image of the Trojan Horse and the heel of Achilles. This period of ancient conflict, has been plausibly, assessed by

Henry T. Aubin, in his book *The Rescue of Jerusalem: The Alliance Between Hebrews and Africans in 701 B.C.* Bruce G. Trigger, wrote in the news release from Soho Press:

Dear Reviewer:

> As someone who has spent much of his professional life studying ancient Egypt and the Sudan, I have read with great interest and admiration Henry Aubin's *The Rescue of Jerusalem.* The author addresses a poorly understood, but historical episode – King Sennacherib's abandonment of the siege of Jerusalem in 701 B.C., an event, which is widely held to have made possible the development of Judaism, Christianity and Islam.
>
> In his powerful wide-ranging analysis, Aubin has demonstrated that a key problem that hindered the analysis of this event is the pervasive racism that led scholars to discount the effectiveness of the Kushite (Sudanese) kings who controlled Egypt during the 25th Dynasty.
>
> By successfully countering this image, Aubin is able to construct a highly plausible argument that it was the arrival of the Egyptian army that saved Jerusalem at the time. He is also able to account for why this explanation does not survive in the Hebrew accounts that are available to us. Aubin successfully achieves his primary goal; he provides convincing explanation of what caused the Assyrians to retreat from Jerusalem. In the course of doing this, however, he accomplishes three other goals that in my opinion are of even greater importance. First, he presents the most persuasive panorama I have read of interstate relations from Babylon all the way to Meroe around 700 B.C. second; his unbiased view of the Kushite rulers of Egypt during the 25th Dynasty completely revises our understanding of Egyptian society at this period. As someone familiar with the evidence he uses, I reproach myself for not drawing the revolutionary and totally convincing conclusions about these rulers that Aubin has formulated. Third, he has unmasked, thoroughly and effectively, the unconscious racism that has mangled the scholarly understanding of Egypt for more than a century.

FOUNDATION OF SUCCESSOR AND RIVAL STATES

<u>Ballana: Successor State</u>. The archaeological evidence to date confirms Ballana as the cultural and social successor to Meroe during its decline. It appeared to have held to the kingly traditions

of ancient Kush at the same time abandoning everything associated with priestly traditions. It appears from the royal regalia of the Ballana kings that they regarded themselves somewhat as heirs of Kush as they adopted the Royal Kushite insignia. When Kushite power was diminished in the North it was the Ballana kings that assumed power during the post-Meroitic period.

This culture could be considered the cultural link between Nubia's dynastic age and its emergence of the medieval age. As a transitional culture, it has been said it resembles the Kerma culture. The origins of the Ballana monarchy remain unknown. It is possible that they were tribal warriors from the south or southwest who settled and established rule over the already established Nobatians who were already settled in Lower Nubia.

According to Adams, the tombs of this period produced the richest archaeological finds ever found in Nubia. The discovery of the twin tomb sites of Ballana and Qustul by Kirwan and Emery, in 1931 revealed enormous wealth. The graves differ from those of Meroe with the largest concentration around the Second Cataract. A second concentration was near the administrative center at Qasr Ibrim in the north and some smaller sites in the territory of the Dodekaschoenos and at Firka another important administrative center or residence of a wealthy family or families.

The remains of the Ballana culture were found from Shellal in the north and to Sesebi in the south. Of the known Ballana sites, four fifths of the sites were cemeteries. The chief difference in the graves from those of Meroe is in the superstructures and the grave goods. They were not the brick pyramid mastaba of Meroe but a low dome-earth tumulus similar to those of Kerma adopted by the commoners at Meroe before its downfall. It was typically 12-40 ft. in diameter with a possible height of 15 feet. Kings or nobles had tombs of larger proportions, which appeared at Qasr Ibrim, Ballana and Qustul, Gemai and Firka. These tombs at Ballana and Qustul represent the most auspicious achievement of the Ballana Culture. When these discoveries were made in 1932 -34 the archaeological world was agog as this was the first discovery of royal crowns from Nubia and the northern Sudan.

The superstructures surpassed the tombs of Meroe with their multiple underground chambers, and the disappearance of offering tables; *ba* statuettes and burial stelae suggest the abandonment of the priestly crafts and the diminishment of their power. There were symbols unearthed that reflected the continuance of the Isis cult in the Ballana graves and elsewhere in the area and the continuance of the Meroitic religion. Conspicuous in the Ballana period were several leveled houses. Female pottery dolls, generally, about five inches tall but noticeably absent in the gravesites.

There seemed to be the cult of the grape as the archaeological remains of the taverns and cellars in several Ballana settlements, indicate a great consumption of wine by the huge quantities of broken amphorae and goblets.

Creeping Christian influence was noted in the imported votive lamps with names of saints and Christian insignia. Imitations were made locally and the insignia was found on some of the pottery in the form of a cross.

Kirwan noted that the discoveries made in Royal tombs illustrated diverse beliefs or superstitions. One of the chambers included a gold cross, a scarab and four rolled up strips of metal lying close together which upon close examination was as Agage, a love charm in corrupt Greek, invoking Isis. He also noted that during this period the Ballana kings continued to worship Meroitic gods, still practiced ritual sacrifice, as they flaunted their jeweled and silver crowns while they set up an opulent state on the Byzantine model.

In spite of the assertion of Hellenized and Byzantine influence, the jewelry, bronze work, and ceramics displayed the inventiveness of the Ballana craftsmen most notably in the crowns and diadems of the kings and queens buried in the royal cemeteries. The ten crowns, obviously from a local workshop, as well, as highly skilled silversmiths familiar with the oldest techniques worked heavy rings, bracelets, silver plates and jugs handed down from antiquity.

The Queen's crown and the king's crown now in the Egyptian Museum in Cairo are examples of Meroitic prototypes transformed to conform to contemporary taste. The crown is a road circlet framed with applied silver roll rims and ornamented with semi-precious stones mounted in silver settings between heavily embossed panels incised with udjat eyes, the pupils inset with glass and cornelian. Five winged Uraei crowned with sun-disks, all cut out of silver and incised are fastened to the rim of the circlet. The crown, according to the excavator was on the body that had fallen off the bier when the roof collapsed. The offerings in the tomb seemed to belong to a warrior queen: spearheads and archers' thumb guards. In the burial chamber were five other burials, including a woman and a child and a cow. The crown was 12.6-cm. high and 19.6 cm. wide with Uraei.

A king's crown was found in a grave along with eight servants and several animals. A woman accompanied the king. The animals included a camel and a dog. A variety of weapons such, as swords, spears arrow- heads, thumb guards, tools and bronze objects were included. One of the objects was a bronze incense burner 18 cm high, 8.7 cm. wide and 18.7 cm. long. The stylization of the burner caused different opinions ranging from Persian, Coptic, and Nubian in origin. The bronze incense burner is shaped as a lion with a detachable head. A tiny tongue is seen as the wide-open jaws show the teeth. The long tail is tucked under the right hind leg in a curl on the right flank. The mane appears schematically fashioned. Loops are at the back of the head and the base of the tail from the chains still hanging from them. Fumes can escape from openings in the jaws, nose, and ears and the sides of the body.

The kings of the Ballana culture abandoned Meroitic script and used Greek as their written language. There was a decline in the use of the high arts as they began importing objects d'art from the workshops of Alexandria and Antioch. It was the claim of Kirwan that the Ballana kings, later, with the introduction of Christianity aped the Byzantium courts almost to the point of mimicry the elaborate ceremonial of the Byzantium court.

Rival state: Axum The rival kingdom of Meroe was the kingdom of the Axumites named after its capital Axum. The Greeks and the Romans knew the kingdom as early as the first century A.D., when a Greek merchant from Egypt wrote a naval and commercial guide, *Periplus Maris Erythraei* (Circumnavigation of the Erythean Sea). The merchants of Meroe knew of the thirst for gold and ivory of the Axumites who penetrated beyond their highlands in search of other commodities as well. The author of *Periplus* describes the port of Adulis and states that eight days' journey inland lay the metropolis of the Axumites, whither was carried all the ivory ... whence it was exported to Adulis and so to the Roman Empire. Adulis was a center for the inland and maritime trade that extended to the Mediterranean Sea and Indian Ocean. Ancient authors wrote of the hippopotamus hide, rhinoceros horn, tortoise shell, gold, slaves, and spices on the lists of exports from Adulis. In addition, was mentioned, Zoscales, the first Axumite king who was already pursuing commerce. It must be noted that Axum and Arabia depended for their prosperity on the control of the Red Sea trade, and Meroe depended on the overland caravan routes to Sea which would ultimately lead to conflict; the loss of the control of the trade by Meroe in the interior of Africa, and diminished trade with her Roman neighbors in the Dodekaschoenos, and finally her demise.

The Axumite king Aezanas was known as the first Christian king of Axum (recorded by Cosmas Indicopleustes) and responsible for the establishment of his country's first religion, which persists to this day. As young disciples from Tyre, Frumentius and his Brother, Aedesius, brought Christianity to the King of Axum by Frumentius and his brother Aedesius, as young disciples from Tyre. They were traveling with the philosopher and relative, when the ship was wrecked as they traveled to the Indies. They were saved and sought asylum at the king's court, winning the heart's of the king, the father of Aezanas, and his family, because their great learning and culture. When Frumentius reached manhood, he went to Alexandria, where he informed the Patriarch of the religious situation. The patriarch, St. Athanasius, consecrated him as Bishop and sent him back to the country that had adopted him, gave him the Abba Salama [Prince of Peace]. He forthwith baptized King Aezanas , the son of Amida.

There are commemorative stelae left by Aezanas, some in Greek, some in old Ethiopic (Ge'ez), and some in Sabean which he claims conquest of large areas of land in Central Africa and Arabia. It is claimed that Axum was a successor state to Sabaea (biblical Sheba). "It is worth recalling that the late monarch of Ethiopia (Abyssinia) still based his claim to rule upon descent from the Queen of Sheba- a legitimizing principle older than that of imperial Japan." [157]

There is another stela of Aezanas dated around 350 A.D., which seems to be one of his last military campaigns where he took his army into the heart of Meroe, sometime after his conversion to Christianity. Budge informs us of the campaign:

"By the might of the Lord of All, I made war upon the Noba, for the peoples had rebelled and had made a boast of it. And they were in the habit of attacking the peoples of Mangurto, and Khasa, and Barya, and the blacks, and of making War on the Red peoples. And as I sent warnings to them, and they would not harken to me, and they refused to cease from their evil deeds, and then themselves to flight, I made war upon them. And I rose in the might of the Lord of the Land, and I fought them on the [Atbara], at the ford of the Kemalke. Thereupon they took flight, and would not make stand. And I followed after the fugitives for twenty and three days killing some and making prisoners others, and capturing spoil wherever I tarried. Prisoners and spoil my people who had marched into the country brought back to me.

Meanwhile I burnt their towns, both those built of brick and those built of reeds, and my soldiers carried off its food, its copper, and its iron. And its brass, and they destroyed the statues of their [temples], and treasures of food, and the cotton trees, and cast them in the River [Nile] and [Atbara]. I came to Kasu and I fought a battle and made prisoners of its peoples at the junction of the rivers [Nile] and [Atbara]. The names of the cities built of brick were Alwa and Daro. The towns built of bricks, which the Noba had taken, were Tabito and Fertoti.I planted a throne in that country at the place where the rivers [Nile] and [Atbara] join.

MADONNA PROTECTING THE NUBIAN PRINCESS
PAINTING OF A FRESCO FROM THE FARAS CATHEDRAL

DAWN OF CHRISTIANITY IN THE KINGDOM OF KUSH

According to tradition, Egypt was evangelized by St. Mark and Ethiopia by St Matthew. The literature relied upon for the history of Christianity in Kush before the fourth century was scant. Acts of the Apostles (8, 26-38) records the conversion of the treasurer of the Meroitic Queen Mother as "Candace the Queen of the Ethiopians". He was apparently a follower of Judaism and reading was from a Greek bible, according to Father Vantini. Phillip the Deacon baptized him on the road to Gaza upon his request. *Life of Apa Aaron*, written in the fourth century mentions some activities of the first bishop of Philae and *Lives of the Theban Monks*, tell the tales of wondrous deeds and specific details of geography. There were many fanciful tales written which was written in the fourth century. Kirwan cites one: "one day the leader of a band of robbers broke into the Church of Saint Pachomius at Faw (in Upper Egypt), stood for a while in silent prayer, then talked with Abbot Anastasias and showed him a miniature portrait of Pachomius which he always carried with him The Abbot was astonished at the sight of the relic and asked; "How could Pachomius be known so far as Nubia?" The robber said: "because a young and very holy monk clad in a woolen tunic crossed country and preached in our lands." [158]

We are indebted to the UNESCO Campaign to Save the Nubian Monuments in the sixties for our expanded knowledge of Christianity and the Christian Church in the Kingdom of Kush, those regions in the southern part of Egypt, and in the Sudan to below the confluence of the two Niles near modern Khartoum .It was in this area that three kingdoms were established as the Meroitic Kingdom decayed and collapsed in the fourth century A.D.

The Kingdom of Nobatia was formed from Nubia proper in the stretch of the First and Second cataracts on the Nile. It included 200 miles inside of the Egypt (UAR) to Aswan and for 110 miles into the Republic of the Sudan to the southern tip of the Second Cataract, commonly known by modern scholars as Lower Nubia. The monumental ruins, dating back thousands of years, indicate that the several towns were at some time seats: the capital was Faras (Pachoras), Kalabsha (Talmis), Ibrim, Gebel Adda and others, perhaps. Regrettably, this area was sacrificed by the waters of the Aswan Dam.

The other two Kingdoms established after the fall of the Meroitic Empire were in Upper Nubia: Makuria with its capital at Dongola (today called Old Dongola) and Alwa with is capital at near modern Khartoum. Makuria extend about 600 miles along the mile to Meroe (Kabushiya) and Alwa extends from Meroe to modern Gezira, possibly to Sennar, for 500-600 miles.

The most astonishing and important information regarding Christianity of Nubia comes the Polish Mission at Faras. To look upon the magnificent frescoes from Faras is indeed an awesome experience. They were carefully taken from the walls of the church treated for the extraction of salt for better preservation. The 169 frescoes hung at the National Museum of Khartoum and the Museum at Warsaw represent the finest collection of Christian art from Africa. There is the possibility that even more treasures would have been found if work had not ceased by 1964 and the waters of the Nile have covered them for posterity.

The Frescoes of most interest to me are:

1. St. Ann "Mother of the Theotokos (Period of Paulos) (700-750.). Colors: Yellow/ purple.

2. Kyros, Metropolitan of Pachoras (Faras) (869-902). Colors: White areas and Black contours. Attempts to realism: thick lips, broad nose, and bony face.

3. Peter The Apostle With Bishop Petros of Faras (+999). Colors /purple, realism: black faced Bishop.

4 Madonna with Princess. The Nubian princess unnamed.

5. Votive Cross. Christ is in the Oval, at the center of the cross. In the four corners, the Symbol of the four Evangels. In clockwise from the top right: the Eagle, the Ox, the Lion, and the Angel. (late 11th century). [159]

The Foundation Stela of Paulos Cathedral confirms the accession of King Merkurios in the year 697 A.D. Knowledge of others was found and a list of 27 bishops, and portraits of 14 were also discovered with names and full titles . The art of Faras revealed the perfection of the Nubian artist and their development eight centuries. It also shows a great deal of realism as people were portrayed as they were. The discovery of pottery kilns by Dr. William Y. Adams made it possible to development a system of dating Nubian pottery.

Qsar Ibrim was a more fortunate site. It was spared because the Fortress rose nearly 80 meters above sea level. Today parts of it are under water, which has risen over 60 meters level. Qasr Ibrim was also a see of the Bishop like Faras, but it did not yield frescoes but possessed a great cathedral, which was the finest of its kind , according to J. Martin Plumley who worked on site for eight seasons form 1961.Another great contribution from Qasr Ibrim was the many manuscripts and other materials in remarkable state of preservation. The archaeological evidence from Faras and Qasr Ibrim is quite important because it suggests that Christianity had become established in Nubia much earlier than the Imperial Missions of the 6th century.

As Christianity began to flourish, the pagan temples were converted to churches. It appears that this was the case of the remains of part of the temple built by the Kushite Pharaoh Taharqa found in Qasr Ibrim in 1972. Plumley states that much later this pagan shrine was transformed into a Christian church. A mud brick apse was built in a chamber at the end of a small-pillared hall. The style of the decoration was very early. Excavations carried out in 1976 revealed that the earliest pavement of the church was overlain by X-group pottery and no early Christian pottery. The Temple church may be the earliest in Nubia having been constructed the second half of the fifth century, as much a century before the Imperial Missions of the 6 th century Another discovery at Qasr Ibrim was finding the fragments of a Greek Gospel of St. Mark written in the 5th century.

The Kushite Kingdom ended with the fall of Meroe and the vast cultural change wrought by the advent of Christianity. However its influence did not wane but was sustained though the emergence of warring elite local families represented by the successor and rival states discussed above. Using the modern vernacular, they had morphed from the throne to the church. The royal tomb was no longer the symbol of power and divine authority. The advent of Christianity wrought an ideological transformation in Nubia unparalleled since the introduction of civilization itself. This assertion was made was made by Adams as Crowfoot brought to his attention that 'Nubia was one of the few countries of the old world which adopted Christianity without having passed under the discipline of Roman law. This hegemony began with the Treaty of Philae of 453 A.D. recognizing the religious rights of the Nubians to the Temple at Philae ,after the Edit of Theodosius (390 A.D.) which closed all pagan temples throughout its empire. It remained in force for a hundred years until closed forever by Justinian.

Priscus, the historian, wrote it was the tradition of the Nubians to have free crossing of the river to the temple. They would remove the statue of Isis from the temple and take it back to their country for the purpose of an oracle. This pagan ritual possibly has been preserved by the folk customs and by the Marian festivals throughout Europe , the Latin American countries and Brazil when the Black Madonna is paraded on a liter throughout the country side .in August.

J.W. Crowfoot described a ritual that is a relic from the Christian past of Nubia in an article *"Angel of the Nile* "dealing with the birth practices in the Nile valley or Nubia:

> "The Rite of Mariya (Excerpt)
> The house of the newborn child is swept, the dirt, the after birth and the midwife razor are all put together are all put together on a small raft made of wheat straw. An oil lamp and a big cake of Wheat flower are also placed on it . First or second day after the birth of the baby is taken to the river by the midwife, accompanied by village women or children. The midwife scatters handfuls of on her way , right and left saying:
> "This is the portion the Mariya, Oh Angels ."

The importance of the texts found were few but very important as it showed the deep religious nature of the Nubia. Father Vantini also states that they are of greater value as literary material for the study of the Old Nubian language. He felt that the "Texts of the Cross were of special interest as a litany in praise of the Cross. Griffith in his transcription of *The Nubian Texts* has left for the Western world a treasure that can be considered another contribution or legacy of the Kingdom of Kush.

...Beloved ,if indeed you desire to know the power , hear its power:

> The Cross the hope of the Christians
> The Cross is the resurrection of the dead
> The Cross is the path of them who have
> The Cross is the guidance of the blind
> The Cross is the staff the lame
> The Cross is the nurse of the sucklings
> The Cross is that which strengthens

There seems to be a connection with The Second Cataract Forts and Kerma. Most of the Kerma burials that were north of Kerma indicate that Kerma troops were used to man the forts at some time. The stele of Sedhefer would validate this conclusion: "I was a valiant commandant of Buhen, and… I built the temple of Horus, Lord of Buhen to the satisfaction of the Lord of Kush" [160] It was further asserted that the rulers of Kerma replaced the pharaoh at the height of her powers. The Lord of Kush was apparently a Nubian king at the time that the Egyptian pharaoh at Phebes uttered his famous complaint, 'I sit united with an Asiatic and a Nubian, each man in possession of his slice of Egypt." [162]

Bibliography

Abuno Philoppos. *Know Jerusalem: On the Patrimonial Rights Ethiopia has in the Holy Land.* Part II, Jerusalem, 1962.

Adams, William Y. *Nubia: Corridor to Africa.* Princeton University Press, 1977.

___*Ceramic Indusrties of Medieval Nubia.*Part-II, University of Kentucky,1986.

Arkell, D. J. *A History of the Sudan to 1821.* Atlone Press, 1961.

Baikie, James. *The Glamour of the Middle East.* Far East Excavation, 1927.

Begg, Ean, *The Cult of the Black Virgin.* London, 1985.

Bellack, Frederick .M. Translator, *The War At Troy: What Homer Did not Tell*, by Quintus of Smyrna. University of Oklohoma , Press, 1968.

Budge, E.A. *The Egyptian Sudan: Its History and Monuments,*vol.I, London, 1907.

The Gods of the Egyptians. 1969.

Carruthers, Jacob.H. "The Vision of Governance" in *Kemet and the African World View.,*eds. Maulauna Karenga and Joseph Carruthers, University of Sangore Press, 1986.

Delaney, Martin R. *Primcipia of Ethnology: The Origins of Racism and Color with a Compendium of Ethiopian and Egyptian Civilization.*Hapers: 1880.

Dickinson, Patrick. *The Aenied,* New American Library, 1961.

Diodorus, Siculus. *On Egypt.* Book III, Translated by Oldfather, 1933.

Diop, Cheik Anta. *The African Origin of Civilization in Reality.* Westport, 1976.

Documentation and Research Centre, The *Salvation of the Nubian Monuments.* Cairo, 1964.

Eide,Tormod et al.*FontesHistoriaeNuborium, vol.I, Norway, 1996.*

Emery, W. B. *Lost Land Emerging.* New York, 1967.

Finch, Charles S. "The Nile Valley Conference": New Light on Kemet Studies, in *Nile Valley Civilizations*, Transactions Pub., 1985

Franfort, Henry. *Kingship and The Gods, Universtiy of Chicago Press,* 1948.

Griffiths,F.LL. *Meroitic Inscriptions.* Part II, London, 1912.

Graves, Robert, *The Great Myths, vol. I, 1959.*

Herodotus. *The Histories*, Penguin Books, *1954.*

Hodkins , G.A. *Travelers in Ethiopia,* London. 1835.

Houston, Drusilla D. *The Wonderful Ethiopians and the Ancient Cushite Empire.* Baltimore, 1926.

James, George W. *Stolen Legacy: The Greeks Were Not The Authors of Greek Philosophy, But People of the North Africa,Commonly called the Egyptians.* San Franciso, 1954.

James, T. J. H. *An Introduction to Ancient Egypt.* London,1979.

Keating, Rex .*Nubian Rescue. London, 1975.*

Ludwig, Emil. *Napoleon.* New York, 1926.

Morehead, Alan. *The Blue Nile,* New York, 1962.

M'Bow, Amadou. ed. *General Edition of Africa,* Abridged edition, vol. II, California, 1990.

Murray, Margaret A. *The Splendor That Was Egypt.* New York, 1967.

O'Connor, David. *Nubia*: *Egypts Rival in Africa.* 1993.

Rawlinson George,Tr.,*The History of Herodotus, Tudor, 1939.*

Robinson, James. ed. *The Nag Hammadi Library in english Harpers. 1978.*

Sattin, Anthony. ed., *Florence Nightingales, Letters from Egypt: a Journey on the Nile,1849-1850.* New York, 1987.

Shinnie, P.L. *Meroe: A Civilization of Africa.* New York, 1967.

Shefter, Henry. ed. *The Iliad of Homer.* 1967.

Sim, J.L. *Burchkhardt: A Biography.* New York. 1897.

Smith, William, *A Smaller Classical Dictionary of Biography, Myththology and Geography.* Harpers, 1885.

Snowden, Frank M. *Blacks in Antiquity: Ethiopians in the Graeco-Roman Experience.* Harvard Press , 1970.

_____*Before Color Prejudice: The Ancient View of Blacks.* Harvard Press, 1983.

Soderburgh, Saeve T. *Temples and Tombs of Ancient Nubia.* London, 1987.

Strabo. *The Geography of Strabo.* Book XVII, Tr. , Horace Jones, The Library of Classical Literature, 1932.

Lazlo, Torok. *The Kingdom of Kush: Handbook of Napatan –Meroitic Civilization.* Leiden, 1998.

Toynbee, Arnold, *A Study of History.* Dell, 1965.

Van Sertima, Ivan. *Egypt Revisited.* Journal of African Civilizations Ltd., 1989.

Vantini, John. *The Excavations at Faras: A Contribution to the History of Nubian a Christianity.* Verona, 1970.

Wesley, Charles H. "The Changing of African Historical Tradition". Journal of Human Relations *vol.VIII, numbers 3 and 4.*

Wenig, S., ed. *Africa in Antiquity* : *The Arts of Ancient Nubia and the Sudan. Vol. I-II,* Brooklyn Museum, 1978.

Wildung,Dietrich, ed. *Sudan: Ancient Kingdoms of the Nile.* Paris, 1997.

Windsor, Rudolph R. *From Babylon to Timbukto.* Exposition Press, 1969.

Williams, Bruce. "The Lost Pharaohs of Nubia" in *Egyp*t *Revisited,* 1982.

Williams, Chancellor, *The Destruction of African Civilization; Great Issues of Race from 4500 B.C. to 2000 A.D.* Third World Press. 1987.

Wilson, John A.*The Culture of Ancient Egypt.* Chicago, 1961.

Woodson, Carter G. *The Miseducation of the Negro.* Associated Publishers, 1933.

Wortham, John. *The Glories of British Egyptology.* Norman, 1971.

ENDNOTES

[1] William Y. Adams, *Nubia: Corridor to Africa*, Princeton, 1977, p. 5

[2] Amadou-Mahtar M'Bow , *General History of Africa*. Abridged Edition, California, James Curry, 1990,vii

[3] Necia Desiree Harkless, *Afrocentrism and Nubian Scholarship,* Second International Sudan Studies Conference, University of Durham , U.K. April 1991: Conference Papers, pp. 62-70

[4] Charles H. Wesley, "The Changing African Tradition" (reprint) *Journal of Human Relations.* Vol.VIII, nos.3 &4, p.323

[5] Jacob H. Carruthers,"The Vision of Governance in Kemet and the African World View" in *Kemet and the African World V,* Eds. Maulana Karenga and Jacob H. Carruthers, Los Angeles, University of Sankore Press, 1986, p.3

[6] Ibid

[7] Charles S. Finch," The Nile Valley Conference: New Light on Kemet Studies" in *Nile Valley Civilizations,* ed. Ivan Van Sertima. New Brunswick, Transaction Publishers, 1985, p.7

[8] Martin R. Delaney, Philadelphia, Harper Brothers, 1880, pp. 3,108

[9] Chancellor Williams, *The Destruction of African Civilization: Great Issues of Race from 4500 B.C. to 2000 AD.*Chicago, Third World Press 1987, pp. 361-366.

[10] Basil Davidson in *Egypt Revisited,* Ed., Ivan Van Sertima, Journal of African Civilizations Ltd., Inc., p.51

[11] W.Y. Adams, *Nubia: Corridor to Africa*, Princeton, Princeton University Press.1977,84 ,p.6

[12] Bruce Williams, *The Lost Pharaohs of Nubia* in *Egypt Revisited,Ed.Ivan Van* Sertima , *New Brunswick,* Transaction Publishers, 1989, Pp. 90-104

[13] Ibid

[14] *New York Times* , February 4,1990.

[15] Frank M. Snowden, Jr. "Publisher's Notes" from Citation, Doctor of Letters, *honoris causa,*Georgetown University, May, 1985

[16] Frank S. Snowden, Jr. *Before Color Prejudice: The Ancient view of Black,* Boston, 1983, p.57

[17] Robert Graves, *The Greek Myths*, New York: Brazilier, 1959 Vol. I p. 9,

[18] Ibid

[19] William Smith, *A Smaller Classical Dictionary of Biography, Mythology and Geography.* New York: Harper and Bro. 1885. Pp. 301-304.

[20] Ibid pp. 681-683.

[21] Robert Graves *The Greek Myths,* New York: Brazilian, 1959, p.302.

[22] Patrick Dickinson, *The Aeneid,* New York, 1961, pp.19-30.

[23] William Smith, *A Smaller Classical Library,* New York, 1885, p.250.

[24] Frederick M. Bellack, Tr. and Intro, *The War at Troy: What Homer Didn't Tell* by Quintus of Smyrna . University of Oklahoma, Norman, 1968. Pp 6-48.

[25] Ibid

[26] George Rawlinson, Tr. *The History of Herodotus,* New York, Tudor Pub, 1939,pp.90-99,

[27] Ibid. pp. 152-153.

[28] Diodorus *On Egypt, Book III,* pp.2-3

[29] Strabo , *Geography , Book XVII* , Tr., Horace Leonard Jones, London :1996 (reprint), Harvard Press , pp. 143-149

[30] James M. Robinson, Ed. *The Nag Hammadi Library in English.* San Francisco, Harper & Row, 1978, pp. 258-259

[31] 2 Chr. 10:2-9

[32] 2 Kings19: 9; Isaiah.37:9

[33] *New Jerusalem Bible*, New York, 1989, Isaiah 18:1-3.

[34] 2 Kings 19:9.

[35] Abuna Philippos, Archbishop of the Ethiopian Orthodox Church, *Know Jerusalem: On the Patrimonial Rights Ethiopia has in the Holy Land*, Part III, Jerusalem, 1962

[36] John Vantini, *The Excavations at Faras: a Contribution to the History of Nubian Christianity.* Verona, 1970, p. 49.

[37] William Y. Adams, *Nubia: Corridor to Africa*, Princeton, 1977, p.2

[38] Gordon Waterfield, *Egypt.* New York, 1987, pp 54-104

[39] Ibid.

[40] E. A. Wallis Budge, *The Egyptian Sudan,* vol. I. London, 1907. pp. 1-63

[41] Ibid

[42] Ibid

[43] Alan Moorehead, *The Blue Nile,* New York, pp.15 –16.

[44] ibid, pp. 34-35

[45] Emil Ludwig, *Napoleon,* New York, 1926, p.11.

[46] Anthony Sattin, ed. *Florence Nightingale, Letters from Egypt: a Journey on the Nile, 1849-1850,* New York, 1987, p.12.

[47] Ibid, pp. 21-208.

[48] Katherine Sim, *J.L. Burckhardt: A Biography.* New York, 1987, p. 12.

[49] William Y. Adams, "*J.L. Burckhardt, Ethnographer*", *Ethnohistory* 20/3. pp.225-8.

[50] Ibid.

[51] E. A. Wallis Budge, *The Egyptian Sudan: Its History and Monuments.* Vol .I, London, 1907, pp. 38-55

[52] G.A. Hoskins, *Travels in Ethiopia,* London, 1835, p.68

[53] James Baikie, *The Glamour of Near East Excavation,* London, 1927, pp.40-49.

[54] Ibid, p.78

[55] Ibid.

[56] John Wortham, *The Genius of British Egyptology*, Norman, 1971, p.106

[57] W. Y. Adams *Nubia: Corridor to Africa* ,Princeton 1984, Princeton University Press, p. 89

[58] Walter B. Emery, *Lost Land Emerging,* New York, Scribner's, 1967, p.32

[59] Ibid, pp.35-38

[60] Adams, op.cit.p.74

[61] Ibid p. 75

[62] Adams, p.180 - 187

[63] Ibid

[64] Walter B. Emery, *Lost Land Emerging, New* York, Charles Scribner's and Sons, 1967 pp.39 –51

[65] Ibid

[66] Ibid

[67] Save-Soderburgh, *Temples and tombs of Ancient Nubia,* New York, UNESCO, p. 54

[68] Ibid p. 76

[69] Ibid p. 124

[70] Ibid

[71] Ibid pp. 137-144

[72] Ibid , p. 210

[73] Save-Soderburgh, *Temples and Tombs of Ancient Nubia, Paris, 1987*, p.50.

[74] James Muhly," Where the Greeks Got their Gifts", *Book World,* 1991, p.3.

[75] Documentation & Research Centre, *The Salvation of the Nubian Monuments, Cairo, 1964*, p. 87.

[76] F. Ll. Griffith, *Meroitic Inscriptions*, Part II, London, 1912, p.33

[77] Documentation & Research Centre, p. 91

[78] Griffith, op. cit.

[79] Documentation & Research Centre, p.134

[80] Ibid, p.9

[81] William Y. Adams, *Nubia: Corridor to Africa*, Princeton, 1977, pp.330-338

[82] Ean Begg, *The Cult of the Black Virgin*, London, 1985, pp.61-68.

[83] Documentation & Research Centre, pp. 92- 94

[84] Ibid

[85] Griffith, pp. 27-32

[86] Wallis Budge, *The Nile,* London, p.71

[87] Save-Soderbergh, pp. 127-8.

[88] Ibid

[89] Documentation & Research Centre, 92

[90] Ibid, p. 97

[91] Ibid, p. 98

[92] Ibid, p.99

[93] Ibid, pp. 100-01

[94] Ibid

[95] James H. Breasted, *Ancient Records of Egypt, Vol. II, New* York, 1906, pp. 309-312

[96] Wallis Budge, pp. 725-730.

[97] E.A. Budge.*The Gods of the Egyptians ,* Vol .2. New York, Dover Publications, 1969, p.46

[98] James Henry Breasted, *Ancient Records of Egypt,*Vol IV, New York , Russell and Russell, 1962, p.55

[99] Wallis Budge, *The Egyptian Sudan*, Vol II, London, Kegan and French, Truchner, &Co. 1902,pp. 343-357

[100] Robert Caputo, *"Journey Up the Nile"*, *National Geographic,* Vol. II, Nov5. Washington, May 1985 ,p.629

[101] Ibid pp. 631-632

[102] Rex Keating, *Nubian Rescue,* London, Robert Holt C., 1975, pp. 88-105

[103] Bruce Trigger , *Nubia Under The Pharaohs,* Colorado, Westveiw press, 1976, pp. 111-114

[104] Breasted, pp. 131-150

[105] ibid

[106] Ibid

[107] William Y. Adams "The Misrepresentations of Nubia," *Sudan Newsletter*, UK

[108] James Shreve "Secrets of the gene" *National geographic*, Vol. 196, no 4, October 1999, p.73.

[109] Christopher Ehret, *The Civilization of Africa*, Charlottesville, 2002, University of Virginia Press, p.7

[110] Frank M. Snowden, *Before Color Prejudice*, Boston, Harvard Press, 1983, p.7

[111] Christopher Frye, *Race, Empire and Post Empire*, The African Horton Memorial Lecture, University of Sierra Leone, 12/13/79

[112] Adams, *Nubia: Corridor to Africa*, pp. 5-6

[113] G.Mokhtar, ed., *General History of Africa:* Vol. II: *Ancient Civilizations of Africa*, California, 1990. pp.390-91

[114] Budge p.505

[115] ibid op. cit. p.119

[116] B.Gratien, *Les cultures Kerma , Essai de classification*, Lille, 1978, pp.307-312.

[117] Ibid

[118] Adams, op. cit. p. 153

[119] Adams, op. cit. p.

[120] Frank M. Snowden, Jr. , *Blacks in Antiquity: Ethiopians in the Greco-Roman Experience*, Cambridge, 1970 Harvard University Press, pp. 189-195

[121] Tormod Eide et al, *Fontes Historiae Nubiorum*, Vol. II, Norway, 1996,University of Bergen, PP.582-584

[122] ibid

[123] William Adams, *Nubia: Corridor to Africa*, Princeton, *1974*, Princeton Press, p. *216*

[124] David 0' Connor, *Africa in Antiquity*, Vol. I: *"Nubia before the New Kingdom"*, New York. Brooklyn Museum, 1978 p. 51

[125] James Breasted, *Ancient Records of Egypt, Vol. I .New York, 1906, Russell $ Russell, pp.131-150*

[126] Ibid

[127] Ibid, pp. 293-295

[128] A. J. Arkell, A History of the Sudan, London, 1955, University of London, pp. 97-107

[129] Timothy Kendall, *"KINGS OF THE SACRED MOUNTAIN: NAPATA AND THE KUSHITE TWNETIY-FIFTH DYNASTY OF EGYPT"* in *SUDAN,* Paris, Flammarion, p. 162

[130] P.L.Shinnie, *Meroe,* 1967, Praeger, 31

[131] Dietrich Wildung, *Sudan, P. 302*

[132] Freidrich W. Hinkel, *"The Royal Pyramids of Meroe, Architecture, Construction and Reconstruction of a Sacred Landscape" in Sudan & Nubia*, Bulletin 10, *pp. 11-26*

[133] G.A. Hoskins, Esq, *Travels in Ethiopia*, London, 1835, Rees, Orme, Brown & Longman, pp. 68-69

[134] Frederick W.Hinkel, *Meroitic Architecture" in Sudan*, pp. 393-416

[135] Hoskins, Ibid

[136] Adams, p.291

[137] Lazlo, Torok, *The Kingdom of Kush: Handbook of Napatan-Meroitic Civilizations,* Leiden, Brill, 1998, pp 154-5

[138] Lazslo Torok, *The Kingdom of Kush: Handbook of Napatan – Merotic Civilizations,* ,

[139] Ibid

[140] . Mokhtar, General History of Africa, UNESCO, 1991, pp. 174-5

[141] Timothy Kendall, *"Kings of the Kushite Sacred Mountain" in Sudan,* Flammarion 1997, p.166

[142] Kendall ,p.185

[143] Karl-Heinz Priese, *Sudan,* Paris, 1997, Flammarion,pp *226-242.*

[144] Dietrich Wildung, *Sudan,* pp. 302 340

[145] ibid, p. 310

[146] ibid ,p. 324-5

[147] ibid .p.306

[148] ibid, p. 308-9

[149] ibid

[150] ibid p.340

[151] W. Y. Adams *"Meroitic Architecture; An Analytical Survey and Bibliography",* Meroitstiche Forschunngen 1980, *Meroitica* 7, 8. 255-279, Berlin 1984

[152] W. Y. Adams *Ceramic Industries of Medieval Nubia* ; *Part One,* Lexington, 1986, University of Kentucky Press, pp. l-11

[153] W.Y. Adams, *"Ceramics,"* in *Africa in Antiquity, Vol. I* , pp. 126-133

[154] Boyce N. Driskell, Nettle K. Adams and Peter French, "A Newly Discovered Temple At Qasr Ibrim: Preliminary Report," *Archaeologie du Nil Moyen,* Vol. 3, 1989, pp. 11, 23-24.

[155] G. Mokhtar, ed. *General History of Africa. Vol. I p.* 78, UNESCO 1981-1990

[156] Arnold Toynbee, *A Study of History,* Vol. I Dell Publishing Co. 1965, p.75

[157] Abune Phillipos , Archbishop of the Ethiopian Church, *Know Jerusalem: On the Patrimonial Rights Ethiopia has in the Holy Land,* Pat III, 1962

[158] Vantini p. 50

[159] Vantini ,143-147

[160] Adams, p.214 -215

[161] Ibid

INDEX

A

Abu Simbel 23
Achilles. *See* Memnon
Afrocentric scholarship 5
Afrocentrism xiv, 5
Agrarian tradition 171
Alwa 192
Amadou Mahtar M'Bow xiii
Ameni 113
Aneiba. *See* Second Cataract Fortress
Animal life 54
Annexation to Rome 81
Apedemak. *See* Lion God
Apocalypse of Adam 17
Art and Architecture 174
Atlanersa. *See* Stand
Axum 150, 189

B

Bed Burial. *See* Kerma
Beit el Wali 40
Belzoni 24
Bible. *See* Genesis, Kings, Isaiah, Psalms
Biblical tradition 16
Bigeh. *See* Temples
Black Nationalists 5
Bonnet. *See* proof of mining in Kerma
Boston Museum. *See* Kerma artifacts
Bow and mercenries 57
British Museum 26
Bruce Williams 8
Budge xii
Buhen. *See* Second cataract Fortress; *See* Second Cataract Fortress; *See* Second Cataract Fortress

C

Caillaiud 22
Cambyses 15
Carthage. *See* Queen Dido
Character 63
Charles H. Wesley 5
Cheikh Anta Diop 7
Chirtianity in Kush 192
Chronoly of Nubia. *See* Nubiocentric
Civil government 121
Classical tradition 10
Climate 53
Conquest of Egypt 124

D

Dakka. *See* Temples
Dead Sea Scrolls 16
Debod. *See* Temples
Dendur. *See* Temples
Derr. *See* Temples
Descendants of Noah. *See* Gen 9:18; *See* Gen 9:18
Diodorus 6. *See* History of Egypt
Divine Kingship 113
DNA, Mitochodrial 62
Domed Tumuli 88
Domeric arts{ Pottery, weaving, and iron 179
Drovetti 25
Drusilla Dunjee Houston. *See* Mc Alister Seminary
Dynastic durability of Kush. *See* 1200 years

E

E. A. Budge 7
Eastern Defuffa 85
Egyptian Exploration Society. *See* Shinnie and Fairman
Emery xii
Ethiopians 13. *See* Diodorus
Ethiopian Dynasty. *See* Conquest of Egypt
Evliya Celebi. *See* Ottoman traveler in Nubia

F

F. LLI Griffith. *See* Pioneer of Christian Nubian Studies
Fertile Crescent 99
Fifth Cataract 49
First Annual Ancient Egyptian Studies Conference 5
First archaeological Survey 27
First Cataract 49. *See* boundaries of Egypt
Firts Intermediate period 75
Flinders Petrie 26
Florence Nightingale 22
Fourth Cataract 14, 49
Frescoes of Faras 36

G

Genesis 2
13. *See* rivers of Eden
George Reisner 27
Gerald Massey 7
Gold of Kush. *See* Upper Nubia
Gold of Wawat. *See* Lower Nubia
Growing seasons 55

H

Hansbury 24
Hapi. *See* God of the NIle
Harkuff 59
Harvard Boston Expedition. *See* Reisner
Hebrew and African alliance 701 BC 186
Henry Salt. *See* British Consul
Herihor 120
Herodotus xiii. *See* Father of History; *See* On
  Kush; *See* First to mention Meroe by name
Homer xiii. *See* Iliad
Hoskins 22
Huy Inscription 118

I

International trade
 Goods and ideas 182
Isaiah 124. *See* Commerce of Ethiopia
Isaiah 36 8-9. *See* Assyria and Libnah
Ivan Van Sertima 9

J

Jacob Carruthers 9
James Baikie 25
James Bruce. *See* Blue Nile
Jebel Barkal 155. *See* Sacred Sites; *See* Cult of
  Amon
John Henry Clarke 7
John Sanderson. *See* mummy powder

K

Kalabsha 40
Kandake. *See* Queens of Ethiopia
Karl Priese 150
Kashta 125
Kemet (KMT) 5
Kemites 5
Kerma 29
Kerma Pottery 88
Khartoum Neolithic 83
Kingdom of Kush. *See* Kerma , Napata , Meroe; *See*
  Kerma, Napatan period and Meroitic Period;
  See Napatan period, Meroitic peroid
Kingom of Kerma. *See* Most Ancient African
  Empire
King Ergamenes 145
King Nastasen. *See* Silver Mirrors; *See* Silver Mir-
  rors
King Natakamani 149
Kiosk of Kertassi 40
Kubban. *See* Second Cataract Fortress
Kurru. *See* Royal Pyramids and Cemeteries

L

Lepsius. *See* inscrption of Nehi
Linant de Bellefonds 24
Lions of Judah 18
Lion Temple 160
Lower Nubia 49

M

Makuria 192
Malauna Karanga 9
Martin Bernal 38. *See* Black Athena
Martin Delaney 6
Maurice Poncet. *See* Voyage to Ethiopia
Memphite Foundation 104
Meriotics. *See* Study of Meroe
Meroe 111. *See* Cult of Apedemak
meroe. *See* Sacred sites
Meroe region 156
Meroitics. *See* new discipline
Meroitic HKIngs and Queens. *See* Forty generations
Meroitic Kings. *See* Meroe
Meroitic period 91
Meroitic phase. *See* Kingship
Meroitic Script 185
Mesopatamian Creation Myth 100
Mesopotamia. *See* Fertile Crescent
Moden Nubia. *See* Kush; *See* Kush
Musawwaret. *See* Lion Frieze,bottom of column;
  See Lion Frieze,bottom of column
Musawwaret es Sufra 162
Museum of Turin 26

N

Napatan and Meroitic royal Cemeteries 29
Napatan Pharaohs. *See* Rulers of Egypt
Napatan region 152
Napoleon. *See* in Egypt
Naqa 162
Native Bed. *See* Kerma; *See* Kerma
Nehi, Viceroy of Thutmose III 118
Neolithic xii
Neolithic Age 71
New Ambassadors Extroadinary. *See* Taffa, Dendur,
  Ellesiya
Nineveh Hore reports 155
Nobatia 192
North pyramids. *See* Meroe
Nubian A Horizon 83
Nubian C Horizon 84
Nubian Pharaohs. *See* XXV th Dynasty of Egypt
Nubian princess. *See* Wall painting ,
Nubian Royal Cemetery of Kerma 28

Nubian Scholarship 5
Nubian scholarship xiv
Nubian Songs. *See* Lepsius
Nubia the land of the cataracts 48
Nubin Kingdom of Kerma 85
Nubiocentric view 8
Nubiology. *See* Study of Nubia; *See* Study of Nu-
    bia; *See* New discipline
Nuri. *See* Pyramid Complex; *See* Royal Napatan
    Pyramids and Cemeteries

O

Old Testament. *See* Cush or Kush

P

Pagan Prayer 41
Palermo stone 71
Period of Transition 7
Persian Dynasty 80. *See* Dynasty XXVII
Philae. *See* Temple of Isis; *See* Sacred sites; *See*
    Cult of Isis
Pianhki 90, 127
Pliny xii, 6
Polish Mission at Faras. *See* INDEX \c
Politics and war 172
Post Colonial Period 8
Priam. *See* King of Troy
Prophet Isaiah. *See* Curse of Kushites
Ptolemaic Dynasy. *See* Hellenistic Monarchy
Pyramid texts 103

Q

Queen Amanirenas. *See* One Eyed Candace
Queen Amanishakheto 147. *See* Jewelry, Beaded
    Necklace Gold Armlet,; *See* Jewelry, Beaded
    Necklace Gold Armlet,
Queen Amanitore 149
Queen Candace 19
Queen Nawidemak 148
Queen of Sheba. *See* Solomon
Quintus. *See* exploits of Memnon at Troy

R

Reisner xii
Reisner's Notes 31. *See* Second Archaeological
    Survey
Religious government 121
Richard Lepsius 22
Robert Graves 10
Royal Cemeteries. *See* Kurri, Nuri, Jebel Barkal,
    Napata region- Northern and Southern cem-
    teries in Meroe

Royal Cities 158
Royal Son's of Kush. *See* vice regal system

S

Sack of Thebes. *See* end of Napatn Pharaohs in Egypt
Sacred Sites 107
Saqia 54
Second Archeological Survey 30
Second Cataract. *See* Nile
Second Cataract Forts. 28
Second Intremediate Period 76
Shadowy Kings. *See* Shabaka and Shabataka
Shaduf 55
Shrine of Apis 161
Sixth cataract 49
Source of the Nile 47
Statue of Memnon. *See* Thebes (Luxor)
Strabo xiii. *See* Geography
Sudan Antiquities Service. *See* Arkell

T

Taharqa 90
Taharqa' s progeny 137
Tarhaqa. *See* teh builder
Ta Nehesu 82
Temples of Philae 38
Temple of Amon 159
Temple of Dakka 41
Temple of Derr 43
Temple of Hathor 44
Temple of Isis 39
Temple of Wadi es Sebua 42
Text Of UNESCO'S Appeal 33
The Association for The Study of Negro Life and
    History 6
The Blue Nile 47
The Colonial Period 6
The Nile Valley Conference 5
Third cataract 49
Third Intermediate period 89
Thomas Hodgkin 7
Tirhaka. *See* Taharqa
Tomb of Pennut 43
Trade and Commerce 171
Trojan War. *See* Memnon
Tyre. *See* Dido ,Queen of INDEX \c ; *See* Modern
    Lebanon

U

UNESCO 33. *See* financial contributions
Uni 59
Upper Defuffa 29
Upper Nubia 49

V

Vegetation 54
Virgil xiii. *See* Aeneid

W

W.E.B. Dubois 6
W. B. Emery 30
Waddington 24
Wad ben Naga 163
Western Defuffa 29, 85
Wilbur Papyrus 120
William Leo Hansberry 6

Z

Zerah. *See* Ethiopian general

ABOUT THE AUTHOR

Dr. Necia Desiree Harkless, a native of Detroit Michigan, is a nationally and internationally known scholar in Early Childhood Education, Curriculum Development, Leadership and Multi-Cultural Education. She has served as an educational consultant throughout the United States, assisting school districts and other organizations develop new programs for children parents and others. She received a fellowship at the University of Illinois to train future teachers.

Education : Prairie View State and Agricultural College,(Hempstead ,Texas) B.A.(Education and Social Science),1942; Detroit Institute of Musical Art, B.A., 1960; University of Illinois, Champaign, Urbana, M.A., 1969; Wayne State University, Detroit, Michigan, ED.D. (Education), 1974.

Memberships: Lexington-Fayette County Historic Commission; Pritchard Committee for Academic Excellence; Kentucky Youth Orchestra Board; Advisory Board of the Governor's School for the Arts; Lay Eucharistic Minister, Good Shepherd Episcopal Church; Prison Ministry, Blackburn Prison Correctional Complex; Advisory Board, Georgetown College Underground Railroad Research Institute; and The International Society for Nubian Studies.

Career: Michigan Department of Social Welfare, Caseworker, 1946-56; Detroit Institute of Musical Arts, Piano and Theory teacher; Detroit Public Schools, Kindergarten Teacher, 1965-1968; Wayne State University College of Education, 1968-74; University of Kentucky, 1974-1981; Georgetown College, 1981-1985; and Donovan Scholar, University of Kentucky 1985-present.

Publications: *Heart to Heart: Poems and Heart Images* by Necia Desiree Harkless; *Childress: Touched Many One Man* by Ann Taylor Wright, published by Heart to Heart and Associates, Dr. Necia Desiree Harkless, Second Edition, University of Kentucky Library Press; 'Three Black Madonnas in My Life' in *She is Everywhere*, iUniverse Press.

May 8, 2002 was awarded Georgetown College's Doctor of Letters honoris causa for her commitment to the advancement of arts and education; exhibitor of her art in Georgetown's Anne Wright Wilson Art Gallery and elsewhere; curriculum development projects in two universities in Nigeria; state delegate to the International Women's Year conference in Houston Texas; The World Conference on Early Childhood Education in Melbourne, Australia.